EMPOWERING PUBLIC SECTOR ENTERPRISES IN INDIA

Empowering Public Sector Enterprises in India

Proceedings of Chief Executive Conference on
Public Sector Enterprises

New Delhi, 8th March, 2007

सत्यमेव जयते

Department of Public Enterprises
Ministry of Heavy Industries and Public Enterprises
Government of India

SHIPRA

ISBN: 978-81-7541-371-9

First Published in India in 2008

Published by:
SHIPRA PUBLICATIONS
115-A, Vikas Marg, Shakarpur, Delhi-110092, INDIA
Phone: 91-11-65277210, 91-11-22500954
Fax: 91-11-22458662
E-mail: info@shiprapublications.com
www.shiprapublications.com

Contents

Foreword

The prominent role played by the public sector enterprises in India, in the industrial and economic development of the country, is well acknowledged. The country today has a strong and vibrant economy. The Chief Executive Conference on Public Sector Enterprises held on the 8th March, 2007 at the Balayogi Auditorium in New Delhi was inaugurated by Dr. Manmohan Singh, Hon'ble Prime Minister of India. He also gave away the MoU Excellence Awards for the year 2004-05 and 2005-06. The Conference was attended by dignitaries, distinguished guests and public sector executives from all over the country. The main theme of the Conference was, *"Empowering Public Sector Enterprises in India"*.

It is heartening to note that a book on this theme is now being brought out for the benefit of all those who would like to go through and use the details. The subject matter of the book acquires greater significance for the Public Sector Enterprises in India in the light of the expanding domestic economy, opportunities abroad and the intense competition in the market. Needless to say, the Government has been providing the enabling environment for these enterprises to perform and flourish. In this context, the remarks of the Prime Minister in his *Inaugural Address* becomes very significant wherein while applauding the contributions made by the Public Sector Enterprises he stated that the Government is committed to empowering the management of PSEs with full managerial and financial autonomy.

Various papers included in the book provide information on different facets of public sector enterprises growth in India, their different corporate strategies, successes and failures, the need for greater autonomy and the challenges before them. The book has been divided in three parts, besides the Introduction. While Part-I covers the Inaugural Session, Part-II has the papers presented during the Technical Session and Part- III includes the Report of Ad hoc Group of Experts on Empowerment of Central Public Sector Enterprises.

Public Sector Enterprises in India have an important role to play during the 11th Five Year Plan in helping the country achieve an average GDP growth of 9 per cent during the Plan period. It has to be recognized that public sector investments will have to be substantial during the 11th Plan and these enterprises are to access market for capital expenditure. The responsibility of the public sector enterprises, in this context, especially in the development of infrastructure (and the core sectors) remains as important as before. Looked at from this perspective, the publication of the book is very timely. I am sure the book will generate a lively discussion on all the issues raised and will be well received.

New Delhi
September , 2007

Santosh Mohan Dev
Minister, Heavy Industries
and Public Enterprises

Acknowledgement

The Chief Executive Conference of Central Public Sector Enterprises held on 8th March, 2007 was organized jointly by the Department of Public Enterprises and the Standing Conference on Public Sector Enterprises (SCOPE). It was a moment of pride for all the Central Public Sector Enterprises in the country. Hon'ble Prime Minister of India, Dr. Manmohan Singh inaugurated the Conference. Mr. Santosh Mohan Dev, Hon'ble Minister for Heavy Industries and Public Enterprises, Mrs. Kanti Singh, Hon'ble Minister of State of Heavy Industries, Mr. T.K. Nair, Principal Secretary to the Prime Minister, Mr. B.K. Chaturvedi, Cabinet Secretary, Dr. R.C. Panda, Secretary, Ministry of Heavy Industries & Public Enterprises, Mr. S. Behuria, Chairman (SCOPE) and Dr. S.M. Dewan, Director-General of SCOPE participated in the Conference. We acknowledge with gratitude their gracious participation in the Inaugural Function.

We also acknowledge with thanks, the august presence of other guests, namely, Mr. Priyaranjan Dasmunshi, Hon'ble Minister of Information and Broadcasting, Justice P.N. Bhagwati, Mr. Abid Hussain (former Member, Planning Commission), Mr. Hiten Bhaya (former Member, Planning Commission), the Members of the Task Force on MoU as well as large number of Secretaries of the Government of India and the CEOs of different Central Public Sector Enterprises.

Mr. Jairam Ramesh, Hon'ble Minister of State for Commerce addressed and chaired the Technical Session. We express our grateful thanks for their presence during the Conference and for their cherished commitment towards the public sector enterprises in India.

This book is the result of the *Proceedings of the Conference on Public Sector Enterprises in India.* The book contains *the Inaugural Address* of the Hon'ble Prime Minister, *the Key Note Address* of the Hon'ble Minister of Heavy Industries and Public Enterprise, *the Special Address* of Minister of State for Commerce and the *Theme Address* by Dr. Athreya. The other papers included in the book are based on the presentations made during the Technical Session. We acknowledge with thanks to all for the contributions made by them.

A great deal of work had also to be done in house to bring out this book. The efforts put in by Dr. Sharat Kumar, Adviser, Mr. K.D. Tripathi, Joint Secretary, Department of Public Enterprises and the team of officers (Mr. S.S. Negi, Mr. V.K. Jindal, Mr. T.P. Singh, Mr. U.K. Swamy and Mr. Jagdish Prashad) are duly acknowledged. Thanks are also due to Mr. Ajay Sareen for his assistance in preparing the manuscript. Finally, we wish to acknowledge the contribution of Mr. D. Kumar of Shipra Publications for publishing the book in such a short time.

Introduction

Public sector enterprises evoke impressions of technologically complex entities engaged in large scale production. The Second Five Year Plan (Government of India) laying emphasis on industrial growth stated: 'the use of modern technology requires *large scale production* and a unified control and allocation of resources in certain major lines of activity'. Indeed, 'nearly all communications, nearly all production and distribution of electric power, much transportation, most manufacturing and mining, a substantial share of retail trade, and a considerable amount of entertainment are conducted or provided by large firms' (Galbraith, 1967). It has been, furthermore observed: 'this is the part of the economy which automatically we identify with the modern industrial society. To understand it is to understand that part which is most subject to change and which accordingly, is most changing our lives' (Galbraith, 1967).

These firms or enterprises are run as 'large corporations'/'large companies'. Corporations, in turn, have been defined as a body (of people) legally united to act as an individual. 'Till the sixteenth century most of the economic corporations were guilds which were little more than trade unions. It was the growth of the great chartered companies during the age of exploration, of which the East India Company was the longest and the most famous, which gave these corporations their modern form. They were joint stock companies issuing shares that could be traded. They also limited the liabilities of the shareholders' (Lal, 2006). The share, of these corporations, both in goods and services, in the total gross domestic product (GDP) in various countries, especially so, in the advanced countries is as high as *fifty percent*. Since there is an increasing trend towards 'corporatization' in the Indian economy, the share of the corporate sector is bound to go up.

PUBLIC SECTOR ENTERPRISES

The *Industrial Revolution* in the 18th-19th century saw the emergence of a new entrepreneur class or 'the bourgeoisie'. Unlike the feudal elite of yesteryears who were largely landowners, the bourgeoisie were owners of capital/capital goods. Since the Industrial Revolution occurred first in Great Britain, countries, such as, France and Germany were left behind during this period, 'The relative late start of Industrial Revolution on the continent of Europe necessitated the need of a quick catch up with Great Britain. Private people could not be expected at once to set the process of industrialization in action and also to close up the gap in development' (Prasad, 1957). Large scale enterprises were, therefore, set up in the public sector in these countries to bridge the gap in industrial development between their own countries and Great Britain. Lack of an entrepreneurial class, absence of financial institutions and fear of western dominations prompted the government of the day in Japan also to undertake the entrepreneurial functions itself. By 1880, the Government owned and operated merchant ships, shipbuilding, railways, telegraph, factories and mines. The Japanese economy was soon transformed into an industrial state over a period of the next twenty five years. Reasons for establishment of *public sector enterprises,* in developing countries, as varied as Africa, Asia and Latin America, in the post-colonial period also lay in their *quest for growth* and the need to catch up with the advanced countries.

II
'ENTREPRENEURIAL' AND 'MATURE' CORPORATIONS

Writing in the 1960s, Prof. J. K. Galbraith observed, 'Seventy years ago the corporation was the instrument of its owners and a projection of their personalities.... The men who now run the large corporations own no appreciable share of the enterprise'. Capital that was a scarce commodity and symbolized "power" *is no more so scarce.* 'Given a competent business organization, capital is now ordinarily available'. (Galbraith, 1967) This has been especially so, for economies with high incomes and greater propensity to save. It is today the middle class in different countries that has become the provider of the much sought after capital, either through its savings in banks, insurance and pension funds or through direct investments in the capital market. On account of relatively unhindered flow of capital across countries, moreover, capital can be accessed globally.

ENTREPRENEUR VS. TECHNOSTRUCTURE

The technological complexity of large corporations has brought to the fore an altogether new factor of production, namely, 'the technostructure'. It is stated to be distinct from the usual four factors of production viz. *land, labour, capital* and *enterprise*. While the traditional owner-entrepreneur presided over firms, employing the best managers and supervisors to direct relatively simple tasks of his firm, *the large corporations* of today require the combined technical knowledge and experience of different people for performing complex tasks. Hence, while an entrepreneur may create the organization that is technologically complex, it is only 'technostructure' (technicians/ professional managers) that can operate it. It has been further remarked, 'The prevalence of group, instead of individual action is a striking characteristic of management organization in large corporations' (Gordon, 1945).

Technostructure, in turn, has been defined as 'the association of men of diverse technical knowledge, experience or other talent which industrial technology and planning require.... It extends from the leadership of the modern industrial enterprise down to just short of labour force and embraces a large number of people and variety of talent' (Galbraith, 1967). Moreover, 'the need for such a *group personality* begins with the circumstance that in modern industry a large number of decisions, and all that are important, draw on information possessed by more than one man. Typically, they draw on the specialized scientific and technical knowledge, the accumulated information or experience and the artistic or intuitive sense of many persons' (Galbraith, 1967).

GOVERNMENT AND TECHNOSTRUCTURE

Large corporations are generally registered under the Company Law as separate legal entity. It is subject to audit by a chartered accountant and is liable to taxation. It functions according to its '*articles of association*' and the liability of the shareholders is limited. Besides abiding by the laid down norms of *annual reporting* to the Registrar of Companies, payment of corporate taxes to the government and other dues, these organizations are to be run as *autonomous bodies* without interference from Government.

The relationship between large corporations donned by *the technostructure* and *the government* is, nevertheless, benign and very great. Unlike the predominantly pecuniary outlook of the *entrepreneur corporation*, where the corporation made attempts to influence the state/government, overtly or covertly, to get tax concessions, win contracts, and other personal favours, the *technostructure* of large corporations depends on the state for ensuring it with supply of qualified young people/skilled manpower and a good macro-economic environment to operate. The state, in turn, looks up to these large corporations for economic growth, higher tax revenue and more employment.

SHAREHOLDERS AND TECHNOSTRUCTURE

While the shareholders are the legal owners of large corporations, they do not necessarily control the decision making process. The traditional owner-entrepreneur held large enough stocks to exercise potential control over the enterprise. Given the nature of large scale production in certain enterprises, the requirement of funds generally far exceeds what the promoter entrepreneur can provide. This necessitates mobilisation of additional funds through stock exchanges and other means. Consequent to increase in the number of shareholders, control of each stockholder in 'the management' only declines. The large number of stockholders, moreover, has no understanding of how the corporation runs. They may not have a lasting interest in the corporation either as they are more concerned about the 'capital gains', which materialises as a result of purchase and sale of shares. During the annual general body meetings of large corporations as well, the large majority of stockholders may either abstain or exercise the voting rights mostly through the Board of Directors (of the Company) as 'proxies'.

Wherever such developments have taken roots in relation to the large corporations, they have *disenfranchised the stockholder* and provided 'the technostructure' the much needed autonomy to operate. Differentiating between various type of corporations, Prof. Galbraith opines, 'it will be necessary to distinguish between corporations in which age, size and simplicity of operation still accord power to an individual who has control of capital and those where the technostructure has taken over. I will refer to the first as '*Entrepreneurial Corporation*' and the second as '*Mature Corporation*'.

III
PUBLIC CORPORATION IN INDIA

India adopted the mixed economy framework soon after Independence and accorded primacy to the role of the public sector enterprises for industrial growth. The *Industrial Policy Resolution (April 1956)* of Government of India, accordingly, made the following policy statement:

'The adoption of the socialist pattern of society as the national objective, as well as the need for planned and rapid development, requires that all industries of basic and strategic importance, or in the nature of public utility services, should be in the public sector. Other industries which are essential and require investment on a scale which only the State, in present circumstances, could provide have also to be in the public sector. The State has, therefore, to assume direct responsibility for the future development of industries over a wide area. Nevertheless, there are limiting factors which make it necessary at this stage for the State to define the field in which it will undertake the sole responsibility for further development, and to make a selection of industries in the development of which it will play a dominant role. After considering all aspects of the problem, in consultation with the Planning Commission, the Government of India have decided to classify industries into three categories, having regard to the part which the State would play in each of them. These categories will inevitably overlap to some extent and too great a rigidity might defeat the purpose in view. But the basic principles and objectives have always to be kept in view and the general directions, hereafter referred, to be followed. It should also be remembered that it is always open to the State to undertake any type of industrial production.

In the first category will be industries, the future development of which will be the exclusive responsibility of the State. The second category will consist of industries which will be progressively state-owned and in which the State will, therefore, generally take the initiative in establishing new undertakings, but in which private enterprise will also be expected to supplement the efforts of the State. The third category will include all the remaining industries, and their future development will, in general, be left to the initiative and enterprise of the private sector.

Industries in the first category have been listed in *Schedule-A* of this Resolution. All new units in these industries, save their establishment in the private sector which have already been approved, will be set up by the State. This does not preclude the expansion of the existing privately owned unit, or the possibility of the state securing the cooperation of private enterprise in the establishment of new units when the national interests so require. Railways and air transport, arms and ammunition and atomic energy will, however, be developed as Central Government monopolies. Whenever cooperation with the private enterprise is necessary, the State will ensure, either through majority participation in the capital or otherwise, that it has the requisite powers to guide the policy and control the operations of the undertakings.

Industries in the second category will be those listed in *Schedule-B*. With a view to accelerating their future development, the State will increasingly establish new undertakings in these industries. At the same time, private enterprise will also have the opportunity to develop in this field, either on its own or with the State participation. All the remaining industries will fall in the third category, *Schedule-C*, and it is expected that their development will be undertaken ordinarily through the initiative and enterprise of the private sector, though it will be open to the state to start any industry even in this category.

It will be the policy of the State to facilitate and encourage the development of these industries in the private sector, in accordance with the programmes formulated in successive Five Year Plans, by ensuring the development of transport, power and other services, and by appropriate fiscal and other measures. The State will continue to foster institutions to provide financial aid to these industries, *and special assistance will be given to enterprises organized on cooperative lines for industrial and agricultural purposes*. In suitable cases, the State may also grant financial assistance to the private sector. Such assistance, especially when the amount involved is substantial, will preferably be in the form of participation in equity capital, though it may also be in part, in the form of debenture capital.

Industrial undertakings in the private sector have necessarily to fit into the framework of the social and economic policies of the State and will be subject to control and regulation in terms of the *Industries (Development and Regulation) Act* and other relevant legislation. The Government of India, however, recognize that it would, in general, be desirable to allow such undertakings to develop with as much freedom as possible, consistent with the targets and objectives of the national plan. When there exist in the same industry both privately and publicly owned units, it would continue to be the policy of the State to give fair and non-discriminatory treatment to both of them.'

SECOND FIVE YEAR PLAN (GOVERNMENT OF INDIA)

The *Second Five Year Plan* was launched in April, 1956 coinciding with the Industrial Policy Resolution (IPR). The Plan thus became the instrument to implement the IPR. Consequently: both the number and total investment in public sector enterprises saw an overwhelming increase in the subsequent years. The public sector enterprises that were subsequently set up have had any of the three organizational forms of (a) departmental undertakings, (b) limited liability companies/ public corporations and (c) statutory corporations. The limited liability or Joint Stock Company has been the most preferred type of organization for setting up public sector enterprises in (post-independent) India. 'One of the important motivations for preferring this form of organization has been the ease with which an enterprise could be set up without the approval or by an Act of Parliament. The other advantage that went with this form of organization has been the convenience it afforded for accommodating private capital through mobilization of additional funds from the stock market' (Prasad, 1957).

'Technostructure' has been an integral part of these public sector enterprises as it brought together highly qualified and skilled manpower. These enterprises have been engaged in the production and supply of a wide range of products, which include basic goods like steel, cement and chemicals; capital goods like pressure vessels, boilers and drilling rigs; and intermediate goods like electricity and gas. They have been also rendering a large number of services, such as, telecommunications, trading, tourism, warehousing etc. However, while these enterprises contributed significantly by way of profits, salaries and wages, interest payments and taxes (besides supplying goods and services), some complacency was visible across sectors in subsequent years.

ECONOMIC REFORMS AND INDUSTRIAL POLICY 1991

The Industrial Policy Resolution of 1956 (and subsequent modifications made therein over the years) was subjected to review in July, 1991. The highlights of the *Statement on Industrial Policy 1991*, in regard to public sector enterprises may be summarized as follows:

(i) Portfolio of public sector investments will be reviewed with a view to focus the public sector on strategic, high-tech and essential infrastructure. Whereas some reservation for the public sector is being retained there would be no bar for areas of exclusivity to be opened up to the private sector selectively. Similarly the public sector will also be allowed entry in areas not reserved for it.

(ii) Public enterprises which are chronically sick and which are unlikely to be turned around will, for the formulation of revival/rehabilitation schemes, be referred to the Board for Industrial and Financial Reconstruction (BIFR), or other similar high level institutions created for the purpose. A social security mechanism will be created to protect the interests of workers likely to be affected by such rehabilitation packages.

(iii) In order to raise resources and encourage wider public participation, a part of the government's shareholding in the public sector would be offered to mutual funds, financial institutions, general public and workers.

(iv) Boards of public sector companies would be made more professional and given greater powers.

(v) There will be a greater thrust on the performance improvement through the Memoranda of Understanding (MOU) system through which managements would be granted greater autonomy and will be held accountable. Technical expertise on the part of the Government would be upgraded to make the MOU negotiations and implementation more effective.

(vi) To facilitate a fuller discussion on performance, the MOU signed between the Government and the public enterprise would be placed in Parliament. While focusing on major management issues, this would also help place matters on day to day operations of public enterprises in their correct perspective.

IV
EMPOWERING THE PUBLIC SECTOR ENTERPRISES

Public sector enterprises have generally been set up in post-Independent India in the core sectors of steel, heavy industries, power, coal and fertilizer. Since most of these enterprises came under Schedule-A industries that created barriers to entry for the private sector, these enterprises had a monopoly status. All this changed with the Statement on Industrial Policy (1991), which reduced the number of industries exclusively reserved for the public sector. Barriers to entry leading to monopoly powers can still be created through 'patenting' and 'copyrights' that protect a new product from new entrants for a specified period of time. A larger share in the market (higher concentration ratio) and the status of 'key player' also accord monopoly power to enterprises. The price elasticity of demand of the product also influences the monopoly power of an enterprise, that is to say, greater the inelasticity of demand to a change in price greater is the monopoly power and vice versa.

PMR AND EMPOWERMENT

One of the advantages of being a monopoly (public sector or private sector) is the ability to charge a higher price for the product compared to a competitive firm. This has, however, been not generally the case in regard to the public sector enterprises in India as they have had to operate under the Administrative Price Mechanism (APM). Very often output prices have not been allowed to be raised under APM even when input prices went up; eliminating/squeezing in the process the expected 'normal profits' to such enterprises. The Industrial Policy Statement of 1991, therefore, emphasized on greater autonomy to the management of public sector enterprises. The APM was gradually dismantled and this has significantly improved the performance of public sector enterprises. Besides APM, there have been various other kinds of product market regulations (PMR), both at the state and at the all-India level, arising from the Essential Commodities Act (1955) under which the public sector enterprises have had to operate.

Consequent to 'economic liberalisation' and the opening of the Indian economy, moreover the public sector enterprises are faced with greater competition from within and without. The only way to survive and succeed is to become competitive. The Competition Act (2002) that was enacted in 2003, in this context, lays stress as much on 'fair trade practice' as on making the Indian industry competitive through removal of various 'controls' that have outlived their utility. It has been further observed that 'innovation and responsiveness to changing market demands require the ability to create new firms quickly. All levels of government should lower the barriers to entrepreneurship by re-engineering procedures to reduce administrative burden on new and existing firms and reduce the extent of inspections as well as the number of returns' (Economic Survey of India, OECD, 2007).

Withdrawal of such product market regulations (PMR) and barriers to trade can significantly improve the performance of public sector enterprises and can be an important source of their empowerment.

AUTONOMY AND EMPOWERMENT

The need for *a high measure of autonomy* by 'the technostructure' or 'the management' arises from 'the group decision making' character of large corporations. 'Decisions are arrived at after pooling information from several decisions and numerous individuals. In the absence of autonomy, the large corporation is vulnerable to any intervention by external authority, for given the nature of the *group decision-making and the problems being solved,* such external authority will always be *incompletely informed* and hence arbitrary' (Galbraith, 1967). Greater autonomy, in turn, refers to the independence in decision making *from the shareholders (whether private or government), other financiers and the labour unions.* Greater autonomy to 'mature corporations' is a common theme that cuts across countries, such as, U.K., U.S.A., Russia, China and France. In this respect, it is also claimed there is not much difference between the public and the private corporate sector if they qualify as *'mature corporations'*. As it has been observed, 'if an intelligent observer from Mars or Venus could come and examine all large contemporary industrial concerns—public or private—as working enterprises, he would notice, I suspect, only their overwhelming sameness' (Palmer, 1960).

MoU and Autonomy

Memorandum of Understanding (MoU), in relation to public sector enterprises, is a policy instrument aimed at providing greater autonomy to the public sector enterprises vis-à-vis the control of the government. MoU combines 'autonomy' of management with 'accountability' of public sector enterprises. MoU or 'performance contract', between the management of the public sector enterprise and the government, was first introduced in France consequent to the submission of the *Simon Nora Committee Report* in 1967. It was originally a medium term agreement (3-4 years) coinciding with the national plan and its targets. However, in line with the system of annual budgeting in the Ministry of Finance, the medium term contract has had to be subjected to annual review. While the MoU reduced the day to day intervention by the government in the functioning of the enterprise, it allowed the government to retain *a priori* control through setting the targets to be achieved by the enterprise in the beginning of the year as well as *a posteriori* control through performance evaluation at the end of the year.

MoU or 'performance contract' in this respect may appear rather restrictive as it compromises the autonomy that might be needed by the management of a large corporation. However, since public enterprises have been the result primarily of state plans; the government may be justified in ensuring that its objectives are achieved through these enterprises. At one level, both the government and the management are on the same side since the objective of higher economic growth is common to both. However, a situation can be visualized whereby the state may want supply of goods and services at a price that is below the economic cost. This will jeopardize the very survival of the enterprise. This will call for a commensurate compensation to the enterprise by way of 'subsidies' based on the subjective-normal price of the output, accounting for a notional level of capacity utilization. The MoU, therefore, provides for obligations on the part of the government in the form of the requisite support, both budgetary, and non-budgetary, to be given to the public sector enterprise.

Retained Profit and Autonomy

One of the important prerequisites *for retaining autonomy* is to be free from dependence on others for the financial support. The management of '*mature corporations*' are able to do this through *earning profits* and retaining part of the profits with the company by deciding not to distribute all profits as dividends to shareholders. A loss making enterprise, on the other hand, is dependent on the government and does not have this independence. The retained profits of a profit making company, in turn, guarantees freedom to the 'technostructure' or the management from the onslaught of all kinds of financiers, whether that be government, banks or financial institutions. 'It has full control over its own rate of expansion, over the nature of that expansion and over decision between product, plants and processes' (Galbraith, 1967). Central Public Sector Enterprises (CPSEs) investiture as 'Navaratna' companies, that is, Navaratna status given to CPSEs who have 'reserves and surplus', is very much akin to this feature of 'mature corporations'. Greater autonomy, under the Navaratna scheme, is delegated , in regard to, capital expenditure, organizational restructuring, diversification and joint ventures.

STRATEGIC PLANNING AND EMPOWERMENT

Since the large corporations are into business of operating on a large scale, *they cannot afford to fail in the market.* Very often, their effort is directed towards supplying product or service at a distant date; the risk of going wrong is far too great since it does not concern the immediate future. Strategic planning, in this context, helps minimize risk and market uncertainty. The three well documented strategies adopted by large corporations for reducing market uncertainty/market risks are noted to be (a) forward contract with buyers or sellers, (b) vertical integration and (c) aggressive advertising to win over customers. *Forward contract* is an agreement between the seller and the buyer in regard to both price and quantity; 'the agreement' thus removes the uncertainty arising from both price fluctuation and change in demand. Under 'vertical integration', on the other hand, the planning unit takes over the source of supply. This may involve merger between two firms. *Vertical integration*, thus, does away with the need for inviting tenders or negotiating price every time the input is required. This removes the associated uncertainty regarding strategic cost factors and makes the supply of input as part of a purely internal decision. *Advertising*, similarly, registers familiarity for the product or service amongst the buyers, and goes a long way in guaranteeing demand.

Diversification (Polyglot Corporation)

Yet, another way of reducing risk and incidence of failure is to diversify. Such a strategy qualifies a corporation to be called 'a polyglot corporation', since its large size combines diverse line of production and services. Numerous examples exist in this category like General Electric producing jet transports, submarines, telephones and refrigerators. Amongst the Indian companies, the Tatas, the NTPC and the Reliance Industries Limited belong to this category. Failure in one line of activity can thus be more than compensated by success in some other activity. The case of Nippon Steel is equally instructive as it reduced its steel output to focus on new activities. It is worth mentioning that public sector enterprises in India have generally focussed on the core sectors, leaving the entire consumer industries to the private sector. The Industrial Policy Statement of 1991 encourages entry of public sector enterprises to enter in areas not reserved for it.

Research and Development

More than competing firms, the large corporations face threat from new products, new way of doing things and new organizations (Ryon, 1994). In view of 'the product life cycle hypothesis', moreover, and the need to phase out products or to renew designs, research and development (R&D) is an integral part of strategic planning and an important source of empowerment. R&D may also be directed towards cost cutting measures enhancing the competitiveness of the enterprise. Technological Development (R&D) has, furthermore, to be supplemented by demand forecasting and market research to assess customer response. Market performance may be evaluated based on (a) stocks to sales ratio and (b) change in market share over time.

HUMAN RESOURCE DEVELOPMENT (HRD)

Recruitment of highly qualified people as engineers, scientists and other experts, has been the hallmark of Central Public Sector Enterprises (CPSEs). In addition to a fair and transparent recruitment policy, the CPSEs have had their own *training institutes* to keep their cadre up-to-date vis-à-vis *'the state of the art technology'*. In recent years, they have been encouraged to send their employees to training institutes other than their own institutes. While CPSEs based institutes are observed to focus on imparting training relevant to the enterprise, the stand alone institutes provide training in specialized fields of general nature. Useful training programmes are a tool for managing change and are seen to contribute more to increase in 'Total Factor Productivity' of an enterprise than increase in capital intensity.

Decision by Committees

In view of the complex nature of large scale operations and the well recognized inter-dependence of people on each other in 'mature corporations', decisions by Committees is considered as the best approach to follow. 'Association in a committee enables each member to come to know the intellectual resources and the reliability of his colleagues. Committee discussion enables members to pool information under circumstances which allow also, of immediate probing, assessing the relevance and reliability of the information offered. Uncertainty about one's information or error is revealed as in no other way' (Galbraith, 1967). This may also encompass the 'bottom-up approach' of consulting the various production units for formulating and finalising the corporate plan. In other words, greater the recourse to taking decisions through different committees/working groups, the more empowered is the organization.

MOTIVATION IN 'MATURE CORPORATIONS'

The motives of 'mature corporations' is observed to be co-terminous with the interests of employees who in turn recognize they are better off being part of the organization rather than when they are on their own. Maximization of profit for the shareholders may not generally motivate 'the technostructure' of large corporations, who may draw a fixed pay scale. Their interest in profits is either for profit linked bonuses, or for enhancing their corporate influence through reinvesting profits for further expansion. This is, however, in conflict with the shareholders/owners interests who are interested in higher dividends. Neglect of shareholders' interests, moreover, jeopardises the capability of the corporation to raise capital from the stock market. The conflicting interest of 'the technostructure' and the shareholders can, nonetheless, be resolved through linking the remuneration of 'the technostructure' to stock options. Higher dividend payout helps push up the market value of shares raising the valuation ratio (v), i.e, the ratio of 'the market value of shares' to 'the book value of the shares. Higher valuation ratio, in turn, provides security to technostructure from the threat of 'takeover' or 'merger' from predators leading to change in management. The interests of the management (the technostructure) and the shareholders in such a case coincide. The management, in such a situation, may have the temptation to manipulate the market value of shares, which leads to the related issue of corporate governance.

EMPOWERING PSEs AND CORPORATE GOVERNANCE

Corporations/Companies in India have to abide by the Companies Act, 1956 and the Securities and Exchange Board of India (SEBI) Act, 1992 etc. Accordingly, audited annual reports have to be submitted to the Registrar of Companies and all safeguards have to be taken to protect the interests of (retail/minority) shareholders. Essentially, the corporations are expected to uphold good business practice. The *Guidelines on Corporate Governance for CPSEs (2007)* acquires significance for public sector enterprises since it lays emphasis on the *professionalization of the Board of Directors*. The *Guidelines* also lays emphasis on transparency in the operations of CPSEs, regardless whether listed or not listed on stock exchanges. Emphasising the same point of view Dr. Manmohan Singh, Prime Minister of India observed, 'we must pay greater attention to how we identify "independent" directors and ensure that they are indeed truly independent "professionals" who bring with them both expertise and a reputation for good governance and high professional conduct" (Inaugural Address of the Prime Minister at the Chief Executive Conference of CPSEs; 8th March, 2007 New Delhi).

V
BRIEF OVERVIEW OF THE CONTENTS

The book has been organized into three parts, besides the Introduction. While Part-I covers the Inaugural Session, Part-II has the papers presented during the Technical Session and Part-III includes the Report of Adhoc Group of Experts on Empowerment of Central Public Sector Enterprises. The Hon'ble Prime Minister of India, Dr. Manmohan Singh inaugurated the Conference of Chief Executives of Central Public Sector Enterprises (CPSEs) on 8th March 2007, jointly organized by the Department of Public Enterprises and the Standing Conference of Public Enterprises. The Inaugural Session was presided over by the Hon'ble Minister. for Heavy Industries and Public Enterprises, Mr. Santosh Mohan Dev.

INAUGURAL SESSION

Welcoming the distinguished gathering, Dr. R.C. Panda, Secretary, Ministry of Heavy Industries and Public Enterprises outlined the main theme of the Conference namely '*Empowering Public Sector for Growth*'. He stated that public sector in India has achieved a great deal over the last half a century and more, especially during the last three years. The growth projection for the Eleventh Plan, moreover, provides a formidable space for the CPSEs in terms of investments. The objective of empowering public sector enterprises has to be to make them more competitive, vibrant and globally recognized.

The Hon'ble Minister, Heavy Industries and Public Enterprises, Mr. Santosh Mohan Dev in his address stated that the CPSEs have come a long way since the First Five Year Plan. He mentioned that as against an investment of Rs. 29 crores in 5 CPSEs during 1951, the investment has gone up to approximately Rs. 4 lakh crores in 245 CPSEs as on 31st March' 2006. He also outlined the performance of CPSEs in 2005-06 in terms of their reserves and surpluses, and contribution to the exchequer by way of dividend, taxes and duties. He further informed that the Government had approved 25 proposals for revival of sick CPSEs with a cash infusion of Rs. 2,000 crores and non-cash financial support of Rs. 5,700 crores. He informed that as many as 11 CPSEs, amongst the erstwhile sick and loss-making enterprises under the Department of Heavy Industries, have started paying salaries and wages to their employees on their own.

Amongst the proactive decisions taken by the Government for improving the CPSEs, he mentioned in particular, the followings: (i) delegation of enhanced financial powers to Navratna/Miniratna/other profit making CPSEs, (ii) provision of substantial budgetary support to sick CPSEs for meeting their salary/wages/statutory dues obligations, (iii) implementation of Counselling, Retraining and Redeployment (CRR) of employees separated from the enterprises with higher budgetary allocation. He furthermore advised the CPSEs to (a) build their risk taking capabilities in order to utilize their increased empowerment for decision making and (b) make larger investment in R&D and technological up-gradation so as to meet the challenge of local and global competition.

The Hon'ble Prime Minister in his inaugural speech stated that CPSEs continue to be the bulwark of our industrial system and are an engine of economic growth. He paid tributes to the competence and the commitment of workers, employees and management of these enterprises. He especially complimented the CPSEs for their improved physical and financial performance in the past two years. He observed that the Government's policy has been to remove all irritants in the way of the healthy functioning of the CPSEs. The Government has already taken several initiatives in this direction and more such initiatives will come in future. In regard to sick and loss-making CPSEs, he hoped that the Board for Reconstruction of Public Sector Enterprises (BRPSE) would come forward with time-bound programme(s) for revival of sick CPSEs so as to enable the Government to take early decisions on all such proposals.

The Hon'ble Prime Minister also advised the remaining non-listed CPSEs to get listed on the stock exchanges. He also advocated for greater professionalization of the Board of Directors and empowerment of Independent Directors. Since Independent Directors on the boards of CPSEs will significantly improve the decision-making processes, greater attention needed to be paid on identifying Independent Directors. He exhorted the CPSEs to evolve their own code of corporate ethics and to ensure adherence to such codes. With a view to enhance their competitiveness, he advised them to learn from the private sector and seize opportunities for mergers, acquisitions, amalgamations, takeovers and creating new joint ventures to become cost effective, increase market share and thereby create wealth for the society. He also advised the State Governments to find viable means to revive and sustain the State Level Public Enterprises. Finally, he congratulated the entire award winning CPSEs of MoU Excellence Awards as well as the SCOPE Awards, which he hoped should encourage them to do still better.

Thanking the Hon'ble Prime Minister for his gracious presence, Mr. S. Behuria, Chairman SCOPE, mentioned that the public sector need a decisive policy push to successfully take-off to a higher growth paradigm. He observed that the time had come for complete unshackling of the public sector to enable it to find its own place in the world market. On behalf of the entire public sector fraternity, he assured the Hon'ble Prime Minister that the public sector would continue to strive for excellence in their business operations as engines of economic growth.

TECHNICAL SESSION

The Hon'ble Minister of State for Commerce, Mr. Jairam Ramesh, chaired the Technical Session of the Conference. He also distributed the *MOU Excellence Certificates* to the selected Chief Executives of the CPSEs for the year 2004-05 and 2005-06. In his address, he stated that the multi-faceted role of CPSEs in India's overall development needs hardly any repetition. They are today into primary, secondary and services sector. Besides providing goods and services of all kinds, they have played a commendable role in the development of backward regions and have created (direct) jobs for more than a million people. He, nevertheless, mentioned that the CPSEs in India have had to work under control of all kinds. Their profit margin was often squeezed due to these overriding controls. In the eyes of the general public, however, the CPSEs were seen as inefficient performers.

He, moreover, observed that alongside the policy of public sector investment, there should be an exit/disinvestment policy. In this context, he cited the example of 'venture capitalists' that finance riskier ventures/enterprises, sit on its management as long as required and exit once the enterprise is successful. In view of a higher projected GDP growth rate in the Indian economy, he stated the country would soon experience shortage of trained manpower. He observed that the CPSEs have been paying greater attention to this aspect and have done great service to the country. The private sector in this respect has been far behind and will not invest in HRD in the near future because of uncertainty over retaining the manpower. The CPSEs can indeed bear the burden of training, but this needs to be done in a much more systematic manner.

Prof. M. Athreya's in his theme address drew attention to the (Indian) economy growing at the rate of 9-10 per cent per annum, which offered tremendous opportunity for the CPSEs to grow. He, however, cautioned that while Indian companies are good at planning, they are not so in the implementation; the CPSEs, in particular, need to reduce the project completion time. They also need to adopt *corporate management models* with global corporate objectives. He suggested a three-tier model for the management of CPSEs that will ensure the followings: (i) Administrative Ministry, Department of Public Enterprises, Cabinet, PMO etc to focus together on macro level Policy formulation, with respect to that sector (ii) Board of Directors, including the executive and non-executive directors, to focus on Governance, as per SEBI and other provisions, covering board committees, reports, disclosure etc. (iii) Day to day management to be left in the hands of the whole time directors accountable to the Board.

Mr. Arup Roy Choudhury, CMD, National Building Construction Corporation (NBCC) in his presentation mentioned about the poor status of the Company in 2001 when the salary unpaid was for almost six months. There was gloom all-round and the government took the decision to disinvest the company, which further demoralized the staff awaiting the *fait accompli* of closure. The management of the company subsequently made SWOT analysis and took various actions such as, (i) building confidence amongst employees, (ii) creating corporate values, (iii) focussing on the needs and satisfaction of customers, (iii) adhering to strict cost control, (iv) changing organizational structure, (v) higher delegation of powers and redrafting procedures to suit faster decision-making and (vi) proper fund management, etc. As a result, the company was able to increase its turnover from Rs.313 crores in 2000-01 to Rs.1,317 crores in 2005-06, with a net profit of

Rs. 28 crorer and a net worth of Rs.73 crores during the year (2005-06). He concluded that NBCC is a living example of how a CPSE on the brink of closure could turnaround through 'empowerment'.

Mr. V.C. Agrawal, Director (HR), Indian Oil Corporation (IOC) Limited in his presentation mentioned how IOC was able to utilize the powers granted by Government in 1986, 1987 and 1997 vis-à-vis 'autonomy' and thus transformed IOC into a Transnational Energy major. IOC was able to convert business opportunities into commercial successes through aligning human resource initiatives with business strategies. Besides earning profits, IOC has taken up a number of community development programmes for promoting education, health, and drinking water in less developed regions, and has also contributed towards preserving and promoting national heritage monuments. IOC has been also pursuing the Green Agenda by promoting Hydrogen-CNG, Bio-diesel, Ethanol blended petrol, etc.

Mr. G. Ojha, Director (Personnel), Steel Authority of India Limited (SAIL) in his presentation touched upon critical issues impinging on the empowerment of CPSEs. He mentioned that SAIL is the largest producer of steel with 32 per cent share in the domestic market and operates in a competitive environment. Its turnover and net profit for 2005-06 were of the order of Rs. 32,280 crores and Rs. 4,013 crores respectively. He briefly discussed the constraints being faced by CPSEs, such as (i) pressure from State Governments/political groups/local communities in the matter of providing employment, (ii) motivated complaints against senior management officials, (iii) difficulty in closure of unviable units due to pressure from employees, (iv) over-governance at operating level, resulting in lack of proactive decision making, etc. In the context of over-governance he drew attention to practical problems, such as, different set of customers who have to be accorded special treatment in a competitive environment. This often calls for subjectiveness in decision making, and uniform norms cannot be applied.

Mr. V.K. Agarwal, MD, RITES Limited in his presentation mentioned that RITES is a Miniratna Consultancy Company. RITES is ranked first in India and 64th in the world amongst the top 200 engineering consultants. It posted an all time high turnover of Rs. 414 crore, with a net profit of Rs. 101 crore during 2005-06. He, however, drew attention to the wide disparity in the emoluments of executives of CPSEs and the private corporate sector. CPSEs today are unable to attract the best talents at the entry level from IITs/IIMs and the high turnout (attrition) in RITES has led to low morale and poor motivation. He suggested that greater functional autonomy to Boards of CPSEs for deciding the compensation package for the public sector employees, especially in regard to (i) incentives like higher variable pay, (ii) stock option, (iii) profit sharing and, (iv) merger of DA with 50 per cent of basic pay.

Dr. R.C. Panda, Secretary, Department of Heavy industries and Public Enterprises in his presentation drew attention to the National Common Minimum Programme (NCMP), which calls for the strengthening and empowering the PSEs with full managerial and financial autonomy. Public enterprises have to be run as the Board-led organizations, having the highest concern for professionalism. Induction of Independent Directors has enhanced this professionalization. He, further, observed that enterprises flourish when there is a premium on 'entrepreneurship'. Too much regulation restricts entrepreneurial drive and makes the management risk averse. There is a need to empower the management suitably to speed up decision-making while at the same time adhering to the code of corporate conduct. He mentioned about the various initiatives taken by the Government, such as, the setting up the Ad-hoc Group of Experts (AGE) on Empowerment of CPSEs. He stated that the various recommendations of the Ad-hoc Group have already been implemented; these include, greater managerial and financial autonomy to the Navratna, Miniratna and profit making CPSEs.

REPORT OF ADHOC GROUP OF EXPERTS (AGE) ON EMPOWERMENT OF CPSES

The Government constituted the Adhoc Group of Experts to consider issues relating to empowerment of CPSEs in November 2004. The Group submitted its Report in April 2005. Amongst the various recommendations, the Report observed that 'the Ministry should not normally review the functioning of the company more than twice a year. Such reviews should be based on the reports of the relevant Board of Directors and selected major performance indicators. Since the profitability of CPSEs is influenced by several factors such as the administered price mechanism and fluctuation in international price of the commodities, the Group recommends that the Ministries concerned should develop CPSE-specific criteria to determine their overall performance, independent of profitability'.

It further stated that 'the Chief Executive should be entirely responsible for the day-to-day management and operation of the company under the overall supervision of the Board of Directors. The Management should be free to exercise all powers explicitly delegated by the Board of Directors. It should function under the supervision of the Chief Executive and Functional Directors on the Board. The Management should be responsible for the implementation of the decisions of the Board of Directors, and compliance of all statutory requirements as well as policy guidelines'.

It also observed that 'subject to statutory requirements, Government policy and regulatory guidelines issued by the RBI, the Board of Directors should have full powers of pursuing new lines of business, deciding on suitable acquisitions and mergers, setting up subsidiaries and exiting from any line of business, as also of making capital expenditure up to the levels indicated, without any prior clearance from the Government'.

In regard to investment decisions it recommended that 'the current restrictions regarding capital expenditures, joint ventures, etc. need to be done away with. Such decisions should be left entirely to the Board of Directors. However, if that is not possible at one stroke, as the first step towards this desirable goal, enhanced powers should be given to Navratna/Miniratna and other profit making companies in respect of capital expenditure, setting up of joint ventures (JVs)/ subsidiaries and subsequent investment in JVs. The Chief Executive of CPSE concerned should be a member of Search Committee for selection of non-official Directors'.

In relation to performance incentives, moreover, the Report observed that 'the Chief Executives and the Functional Directors should also be entitled to the performance linked bonus/incentive within the permissible limit of 5 per cent of the distributable profit. The Compensation Committee of the Board, as constituted under the 'Listing Agreement', should have the authority to decide on the quantum of such performance-linked incentives on the basis of individual's performance and contribution during the year under review. Such bonus/incentive would, however, be governed by the limits prescribed in the Companies Act'.

Part I
Inaugural Session

Inaugural Address

Hon'ble Dr. Manmohan Singh
Prime Minister of India

"I am delighted once again to have this opportunity to interact with some of the captains of our Public Sector Industry. Public Sector Enterprises constitute even today a bulwark of our industrial economy. At one time it was said that the Public Sector occupied the "commanding heights" of our economy. Today you share this space with a very dynamic entrepreneurial class and, in some sectors, with global multinationals. It is a testimony to the competitiveness of our Public Enterprises that in many of these sectors you have been able to stand your ground against fierce competition both internal competition as well as competition from abroad. This is a tribute to your managerial competence, to the dedication of your workers and employees and management to our joint national commitment to the revitalization of Public Enterprises as a major engine of India's economic growth.

I am happy to say that in these past two years you have done a creditable job in turning around many of our Public Enterprises. There has been an improvement in their financial and physical performance. I compliment you all for this solid achievement.

The revitalization of our Public Sector is an integral part of our strategy of promoting 'inclusive growth'. We regard the Public Sector truly as an engine of growth, a source of employment generation and as an important source of R&D in our industrial sector. Our Government's policy has been to remove all irritants coming in the way of the healthy functioning of our Public Enterprises. The National Common Minimum Programme (NCMP) outlines our commitment in this regard in unambiguous terms.

We recognize that the basic environment in which PSEs operate now has undergone tremendous and rapid change. I am glad that despite apprehensions on their survival, Public Sector Enterprises have valiantly accepted the challenge of competition, the challenge of rapid economic and social change, the challenge of rapid and often unpredictable technological change. This has helped them emerge stronger and more competitive.

The latest Annual Report of the Public Enterprises Survey for 2005-06 highlights growing importance and significance of the Public Sector in our economy. It also highlights the changing dynamics of their functioning. The management of change is the greater challenge facing our economy and the manner in which we meet this challenge will determine our responses to the challenges of change that Indian economy must learn to cope with in the years that lie ahead.

I am happy to see that many PSEs have registered handsome growth in their net profit, turnover, as well as contribution to national exchequer, and foreign exchange earnings. I am also happy to learn that the total number of loss making PSEs has fallen from 79 to 58 last year. I hope the Board for Reconstruction of PSEs (BRPSEs), will come forward with time bound programmes for revival of sick PSEs. It must help the Government take an early decision on all pending proposals.

Our commitment towards a stronger and vibrant Public Sector means we are committed to empowering the management of PSEs with full managerial and financial autonomy. Our Government has taken several initiatives to revitalize Public Enterprises and offer them greater financial and managerial autonomy. Autonomy is, of course, directly co-related to the issue of accountability. I am, therefore, happy to note that SCOPE has been emphasizing the need for improved corporate governance in our PSEs.

It may be useful for more Public Enterprises to be listed on the stock exchange, as this would enhance professionalization of the Board of Directors and empower Independent Directors. Induction of Independent Directors on the boards of PSEs would, I believe, ensure greater efficiency and effectiveness in decision-making processes as well. We must therefore pay greater attention to how we identify "independent" directors and ensure that they are indeed truly independent "professionals" who bring with them both expertise and a reputation for good governance and high professional conduct and also a faith in the continuing growth of the Public Sector in the service of our people.

It is wrong to assume that entrepreneurship is to be found only in the private sector. Public Enterprises too can and must foster entrepreneurship. But this requires an environment that encourages risk-taking, empowers professionalism and offers adequate freedom to the chief executive and his or her senior management to take quick and difficult decisions. Excessive regulation restricts entrepreneurial drive and makes management risk averse. That is not the way to go forward in the fast changing world full of uncertainty—the overall environment in which our Enterprises operate.

Public Enterprises should also evolve their own code of corporate ethics and conduct and ensure adherence to such codes. Our Government is working towards limiting the administrative ministries' role in the day-to-day management of Public Enterprises. I hope the steps we intend to take will help our Public Enterprises to become more globally competitive. That should be the ambition of all PSEs.

Going beyond organizational issues, Public Enterprises also need a new strategic vision. In the increasingly globalized world that they operate in now, they must learn from the private sector and seize opportunities for mergers, acquisitions, amalgamations, takeovers and creating new joint ventures. This should be an integral part of their business strategy to create value for their shareholder, become cost effective, reduce the cost of finance and increase their market share. I believe that many joint ventures and alliances both between Public Enterprises and between public and private enterprises are being worked out. That truly is a healthy development. Such joint ventures and public-private partnerships can help the Public Sector benefit from the private sector's competitive advantages wherever it might exist.

Apart from central Public Enterprises, there are hundreds of State Level Public Enterprises with vast sums of public money invested in them. They must also change and adapt to the needs of times. Given the state of State Government finances, many State Governments are unable to afford luxury of large number of loss making enterprises. We must therefore find viable means to revive and sustain such enterprises and ensure that the interests of workers and employees are not hurt due to political interference and bad management.

I am very happy to have given away the MoU Excellence Awards and SCOPE Awards to some of our best central Public Sector Enterprises and their top management. These awards should encourage our Public Enterprises to do better and aim higher. I congratulate all the Award winners."

Thank you! Jai Hind!

Keynote Address

Hon'ble Shri Santosh Mohan Dev
Minister of Heavy Industries & Public Enterprises

It is a great privilege and honour for us to have Hon'ble Prime Minister amongst us on this inauguration of the Chief Executive Conference and agreeing to give away the awards. Hon'ble Prime Minster's presence is a great source of inspiration. Prime Minister has guided the Public Sector development and growth in the past in his various capacities working in the Planning Commission, the Reserve Bank of India and the Ministry of Finance. Presently, as the Prime Minister, we look forward to his continuous guidance in relation to the Public Sector Enterprises in the country.

The CPSEs have come a long way since the First Five Year Plan. Beginning with 5 Public Enterprises in April 1951, numbers of CPSEs have reached 245 in April, 2006. Investment went up from Rs. 29 crores in 1951 to about Rs. 4 lakh crores in 2006. In 2005-06, the Public Enterprises with a turnover of about Rs. 8.3 lakh crores contributed to about 11 per cent of GDP.

The aggregate reserves and surpluses of all the CPSEs have reached about Rs. 3.6 lakh crores in 2005-06. The accumulated loss of the loss making CPSEs declined from about Rs. 84 thousand crores in 2004-05 to about Rs. 73 thousand crores in 2005-06.

The contribution of CPSEs to the Central exchequer by way of dividend, interest and taxes went up from about Rs. 1.25 lakh crores in 2004-05 to Rs. 1,25,384 crores in 2005-06. Dividend payment to Government showed the highest increase of 28 per cent over last year.

The Public Enterprises, on the whole, performed well during 2005-06. Under Prime Minister's leadership, there has been favourable economic environment for the Public Sector Enterprises. This calls for renewed thrust on the part of the Public Sector to face the challenge of competition. My Ministry will take proactive steps to facilitate improvement in the performance of Central Enterprises.

The Government has granted greater autonomy to the Navratna,

Miniratna and other profit-making enterprises as per the recommendations of the Ad-hoc Group of Experts (AGE). The Public Sector, in general, is required to go for financial restructuring and in-house improvement.

They also need to build the risk taking capabilities in order to effectively utilize their increased empowerment for decision making. This would require innovative thinking and strategic action for growth and development. Larger investment in R & D and technological up-gradation of the production range should be the priority for the enterprises to reach greater efficiency and meet the challenge of local and global competitiveness.

Sickness in Public Enterprises is being addressed by the Government. We look into the revival and restructuring of the sick and loss making Public Sector companies through a Board and take decisions. So far 25 such proposals under various Ministries have been approved by the Government with a cash infusion of about Rs. 2,000 crores and non-cash financial sacrifices of about Rs. 5,700 crores. Given this support and dedication of the workers and management, 11 CPSEs under the Ministry of Heavy Industries have started paying salaries and wages on their own.

Hon'ble Prime Minister has been pro-labour welfare. Substantial amount as, budgetary support, has been provided by the Government to sick Public Enterprises towards meeting their salary/wages and statutory obligations.

We have the responsibility towards the employees who take VRS. We provide financial and training support to mitigate their hardship in the best possible manner. In order to provide facilities for the rehabilitation of rationalized manpower separated from the Enterprises, my Ministry has been implementing the scheme of Counselling, Retraining and Redeployment (CRR). We have used about Rs. 100 crores under this scheme for about 1.1 lakh separated employees since inception of this scheme.

Hon'ble Prime Minister has been promoting the idea to delegate more powers to strengthen these enterprises. The Conference of Chief Executives of Public Sector Enterprises will debate some of the issues today and the theme of the deliberations is "Empowering Public Sector for Growth".

I am glad that SCOPE, as the apex Public Sector organization, has been proactive and progressive in facilitating further development of the Public Sector. Its initiatives on corporate governance, training and certification of directors, leadership for the Enterprises has been in the right direction. We assure all the PSEs of every support and cooperation in their endeavour to become globally competitive.

I congratulate the MoU Excellence Award Winners and SCOPE Award winners for the last 2 years, who will be receiving their awards from the Hon'ble Prime Minister.

Thank you! Jai Hind!

Welcome Address

R.C. Panda
Secretary, Ministry of Heavy Industries & Public Enterprises

It is my privilege to welcome Hon'ble Prime Minister to the annual Chief Executives Conference of the Central Public Sector Enterprises here today. Sir, you have been the guiding light of India's economic reform saga that has transformed our country into a potential economic super power. Sir, under your leadership, the government has reoriented its approach towards the Public Sector, opting to make it strong and vibrant. The Public Sector fraternity looks forward to your enlightening views and vision for empowering the Public Sector for its greater role in achieving higher and sustainable growth.

I welcome Hon'ble Minister for Heavy Industries and Public Enterprises Shri Santosh Mohan Dev Ji, He has been proactively promoting many policy improvements for creating conducive and favourable working environment for the PSEs and helping them to become more competitive and effective.

I welcome the Hon'ble Minister of State, Smt. Kanti Singh. Your presence is of immense importance to this Conference as you have been a source of guidance to these Enterprises.

With long active association with the Public Sector Shri T.K.A. Nair, Principal Secretary to the Prime Minister has become Friend, Philosopher and Guide to the Public Sector Enterprises, I welcome you Sir, to this function.

I welcome Shri B.K. Chaturvedi, Cabinet Secretary, Government of India for being a great source of inspiration and encouragement to all of us. Sir, you have been guiding the growth of CPSEs in many decision-making bodies. The Chief executives look forward to your continued support.

I take this opportunity to welcome Shri Sarthak Behuria, Chairman, SCOPE, Dr. Dewan, Director General SCOPE, all the Award Winners, distinguished Chief Executives and all eminent guests to this function.

The Public Sector has achieved a lot over last half a Century and more specifically during last three years. Many of these enterprises have won many accolades for their role in building nation's industrial and economic infrastructures. Sir, the country has been able to break through the Hindu rate of growth, and marching towards double digit growth rate. This is possible due to economic reforms and superlative performance of the Public Enterprises. The turnover of 245 enterprises has reached Rs. 8 lakh 32 thousand crore. Net profit grew by 23.26 per cent to reach Rs. 52 thousand 430 crore; they have earned Rs. 42,625 crore of foreign exchange and contributed Rs 1 lakh 19 thousand 6 hundred crore to Union exchequer.

The performance of the Central Public Enterprises is showing a northward trend. Result is visible. Twenty-five companies have been revived. Numbers of profit making enterprises are on the increase. Loss of the loss making corporations is on the decline. Sir, the executives of the CPSEs have been looking for their Pay Revision. They are extremely happy since you have set up the 2nd Pay Revision Committee.

The growth projections for the Eleventh Plan provide a formidable space for the CPSEs in terms of length, the investments and the momentum that they are required to provide to the growth agenda for the country. The approach paper to eleventh five-year plan has sought increased investment from the Public Sector in crucial infrastructure sectors of power, energy, communication and transport.

Today, doyens of the Public Sector have assembled here. 5 of them will receive MoU Excellence Awards for both 2004-05 and 2005-06 and 10 of them will get the Awards for either of the years and twelve will receive SCOPE Excellence Awards from the Honourable Prime Minister. Our heartiest congratulations to the Award winners. Sir, the inaugural function will be succeeded by a Technical Session of the Conference. Theme is "Empowering the Public Enterprises for Growth".

Once again I extend our warm greetings to dignitaries and welcome Hon'ble Prime Minister, Hon'ble Ministers, Principal Secretary to the Prime Minister, Cabinet Secretary and all the distinguished participants to this Conference.

Vote of Thanks

S. Behuria
Chairman, SCOPE

I consider it a privilege to propose the Vote of Thanks at the conclusion of the inaugural session. We are very fortunate and deeply honoured to have the Hon'ble Prime Minister amidst us this morning. Sir, your profound wisdom in matters of economic growth and industrial development has infused us with new optimism and ideas.

In your speech, we are extremely grateful to you for acknowledging the managerial competence and dedication of our employees in the face of fierce competition and the change management initiatives that we have taken in the public sector undertakings. Your thought of professionals on the board of directors and greater attention in induction of independent directors is extremely encouraging.

We are also grateful to you, Sir, for reposing your confidence in the capabilities of the public sector to face the challenges of global competition. On behalf of the entire public sector fraternity, I assure you that the public sector enterprises would continue to strive for excellence in their business operations as engines of economic growth of the country.

Sir, under your dynamic leadership and futuristic vision, public sector policy has become more favourable and proactive so as to make public sector enterprises strong, dynamic and vibrant. This enabling ambience has instilled a sense of confidence and trust among the central public sector enterprises, prompting them to perform even better. However, we feel that more changes are needed to make the public sector, as a whole, highly competitive and truly global. We have the opportunities, and we have the wherewithal, as demonstrated by our performance. We are, in fact, poised to soar to new heights of success. What we need is a decisive policy push to successfully take off to a higher growth paradigm.

"Sir, We at SCOPE believe that the time has come for complete unshackling of the public sector to enable it to find its own place in the world market. This would presuppose a higher degree of accountability, transparency and high standards of corporate governance. At public sector we feel that accountability would ensure greater transparency. As for corporate governance, we are progressively adopting the best corporate practice on our own. Similarly, it is not only the speed but the quality of decision-making that needs to be improved as well. And that can happen with greater empowerment of the Boards."

Our special thanks for your gracious presence of Honourable Prime Minister, we are indeed honoured sir.

Dear friends, we have in our midst today the Hon'ble Minister for Heavy Industries and Public Enterprises. We in the public sector fraternity are really fortunate to have a committed and forward-looking Minister in him to guide us. Sir, your foresight and pro-active approach have greatly helped us in ushering in favourable and conducive policy changes. We look forward to your continued support and guidance.

The presence of Smt. Kanti Singh has added value to this forum, we are all indebted for your kind presence Madam. Shri T.K.A. Nair has been a pillar of strength to the public sector undertakings. His passion and commitment to public sector undertakings has helped us immensely. We are indeed thankful to Shri B.K. Chaturvedi who has been facilitating the growth of Public Sector enterprises through empowerment. His presence here has reinforced the commitment of Government for the cause of Public Sector Enterprises.

The public sector enterprises have been looking at the light at the end of the tunnel, which was lit by none other than Dr. R.C. Panda. We are extremely thankful to you sir, for all your initiatives to make Public Sector Enterprises a global giant.

Today the Government has renewed its focus on agriculture and infrastructure to achieve higher GDP growth. The public sector is already very active in the infrastructure sector and ready to shoulder the responsibility of speeding up infrastructure development in the country. The Hon'ble Prime Minister's first interaction with PSE Chiefs at this very forum in the year 2004 brought about positive policy orientation. Sir, your visit here today has raised our hopes further and we look forward to consensual, continuous and consistent policy decisions to set the public sector on a journey to revitalize itself and become an effective catalyst of higher, sustainable and inclusive growth in the service of the nation.

Part II
Technical Session

Special Address

Hon'ble Shri Jairam Ramesh
Minister of State for Commerce

Dr. Panda, Secretary, Department of Heavy Industries and Public Enterprises, Dr. Athreya, Chief Executive Officers of Public Sector Enterprises and friends,

It gives me great pleasure to inaugurate this *Technical Session* on 'Empowering Public Sector for Growth'. First of all, congratulations to all the Chief Executives of CPSEs who have received the MoU Awards for their excellent performance during 2004-05 and 2005-06. I may mention here my long association with the MoU system. I am indeed very proud for having suggested the concept of 'Navratna Companies' amongst the CPSEs that continues to enjoy wide acceptance.

The multi-faceted role of Public Sector Enterprises in India's overall development needs hardly any repetition. They are today into primary, secondary and services sector. Besides providing goods and services of all kinds, they have played a commendable role in the development of backward regions and have created (direct) jobs for more than a million people.

The Public Sector Enterprises in India, however, have had to work under control of all kinds. For instance, the Administrative Price Mechanism (APM) did not permit the CPSEs to raise the output prices even when the input prices went up. Their profit margin was thus often squeezed due to these overriding controls. In the eyes of the general public, however, the Public Sector was seen as inefficient performers. There is, today, a paradigm shift in this respect as the APM has been lifted. The management of Public Sector, nevertheless, continues to be in shackles. The Public Sector Enterprises, like any commercial venture need to take risks. If, however, the management is in the fear of the Damocles sword of vigilance, no initiative will be taken. The Public Sector, therefore, needs to be made free from such restrictions. The Chief Vigilance Officer of CPSEs in any case, ought to be a person with commercial experience.

The MoU system was introduced in the late 1980's to introduce the necessary balance between *accountability* and *autonomy*. Although, there is a good deal of improvement in according autonomy to CPSEs, a lot more needs to be done if they have to become competitive and grow in the global market economy. There is need to change our mindsets and act quickly. If that cannot be done and these 'temples of modern India' have to survive, the only way out would be to privatize them!

I am also of the opinion that along with *investments in Public Sector Enterprises*, we should have a strong exit/disinvestment policy for Public Sector Enterprises. Public Sector Enterprises have been a *historical necessity*; the State in diverse countries have had to step in to make such investments because the private sector either did not exist or else it was not forthcoming to make the desired investments. Even today, the private sector may shun from making investments in backward regions. Under the circumstances, if a Public Sector Enterprise has been put on firm grounds and if there are people (private sector) willing to take it over, the Government may decide to sell the enterprise and exit. The role of the State under such a policy regime becomes similar to that of 'venture capitalist', who finances riskier ventures/enterprises with high returns, sits on its management as long as required and exits once the enterprise is successful. *The capital thus recovered from such sales is reinvested in newer enterprises*. The Government of India may consider emulating this model vis-à-vis its CPSEs.

Besides the commercial objective of wealth creation, the Public Sector Enterprises in India have had to achieve many a social objectives. To the extent the social objectives are in conflict with the commercial objectives, the State should subsidize the CPSEs for the same. The social overheads of the CPSEs should be quantified and the Government should provide the requisite *budgetary support* for compensating the CPSEs for meeting its social objectives.

Indeed, the record of Public Sector Enterprises in India, in some respects, has been much better than the private corporate sector. Many a CPSEs have been model employers, and the emphasis laid by them on training of their employees in various skills and management is something for the private corporate sector to learn from. In view of the higher GDP growth of the Indian economy, the country will soon face the shortage of skilled manpower. The contribution of the private corporate sector in this respect is almost negligible compared to the

Public Sector and the latter have often depended on the Public Sector for the trained manpower.

In the recent past, the issue of public-private-partnership (PPP) has also come to the fore. In my opinion, PPP should imply private finance for public projects. The aim should be to create public assets through private funds. Very often the opposite is happening, that is, public funds are being made available for private projects. There is no denying that there is a difference between *'infrastructure projects'* and *'social sector programmes'*, and there is no fault in public funds being made available for social programmes like 'education' and 'health services' if the results are better under PPP. PPP in 'infrastructure projects' is, however, commercially viable and these should have the major component of private financing.

Finally, I take this opportunity once again, to thank Dr. Panda, Secretary, Department of Public Enterprises for having invited me to speak on this occasion *and to thank you all for the patient hearing.* I am sure the different speakers will be touching upon other issues related to the theme of 'Empowerment of Public Sector Enterprises' during the Technical Session. I wish the Technical Session a great success.

Thank you. Jai Hind !

Empowering PSEs for Growth

*Mrityunjay Athreya**

The economic reforms in India can be broadly interpreted as the empowerment of Indian citizens as consumers, shareholders and employees; and of Indian entrepreneurs and managements. Public Sector Enterprises (PSEs) are very important national assets, accounting for a significant share of capital, sales, profits, jobs, social welfare etc. Their autonomy has been increasing over the years. There is scope for more empowerment, especially as the economy is on the threshold of sustained high growth. This paper is divided into six parts.

i) It begins by noting the globally acclaimed new "*story*" of not just the growth, but "*mega*" growth of the Indian economy.
ii) I share some personal *reminiscences* of my early involvements with PSEs, since 1967, when I joined the faculty of the Indian Institute of Management, Kolkata, on return from Harvard, after completing my Doctorate in Business Administration.
iii) I present my Corporate Management *Model*, with ten important, sequential elements.
iv) I hail *entrepreneurship* as part of the Indian DNA; and our national *competitive* advantage.
v) I look at what *more* and *better* PSEs can do, if they are more *unbound*.
vi) I conclude with *strategies* for further empowerment of our PSEs.

1. MEGA GROWTH STORY

An Indian Century

There are strong *domestic* forces of rising Indian productivity, savings,

* Formerly Professor at IIM, Kolkata; London Business School; and Scottish Business School. Chairman and Member of several GoI Committees. Fellow ICWAI, AIMA, HRD Network, ISTD, IMCI. Currently, Independent Management Advisor.

technology, management etc; and supportive *global* forces of demand, access, funds etc. which can sustain the Indian *mega* growth story for the next ten to twenty years. When I was invited to speak at an International Finance Conference in Hong Kong in 1995, I ventured a scenario of the 21st century being an Asian Century, while the 20th had been an American Century; and the 19th had been a European one. By 2000, in another Conference in Singapore, I could be more specific and speak of an India-China Century. More recently, it is being recognized that the Chinese government is attempting to moderate growth; and deal with issues of reserves; inflation; rational pricing; equity; civil liberties etc. The very lag in India's comparative growth is also now the great opportunity. There is talk of a trillion dollar opportunity in Indian infrastructure alone. Drilling down to another level, out of this trillion, the Power sector alone could absorb 300 billion dollars. At the next level, there are enormous opportunities in power equipment for a PSE like BHEL; in generation and transmission for a sister PSE like NTPC; and in distribution for several national, regional, state and metro enterprises. It is no surprise; therefore that the Prime Minister is reported to have suggested that BHEL should work three shifts.

Towards 10 per cent Growth

I said in the National Management Convention of the All Indian Management Association in 1980 that India was already capable of 8 per cent p.a. GNP growth rate, based on then rate of savings of about 24 per cent of GDP, if only we could achieve a capital output ratio of 3, based on a freer economy, less bottlenecks, better project management, and trade. Alas, that was not to be, for another decade or two. But now that we have liberalized; reduced procedural delays and transaction costs, 8 per cent has become the norm. We can now look at 10 per cent p.a. sustained growth. There are two major caveats. The double-digit growth has to be achieved without *inflation*. The RBI has been talking of lower and *lower* target rates of 5.5 per cent , 4 per cent and 3 per cent . Some are even arguing why not aim at the US and EU rates of about 2 per cent . The other caveat is that the growth has to be "*inclusive*", bringing benefits to the common people of all regions; communities, age groups etc. The CII Annual Conference of 2007 was on the theme of "Inclusive Growth". The Prime Minister presented his 10-point Social Charter, which has led to lively debate.

The PSEs have been, from the beginning committed to *social* objectives. They have been strengthening their record on the *commercial* objectives also.

Global Growth of 4 per cent Plus

Despite the long series of problems, such as the oil crisis, cold war, Afghanistan, 9/11, Iraq, Darfur, Iran, North Korea etc, the world economy has been remarkably resilient. The 4 BRIC economies of Brazil, Russia, India and China have emerged as new "locomotive economies". Japan is reviving from a decade of recession and deflation. The Eurozone is larger, with 27 countries, and growing faster. Germany is reviving up, shedding the tag of the "new sick man of Europe". The US is weathering the sub prime loans; huge trade deficits; and a falling dollar. The World Bank, IMF and OECD are optimistic on the world economy growing at an average of 4 per cent p.a. Even Afro pessimism is changing to some hope.

Rise of Emerging Markets

It is possible that without the high costs of Fascism, Stalinism, Maoism and the cold war, the world may have grown earlier with trade and shared prosperity. The underlying strengths and urges of the people of the world led to a number of growing emerging markets. First came Germany and Japan, rising from the ruins of the Second World War, in the 1950's. They were followed by the Asian Tigers; also called the NICs, the newly industrializing countries, in the 60's and 70's. With Deng's reforms, since 1979, China has emerged as the world's second largest economy, with massive exports, FDI, and GDP growth in double digits. India is now the hottest news, a large EM. There are others like Vietnam, Nigeria and South Africa.

Global Inter-Dependence

Like any system, globalization is not flawless. It has its pros and cons, advocates and critics. But, on balance all countries want to be in the trading system and not be left out of it. The presence of WTO and its dispute settling mechanisms help. While regions and countries bargain for own advantage, to the point of brinkmanship, in the current Doha round, they really have no option, but to conclude it soon, and live with the compromises till the next round. Similarly, the recent G8 plus Outreach 5 conference in Germany brought US commitment to be the part of a Global strategy to deal with warming. The next US administration appears likely to be a Democratic one, and even more cooperative on global issues. There is much at stake for all. So, India need not fear a sudden closure of export markets, and import sources.

2. PERSONAL REMINISCENCES

My interactions with PSEs have spread over four decades; from the time I joined the faculty of IIM, Kolkata in October 1967. I have seen their ups and downs; joys and sorrows; hopes and disappointments. But, overall it has been a journey of progress and great national contribution.

Involvement with PSEs

My exposure to PSEs was in myriad ways. Executives from PSEs came to the Management Development Programmes at the IIMC. That exposure led some of them to invite me to do in-house training programmes in their enterprises. That triggered, in some cases, a consulting assignment on their Corporate Plan; Organization Structure, Planning & Control Systems, HRD etc. Based on these enterprises, I could contribute to the seminars and conferences of the Management Associations, Chambers and other professional institutions like CA, Costing, and CS etc. The visibility led to invitations to be a Member of Government Committees on PSEs. An early experience was to be on the Committee on Indian Airlines, in 1971, when Dr. Karan Singh was the Union Minister for Civil Aviation and Tourism. Membership followed on the Fazal, Dutt and other committees. In 1991, I was Chairman of the Telecom Restructuring Committee, which has led to the telecom revolution and aided the IT boom.

Golden Ages of PSEs

Individual PSEs have had their golden ages. 1960s and 70s were great for steel. I remember consulting with Mr. Mantosh Sondhi and his top team in the structuring and training for the new Bokaro Steel Plant. The individual steel plants had their strengths and weaknesses. Under Mohan Kumaramangalam, Steel Minister, the Holding company idea was adopted. SAIL was formed. Today it is a listed company, with a good market capitalization. Considering the power needs of the growing economy, government decided to set up NTPC as a central

PSE for thermal power generation, with understandable opposition from the State Electricity Boards. I have worked with the founder CMD Mr. D.V. Kapur, and several of his successors till today when it is becoming a broader power company, using several different fuels—Coal, Gas, Hydro, and hopefully nuclear, after the historic Indo-US Nuclear Agreement. I enjoyed working with BHEL in the preparation of its Growth Perspective, 1981-1990, and later exercises of Mission, Vision, Values and Structures. I had a long association with IOC, implementing my Corporate Development Model, as a blend of the more rational Strategic Management component, and the more behavioural, people oriented Organisation Development component. Thousands of IOC executives knew the equation SM+OD = CD. These are by way of examples, and far from exhaustive.

Growth–Decline–Turnarounds

Even during the pre-reform period of 1950-1990, there has always been some competition. PSEs have done well against such competition, during some periods; but have also gone down at other times. In the 1970s and 80s HMT for example, was a national byword for machine tools, tractors, watches etc. It was sad to see its decline in the 1990's, followed by restructuring and recovery of some of the businesses. Similarly, SAIL ran into high-accumulated losses by 1985. Government of India brought in Dr. V Krishnamurthi as Chairman. I had earlier interacted with him in BHEL and Maruti. It was a great challenge and a task of deep satisfaction to help him and his Corporate and plant top/senior management teams in a massive turnaround. It involved interactions with large groups of engineers, executives, supervisors, workmen, unions etc. The system of MOU between SAIL and the Ministry was extended to the next level, between SAIL and each plant. It was based on the concept of APP, an Annual Performance Plan, not just a Production plan. Performance metrics included equipment availability, utilisation, energy consumption, quality, cost, customer service etc. The employees well understood that the top management can not ask the government for funds for Modernization of the old plants, without a substantial improvement in the work culture and results. There was a revolution in belongingness, ownership, discipline and performance. Even good PSEs like IOC, ONGC, and NTPC etc. have gone through bad patches when there were succession battles, gaps etc.

Membership of Committees

Even within an enterprise, there are differences in views about the values and dangers of committees. The scepticism is even more with respect to government committees. Some perceive it as a way of sidetracking or burying an issue; postponing or avoiding difficult decisions, playing for time etc. With a good leader and committed members, committees make valuable contributions. I have joined all the government committees, whenever invited, with passion and enthusiasm. Although not all recommendations are implemented; even those implemented not fully, not on time, still over the decades, one has seen positive changes. I believe the duty of a Chairman and members is to put the best recommendations on the table. The seeds are sown. They will sprout sooner or later. Initial progress may be slow. Then, it could become exponential and catch up. This is what has happened to the recommendations of the Athreya Committee on Telecom Restructuring in 1991. The report appeared to be shelved for about a year. Then in 1992, the Value Added Services of Pagers and Cell phones were opened up. MTNL survived as a PSE, without being merged back into the DoT, as some wanted. The rest of DoT operations have been corporatized into the massive BSNL. Heavens have not fallen. On the contrary Indian telecom has undergone a revolution. It is the world's hottest cell phone market now. There is healthy public-private competition, as well as partnership. It is the kind of change we need to see in Power and other infrastructure areas.

Disappointments and Hopes

The main disappointment, from a professional management perspective is that while our PSEs have done well, they could have done better, much better. It is the difference between "*satisfactory*" performance and "*optimal*" performance. There have been three major constraints on PSE's—their own internal *weaknesses*; an overly controlled Indian economic *environment*; and complexities in their *governance*, due to a multiplicity of agencies—the Board, Ministry, Cabinet, Parliament, CAG, CVC etc. Many PSEs have developed their Vision, Mission, Values, Strategies, Structures, Systems, Processes and talent. The Indian environment is now liberalised and globalized, with lot of opportunities. It is the third factor that is a *relative* handicap to PSEs, vis-à-vis their private sector competitors and MNCs. This Theme Address, therefore, is well chosen to deal with this crucial issue of *empowerment* of PSEs.

3. CORPORATE MANAGEMENT MODEL

In my consulting work in India and abroad, I have followed a comprehensive model, shown in Figure 1. The logic flows as follows:

Corporate Management Model

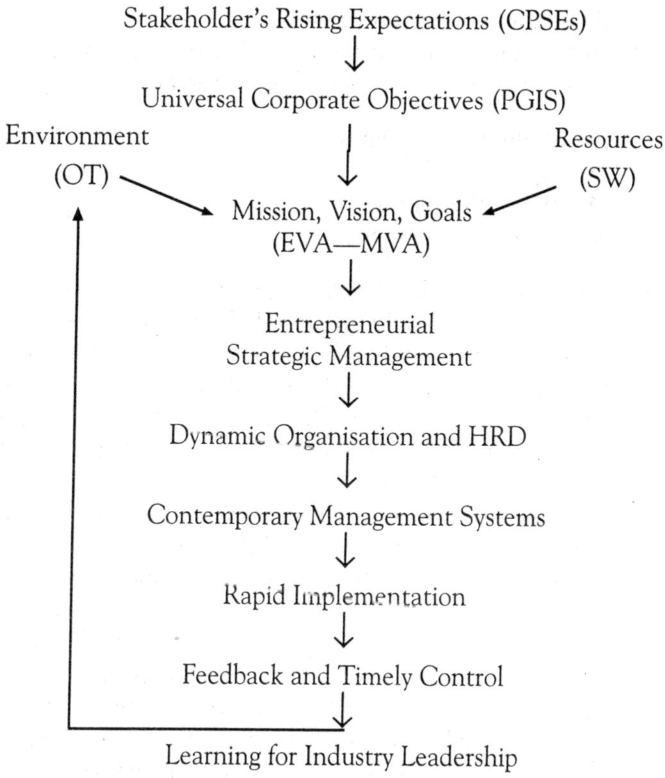

FIGURE 1

i) All businesses have the following stakeholders:

- ❖ Customers
- ❖ Shareholders
- ❖ Employees
- ❖ Society

Indian PSEs were probably more *Government* focused in the 1960's; and *employee*-driven in the 70's and 80's. For their sheer survival, now they have to meet global *Customer* needs and satisfy *shareholders* to attract more funds. There has to be an internal *partnership* between management and employees, as *Trustees*, serving the *external* stakeholders, and thereby deserving their own rewards.

ii) Independent of a promoter, private or government, all enterprises have to achieve four universal objectives.

- Profitability/Viability
- Growth
- Image/Reputation
- Survival/Continuity

iii) There are countless business opportunities. Every enterprise has to choose. Results are a product of focus and energy. The Mission statement defines the business we are in. PSEs tend to be large. They need to be guided by a long term Vision, for the next ten years plus. The Annual Budget is not enough. They should have Sales, Profit and a few other key goals for the next 3 to 5 years, as milestones.

iv) The ultimate summation into a single convenient numerical goal is the Market Value Added (MVA) for a listed PSE. As a surrogate, it should also look at the Economic Value Added (EVA), which is independent of short-term share price variations. The degree of stretch in the goals will depend on the opportunities and threats in the environment.

v) The longer the time frame, resources can be mobilised. But organisational weaknesses will erode the resources. Strengths have to be developed into competitive advantages.

vi) India's national planning was initially more *directive*. It has become more *indicative* for the market sector. Leaders in politics and administration need to appreciate that the PSEs are more and more in the market sector. Therefore, they need to display *entrepreneurial* strategic management. For this, they need more empowerment.

vii) PSEs also need freedom to structure and restructure their organisations and human resource systems and politics to cope with domestic and global competition.

viii) PSEs need to leverage the best of IT in their Planning, Operating, Information and Control Systems.
ix) PSEs also have a systemic disadvantage in the speed of execution of projects and programmes.
x) PSEs should be free to learn and act on the lessons from market feedback.

4. ENTREPRENEURSHIP, OUR NCA

At the PSE level, we talk of a firm's competitive advantage. At country level, we need to identify "National Competitive Advantages" (NCA). One of these, for India, is "entrepreneurship". A major challenge in rebuilding the Russian economy, after Glasnost and Perestroika, has been the slow process of developing entrepreneurship. China had lost this strength during the GPCR of Mao. Much of their business thrust and FDI have come from Hong Kong, Overseas Chinese, and PRC-Returnees.

Shiva-Schumpeter Economics

While some of Marx's critique and social goals are relevant, his core economic ideas, especially the hypotheses of impoverisation of the workers, irreconcilable class conflict, and dictatorship of the proletariat have been tried and given up by history. After World War II, the economics of Keynes gained some currency. It came under question because of the perceived fears of lower motivation and productivity, and higher inflation, or worse, stagflation. The Monetary economics of Friedman has had its run. Money supply is an important variable, but it is not all. Growth and price stability are both important. In the current borderless, globally open, competitive, single market economy, the economics of Joseph Schumpeter appears more relevant. He stressed innovation, and creative destruction for re-creation. This is very much the grand principle of Shiva, the Destroyer, as well as the Cosmic Dancer. National and global economies now grow through a process of research, new products and processes, in response to customer needs. Financial, Human and other resources flow into the successful players.

Entrepreneur at the Core

Today's business can not be run purely by the administrative processes. The corporate locomotive is entrepreneurship. The traditional promoter and his successors are steeped in this environment of entrepreneurship. But it is not limited to them. Senior/top executives have to become "*intrapreneurs*", i.e., entrepreneurs incubated within the enterprise. Such intrapreneurs are needed not only at the corporate headquarters, but in each of its Businesses; and major locations. As PSEs go global, they will need Regional Directors, who are their entrepreneurs for each Region, and Country Managers, likewise for their countries of responsibility. In a bottom-up and top-down interactive process, it is the Business and Geography heads who have to enrich the basket of strategic options.

Entrepreneurship in the Indian DNA

It is a known historical fact that India was a great trading nation, millennia ago. At one point it had a 25 per cent share of world trade. *Vaishya dharma*, the duties of the business community, has been a recognized element of multi-layer, multi-faceted *dharma*, that which upholds the entire social fabric. It was part of *Raja dharma* to create the environment conducive for business. So it was not an accident that during the freedom movement, not only political leadership, but also business leadership was thrown up, in the form of Jamshedji Tata, GD Birla, Singhania, Bajaj, Walchand, Chettiar and others. At the individual level, *artha*, wealth is a legitimate, unapologetic element of the four *Purushaarthas*, human life goals.

Latent in PSEs

At first sight, one may wonder where is entrepreneurship in PSEs?; is there any scope for it?; is there is even a need for it?! Indeed, there is entrepreneurial *agni* (fire) in PSEs. It is latent. Some of it has got out. Much of it is still struggling. Mature PSEs have gone through the following phases:

Phase 1 —	1950 & 60's —	Merely the 'Implementers' of Projects already 'decided' by the GoI, Ministry or Planning Commission.
Phase 2 —	1970's —	"Conceptualising" Projects for the country's needs felt by the Government.
Phase 3 —	1980's —	Proposing Expansion and Diversification Projects.
Phase 4 —	1990's+ —	Proposing Strategic Alliances, JVs and Projects overseas.

As shown by the freer Indian private sector sister corporations, there is scope & great need for the actualisation of much more of the entrepreneurial potential of PSEs.

Unleash it for Growth

This latent entrepreneurial DNA in PSEs needs to be unleashed. They are, by and large, in Core Sectors—Power; Hydrocarbons; Steel; Non-Ferrous; Fertilisers; Capital Goods etc. For India to reach and sustain a 10 per cent growth rate, the removal of infrastructure bottlenecks; provision of capital equipment; revolutionising agriculture etc are needed. To offset the rising trade deficit, PSEs also need to raise their share of exports, and remittances of dividends from their overseas operations.

5. PSEs UNBOUND

If more empowered, our PSEs can contribute much more, from their huge base of knowledge, human, capital and physical resources. The following is an indicative list.

20 per cent + Growth with 3 BL

Many PSEs can achieve 20 per cent or more growth in their sales turnover value, net of inflation, in real terms. That will contribute towards a industrial growth rate of 14 per cent for the economy, moving it towards the 10 per cent GNP growth. They have to not only achieve the above top line growth, but also do it efficiently and profitably. They should fulfil the expectations of the Triple Bottom-line Model (3BL). These are:

i) Financial BL, as reflected in RoCE, EVA, MVA etc.
ii) Social BL, in terms of their CSR, Corporate Social Responsibility, to make the growth more inclusive.
iii) Ecological BL, to help preserve the physical environment, under threat of global warming.

Multiplier Impacts

When our leading PSEs grow at nearer their potential, they will carry with them their several hundred, or even thousands of vendors and dealers, who will grow along with them. As is well known, the medium and smaller businesses tend to create more jobs per unit of capital investment. The jobs will bring not only earnings, but also dignity and hope, to more of the population, in a decentralised manner.

Global Markets and Sources

A major potential benefit for all national economies of the world, from globalisation is that they can optimise their performance in two more ways—

i) Export to overseas markets where there is a combination of demand, better prices and margins.
ii) Import from anywhere in the world; where one gets better prices, delivery, service etc. consistent with a specified quality level.

During the licence raj, a belief system had developed in India that importing was *paapam* (sin) and exporting was *punyam* (virtue). If all countries took this view, there will be much less trade, and all will be losers. The PSEs had been susceptible to another belief, that of self-sufficiency, making everything in house, or at least indigenously. This is beginning to give way to more openness. With empowerment, they can become more aggressive on exports and global procurement.

Mergers and Acquisitions (M&A)

When PSEs are more empowered they can grow faster not only through organic, internal effort, but also by mergers and acquisitions. For this, they need three kinds of strategic freedom. First, corporate strategy to identify the right targets for takeover, whether in India or in any part of the world. Secondly, the Financial strategy, to fix the right price to pay for the chosen target; the mix of payment of shares, cash etc; and the mode of financing, internal funds, FPO, debt etc. Thirdly, the HR strategy to integrate the two organizations, rightsizing, offshoring etc.

Industry Leadership

Given their early start; long learning curve; cumulative investments etc., PSEs ought to be leaders in their respective industries. With the new found dynamism in the Indian private sector, and the rush of MNCs, it may not be possible for a PSE to be "the" leader in its industry, but it can be one of the top, say 3 or 5 players, depending on the structure of that sector.

6. EMPOWERING STRATEGIES

Having made the *case* for more empowerment of PSEs and what they can *deliver* to the Indian economy, I conclude with *recommendations* of the Strategies that Government should adopt and implement, as fast as possible, for such empowerment.

3 Tier Model

I advocate the 3 tier model, shown in Figure 2 with clear and distinct roles:

Figure 2

i) The Government of India, including the Administrative Ministry, DPE, sister Ministries, Cabinet, PMO etc together to focus on macro level *POLICY* formulation, with respect to that sector.
ii) The Board of Directors, including the executive and non-executive directors, to focus on *GOVERNANCE*, as per SEBI and other provisions, covering board committees, reports, disclosure etc.
iii) The day-to-day *MANAGEMENT* to be left in the hands of the whole time directors, leading the executives and employees; accountable to the Board.

Out of CAG and Vigilance

Most PSEs have CFOs, Chief Financial Officers, with contemporary qualifications, with teams of qualified accountants and staff. There is Internal Audit, as well as the Statutory Audit, by a firm of CAs. The Board's Audit Committee is charged with the role of helping the Board with all financial aspects of Governance. In addition, the pressures of competition and the adoption of core values, culture, code of conduct etc will greatly reduce the scope for errors and malpractices. The CAG and Vigilance have played their role in the earlier decades. They may now be relieved of this additional load, so that they can focus on the rising central, state and local public expenditures, projects and programmes. Necessary amendments of laws should be made. The courts will, naturally, go by the new laws, exempting PSEs from CAG and Vigilance. Equity demands that the Board and Management be already accountable to multiple stakeholders, including especially, customers; institutional and individual, Indian and foreign shareholders; the local communities, where they operate; the broader public, etc.

Dividends and Disinvestment

PSEs will, of course, continue to contribute to the government coffers, to help fund important social programmes for inclusive growth. Indeed, as they grow, domestically and globally, more aggressively, through empowerment, their contribution will rise even more. As corporate, they will pay more direct and indirect taxes and levies. There will be two other rising streams—dividends; and disinvestment.

i) Dividends have to be assessed in terms of the "yield", percentage on the market price of a listed PSE; or similar shadow price of an unlisted one. The par value of a share has no real meaning. Dividend is more meaningful, not as a percentage on the par value, but as rupees per share, which can, then be related to the share price. Listed PSEs can also increase the actual dividend amount by issuing bonus shares; doing share splits etc. The upper limits are provided by the need for investment in research, brand building, HRD and expansion. Government would not want to erode the growth capacity and market leadership of the PSEs.
ii) It has been well recognised that 100 per cent ownership, or even 76 per cent is not needed for policy control of a PSE. Currently, the GoI policy appears to be to retain 51 per cent. In many PSEs, this gives tremendous scope for raising funds, as and when needed, for important social programmes. In some PSEs, even a 5 per cent sale can raise a significant sum. In the longer run, as share ownership get broader based in our deepening capital markets, even a holding of 26 per cent is enough for veto power.

Compensation, Values and Joy

In the current environment, PSEs face several kinds of competition. Of these, two are fierce. One is for the customer. The other is the "war for talent". Part of the talent for the rapid growth of the private sector, in almost all industries, has come from our PSEs. In the case of sectors recently thrown open for private sector participation, much of the senior management has come from the PSEs. While this may be a gain for the nation, as a whole, it is a drain on the PSEs. They should not only be able to retain existing talent, but attract more, especially at the entry points, against competition, in a market of overall shortage of the desired competencies. For this, they have to offer competitive compensation; not necessarily the highest, but governed more by the market than by the Pay Commission and other administrative awards and comparisons. They should also be allowed to create wholesome corporate cultures, with values congruent with talent, and untainted by extraneous influences. They should be able to offer QWL, quality of work life, including job satisfaction, scope for professional development and joy at work.

Parliament Questions

In a democracy, a government in power is accountable to the legislature on all policy matters. A convention should be developed, between all our political parties and their MPs, as in France, Britain, Scandinavia and elsewhere, that no operational questions about PSEs will be raised in Parliament. The management should feel empowered to make sound business judgements, without fear of repercussions from certain groups, outside and inside and enterprise, by misleading some legislators, for their sectional gains. All legitimate expectations should be taken care of by the PSE's own projects and CSR, and the government's social programmes. The cost of Parliamentary questions on details is much more than the time and effort taken to answer them, but the hidden cost of paralysis of sound business decision-making, as in the case of vigilance and CAG audit.

CONCLUSION

As a nation, we have done all the hard work in building a fine set of PSEs. Their potentials to contribute to national growth; jobs; exports; revenues; innovation etc are still underutilised; although better utilised than about ten to twenty years ago. We have before us the grand, historic opportunity of creating an Indian century. We can sustain double-digit growth, with acceptable inflation. For this we have to improve infrastructure, capital goods supply, human development, IPR, etc PSEs can make a greater vital contribution. It will be great statesmanship to empower them. In this Theme Address, I have tried to suggest ways of igniting their entrepreneurial energies for growth, through creative destruction, innovation, and recreation, like the cosmic dance of Shiva.

A Road Map to Success: The Story of NBCC

Arup Roy Choudhary[*]

National Buildings Construction Corporation Limited was incorporated as a Public Sector Undertaking in 1960 under the aegis of the Ministry of Works and Housing; now renamed as Ministry of Urban Development. In 2001 the Corporation had almost been written off, the order book was just sufficient for a years' working and there were a plethora of disgruntled Customers, Clients and Employees. The bleak prospects that waited were underscored as unpaid salary bills, notices for non-payment of statutory dues and works which were grinding to a halt all existed together.

It was from this certain brink of doom that the Corporation was steered to be a successful and sustainable organization. From a meagre turnover of less than Rs. 0.50 Crores in sixties, NBCC has grown to a premier construction company of the country with a turnover of around Rs.1,513 Crore as on March 07, having an order book of Rs.3,523 Crores as on date. The authorized and paid-up capital have also enhanced to Rs.120.00 Crores from Rs. 19.95 Crores as in 1997-1998. In a short span of five years the Earning per Share (EPS) has grown ten-fold from Rs.30.46 to Rs.311.50.

NBCC presently operates in a wide spectrum of projects of construction industry such as mass housing projects, institutional buildings, runways and roads, hospitals, bridges and flyovers as also in highly specialized works like power plants, chimneys and cooling towers, ash/material handling systems, sewage treatment plants, water treatment plants, water supply pipeline networks, and marine structures. The Corporation executes Engineering Procurement and Construction (EPC) projects, Project Management Consultancy Services. Projects including construction of large value projects on

---

* Chairman-cum-Managing Director, National Building Construction Corporation Limited.

turnkey basis, etc. not only in the domestic front but also in the international arena in competition with various international companies. It is the Corporation's privilege to have been entrusted with priority works of the Ministry of Home Affairs such as Indo-Bangladesh and Indo-Pakistan Border Fencing and Road Works, Married Accommodation Project (MAP) of the Ministry of Defence etc. The Corporation also operates in the North-Eastern Region of our country where it is currently executing 68 projects valued at Rs.1,014 crore as on 31.3.2006. Due to vast experience and quality of services rendered by NBCC a number of Central Government Ministries and various State Governments have entrusted NBCC with a variety of projects and consider it as their extended engineering arm.

Since inception NBCC has executed work valuing Rs.7,314 Crores in the domestic as well as international market as on 2005-06 as per the Rupee rate prevailing at that time. Half of this has been contributed by a resurgent corporation in the last 5 years.

The performance of NBCC was sluggish, however, from the financial year 2001-02, it has made a complete turn around and this period witnessed spectacular growth in turnover and financial performance. The major financial parameters have demonstrated treble and quadruple growth as under:

	2000-01	*2006-07*	*% age growth*
Turnover (Rs Cr)	313.29	1512.87	382.90
Gross Profit (Rs Cr)	15.49	129.65	736.99
Profit before Tax (Rs Cr)	124.58	2.55	4785.49
Profit after Tax (Rs Cr)	80.58	2.49	3136.14
Net worth (Rs Cr)	(-) 4.03	151.79	3866.50
EPS (Rs)	30.46	895.33	2839.36
Income per Employees (Rs Cr)	0.10	0.62	420.00
Bank borrowing (Rs Cr)	35.83	Nil	(-)

Although the Corporation has 9 recognized unions, not a single man-day was lost during last seven years due to any industrial dispute.

The growth in the performance of NBCC has been due to the efforts made in:

- Goal reorientation of the Organization.
- Creation of vibrant teams with clear-cut goals & measurable targets.
- Decentralization of Operations.

- System of obtaining Customer Feedback Form so as to understand the areas for improvement.
- Composition of two-level committees for evaluation and recommendation for tenders.
- Diversification of activities in the areas of strength and gradual reduction in activities from areas of weakness.
- Greater participation at junior management level by increasing the number of profit centres from 10 to 75 through introduction of modern management techniques in laying down targets and monitoring their achievements.
- Streamlining operations, procedures and induction of modern quality management backed by a Quality Manual.
- Improving clients & customer interaction and paying special attention to customer feedback.

The aforesaid efforts have resulted in up-gradation of MOU rating of the Corporation from Good to Excellent for the last three consecutive years. Prior to setting goals, a process of retrospection was initiated. One strong factor that emerged was that the Administrative Ministry, Ministry of Urban Development was very supportive; a "hands off" policy prevailed. This was a great fortune as it enabled a Board of Directors who were fully empowered to take decisions based on professional and commercial interests. A SWOT analysis for the organization was undertaken to understand the Strengths, Weaknesses, Opportunities and Threats.

From an environmental scanning the opportunities that presented themselves were prioritized. "Success of Honest Intentions", which was a universal phenomenon, was relied upon for convincing clients who were on the fence to entrust works to NBCC. Individuals were chosen as change agents and their self-goals were aligned with organizational goals. The middle level management which seethed with feelings of helplessness, bitterness, inadequacy and loss of self-confidence were nurtured and a pride of accomplishment was drilled into them.

A detailed and intensive interaction was held with employees at all levels as also with trade unions. Separate discussions were also held with NBCC's clients, those who had stayed with the organization and also those who had over the years withdrawn from it. From the findings, the following goals were set and the CMD personally engaged himself working on these goals relentlessly to achieve an impressive turnaround of NBCC to be one of the Industry leaders.

- To ensure good governance practice emphasis was given on observing transparency, accountability and proper disclosure. This resulted in employees following rules and procedures and paying attention to proper documentation at all levels.
- To improve Unique Selling Preposition (USP) of the Corporation for delivering high quality projects within time and cost. There has been an appreciable improvement in the USP of the Corporation and the client organizations have started approaching the corporation for taking up their works on repeat order basis. Now clients are calling NBCC and visiting our Head Office to pursue us to undertake their prestigious projects.
- To improve customer relationship and strive for customer satisfaction by a proactive approach. Now a number of Central Government Ministries and Departments, PSEs and various State Governments are utilising NBCC as their extended engineering arm.
- Selective and accurate tendering, operating in large value projects and in high-profit sectors like Energy, Transportation and Environment which have less competition and involve modern technology. The result has been to procure large value projects in lesser number of locations enabling better control, faster completion and increased margin.
- Expansion of business in Project Management & Consultancy including execution of projects on turnkey basis resulted in high liquidity and increased profitability by capitalizing on ISO 9001 accreditation.
- Entering in the field of large value Engineering Procurement & Construction (EPC) projects utilizing NBCC experience and core competence in power sector and improved market image, resulted in increased marginal profitability in addition to professional satisfaction.
- Changing mind set of the organization and improving its credibility as a techno-professional body with a defined commercial culture and outlook. Now all levels of employees have a sense of belonging to the organization and will generally comply with requirements of projects specific mobility.
- 180° reversal in operation style shifting the order of importance and priorities to SUZH (site-unit-zone-head office) from HZUS (head office-zone-unit-site) since it is sites and units

who actually execute projects and earn profits. This participative management involving units in the decision making process has led to better all round performance.

- Modernization of monitoring and communication system by introducing Modern Project Management Concepts and exploiting development in information technology sector by adopting computerized monitoring through Local Area Network, Web based online monitoring systems etc.
- Mandatory introduction of Cost-to-Completion (CTC) concept at the time of start of projects and reviewing the same at intermediate stages of project. Focus thus always remains on the bottom-line for improved cost control and increase in profitability.
- Improving the financial health of the organization by laying thrust on Real Estate Development. Significant numbers of Real Estate projects are under execution and in the pipe line.

Gradually the Corporation changed from an unviable PSE to a megalith in the construction field, along the way several strategic actions were initiated:

a) Reduction in bank borrowing from Rs. 35.83 Cr. to NIL within a period of 3 years. Clients are confident that the funds deposited by them are not diverted for interest payments;
b) Forming joint ventures with foreign collaborators to get new high value prestigious projects and gain technology transfer;
c) Categorization of projects in 'A','B','C' relating to their criticality for close monitoring and timely completion for better control, timely proactive action and completion for enhanced client's confidence;
d) Ensuring accountability of the functionaries in terms of achievement of defined targets, regular reviews based on agreed Memorandum of Understanding entered into with Zones and Regions;
e) Promotion and Maintenance of Corporate image by proactive approach and constant liaison with the clients;
f) Introduction of Centralized Fund Management for equitable distribution of financial resources on need basis to various projects. This has resulted in timely payments through e-transfers, timely depositing of statutory dues and an improved

market image. Reputed contractors are coming forward to work with NBCC at competitive rates;

g) Emphasis on introduction of quality system in the organization and its implementation at grass root level;
h) Providing all possible incentives to employees and implementing welfare measures for them to enhance motivation and increase in productivity;
i) Improving the profitability of the organization and achieve bankable balance sheet;
j) Implementation of quick decision making process by removing multi tier system to achieve completion of projects on schedule.

Over the years there is a growing feeling of satisfaction that there is a perceptible increase in Market good will. Clients ask NBCC to take up work based on negotiations, associates have a sense of security and thus offer competitive pricing which is passed on to NBCC's customers and NBCC employees have also seen promotion and transfer policies being positioned by management without the adhocism that prevailed earlier.

Indian Oil's Vision and Mission

*V.C. Agrawal**

"Throughout the centuries there were men who took first steps, down new roads, armed with nothing but their own vision".

Ayn Rand

Before independence, there was almost no 'Public Sector' in the Indian economy. The only instances worthy of mention were the Railways, the Posts and Telegraphs, the Port Trust, the Ordinance and the Aircraft factories and a few Government-managed undertakings like the salt and quinine factories, etc. After independence, and with the advent of planning, India opted for the dominance of the public sector, firmly believing that political independence without economic self-reliance was not good for the country.

The passing of the Industrial Policy Resolution of 1956 and adoption of the socialist pattern of society led to a deliberate enlargement of public sector in the country. It was believed that a dominant public sector would reduce the inequality of income and wealth by helping in the rapid economic growth and industrialization of the country and creation of necessary infrastructure for economic development, and advance the general prosperity of the nation. The planners also seemed to believe that by placing the management and workers in public enterprises in a position of responsibility and trust, they would be so imbued with a sense of public good that their actions and aspirations would naturally reflect what was best for the country.

In tune with the widespread belief at that time, the 2nd Five Year Plan stated very clearly that ' the adoption of socialist pattern of society as the national objective, as well as the need for planned and rapid development, require that all industries of basic and strategic importance, or in the nature of public utility services, should be in the public sector. Other industries, which are essential and require investment on a scale, which only the state, in the present

* Director (Personnel) Indian Oil Corporation Limited.

circumstances, could provide, have also to be in the public sector. The state has, therefore, to assume direct responsibility for the future development of industries over a wider area '.

The Second Plan further emphasized that 'the public sector has to expand rapidly. It has not only to initiate developments which the private sector is either unwilling or unable to undertake, it has to play the dominant role in shaping the entire pattern of investment in the economy, whether it makes the investments directly or whether these are made by the private sector. The private sector has to play its part within the framework of the comprehensive plan accepted by the community.'

However, as the Indian economy grew and winds of globalisation swept the country, it was increasingly felt that there should be a gradual paring down of the State's intervention in the functioning of the public sector enterprises (PSEs) and they should be empowered. In the year 1986, profitable PSEs were empowered to sanction *capex* without prior approval of the Government. As one of the measures to give greater autonomy to PSEs, the Government entered into Memorandum of Understanding with a number of PSEs. For the year 1988-89, MoUs were signed with 11 PSEs. This resulted in delegation of enhanced financial and administrative powers to these companies with respect to areas such as wage revision, incentive schemes, voluntary retirement scheme, transfer and foreign tours of functional directors.

With a view to further empowering PSEs with greater financial and operational autonomy and to transform select PSEs into global giants, the concept of *Navratna* and Mini-*ratna* was introduced in 1997. In order to arm the *Navratnas* with competitive advantage, full Government support was accorded in matters related to incurring capital expenditure, formation of joint ventures/subsidiaries/strategic alliances, organizational restructuring and implementation of HRD policies. The pre-requisite to the *Navratna* status was non-requirement of budgetary support/guarantees from the Government, and development & articulation of a clear vision, strategies as well as an effective internal control mechanism. The professionalization of Boards was also made a pre-condition to ensure that the enhanced powers were used prudently. Professionals were inducted in the Boards of Directors of these PSEs and audit committees were set up.

INDIAN OIL—A NAVRATNA PSE

Indian Oil was one of the top-ranking Indian corporates to make the leap to the ivy league of *Navratna* companies. The prestigious status significantly impacted the 'empowerment to execution' cycle in India's leading *Fortune* 'Global 500' corporate. Indian Oil's *Navratna* Board was constituted with representation from Functional Directors, Government nominees, and part-time non-official Directors. All the above measures resulted in more objective and quicker decision-making, and observance of the highest standards of corporate governance. The reconstituted *Navratna* Board of Indian Oil set the ball rolling at its maiden meeting held on 29th January 1999.

Indian Oil's Philosophy on Corporate Governance

Indian Oil strongly believes that good Corporate Governance practice ensures efficient conduct of the affairs of the Company and helps maximize stakeholder value. The Company endeavours to uphold the highest principles and practices of Corporate Governance to ensure transparency, integrity and accountability in its functioning, which are seen as vital for achieving the corporate Vision of becoming a major, diversified, transnational, integrated energy company.

Indian Oil fully complies with the requirements of the revised guidelines on Corporate Governance as stipulated in Clause-49 of the Listing Agreement, except the provision relating to composition of the Board of Directors with respect to the number of Independent Directors, for which the Government of India is taking necessary action, Indian Oil being a Government company.

Corporate Governance in the Corporation has been further strengthened through adoption of the following:

- Code of conduct for Directors and senior management personnel,
- Code of conduct for prevention of insider trading, and
- Policy on risk assessment and minimizing procedures.

Board of Directors

The Indian Oil Board has set certain strategic goals in line with the Corporation's Vision and Mission statements. The Board defines the corporate policy and oversees its implementation in attaining these goals.

The Board of Indian Oil consists of an optimum combination of executive and non-executive Directors. It has part-time non-executive Independent Directors with proven record in diverse areas such as energy policy, academics, marketing, Government and public sector, etc. At present, the Board comprises 15 Directors. These include

Chairman and six whole-time Functional Directors, five part-time non-executive Independent Directors, two part-time non-executive nominee Directors from the Ministry of Petroleum & Natural Gas (MOP&NG), Government of India, and a part-time non-executive Director, a nominee of ONGC Limited.

The Government Directors facilitate a strong channel of continuous communication with our major stakeholder—the Government of India. Besides engaging in brainstorming sessions on strategies, they render valuable guidance in promoting commercial interests of the Corporation while operating within the statutory framework. The Independent Directors bring in professionalism and a fresh line of thinking as well as expertise in their respective areas. With greater thrust on performance management, they render invaluable contribution in value creation and maximizing stakeholder value.

The Code of Conduct for the Directors and senior management personnel of the Corporation has been laid down by the Board and circulated to all concerned. It is also hosted on the Corporation's website. The decision-making process is streamlined and works through several mandatory committees, which are listed below:

a) Audit Committee

The Audit Committee of Indian Oil has been constituted in line with the provisions of Clause-49 of the Listing Agreement and also meets the requirements of Section 292A of the Companies Act, 1956. The members of the Audit Committee have requisite financial and management expertise. The Audit Committee comprises three part-time non-executive Independent Directors as members. The Audit Committee meetings are also attended by Director (Finance) and the head of Internal Audit as special invitees. The representatives of the Statutory Auditors are invited to the meetings as and when required. The Company Secretary acts as the Secretary of the Audit Committee. The terms of reference of the Audit Committee cover all matters specified under Clause-49 of the Listing Agreement of the Stock Exchanges.

b) Remuneration Committee

The remuneration of the whole-time Functional Directors is decided by the Government of India since Indian Oil is a Government company. The part-time non-executive Independent Directors are not paid any remuneration except sitting fees for attending the meetings of the Board or Committees thereof. However, the Board has constituted a

Remuneration Committee to approve certain perquisites for whole-time Functional Directors and below Board-level executives, which are within the powers of the Board.

c) Shareholders'/Investors' Grievance Committee

Shareholders'/Investors' Grievance Committee examines and redresses the grievances of shareholders and investors. The Committee comprises three members with a part-time non-executive Independent Director as Chairman, and Director (Finance) and Director (HR) as members. Indian Oil accords top priority to resolving the complaints, grievances and queries of shareholders within a reasonable period of time.

In addition to the above mandatory committees, the Board has delegated certain powers to various committees with distinct roles and responsibilities, the details of which are as under:

S. No.	*Name of Committee*	*Role and Responsibilities*	*Members*
1.	Planning & Projects Committee	For approval of capital investments of up to Rs.100 crore.	Chairman and all whole-time Functional Directors
2.	Contracts Committee	For award of contracts and implementation thereof.	Chairman and all whole-time Functional Directors
3.	Projects Evaluation Committee	For evaluating and recommending for Board approval, projects costing over Rs. 250 crore	Three part-time non-executive Independent Directors, one part-time non-executive Government Director, Director (Finance) and whole-time Functional Director concerned.
4.	Establishment Committee	To take decisions in respect of creation, selection, appointment and promotion to the posts of General Managers and above and Conduct, Discipline & Appeal Rules.	Chairman and all whole-time Functional Directors, One part-time non-executive Government Director and one part-time non-executive Independent Director.
5.	Committee for De-leasing of Immoveable Properties	To consider requests for de-leasing of Company-leased immoveable properties	Chairman, Director (Human Resources), Director (Finance) and a part-time non-executive Government Director.
6.	Marketing Strategies Committee	To provide direction to the Corporation on marketing strategies and policies.	Two part-time non-executive Independent Directors, Director (Finance) & Director (Marketing)
7.	Upstream Activities Committee	To take all decisions regarding upstream acquisitions.	Two part-time non-executive Independent Directors, Director (Finance) and Director (Planning & Business Development).

Indian Oil's Corporate History

To share the Indian Oil experience, it would be appropriate to start with its inception in September 1964 when Indian Refineries Limited and Indian Oil Company Limited merged to form Indian Oil Corporation Limited (Indian Oil).

From a fledgling company having a net worth of just Rs. 45.18 crore and sales of 1.38 million tonnes valued at Rs. 78 crore in the year 1965, Indian Oil has grown over 2,000 times in just over four decades! It is currently India's largest company by sales with a turnover of Rs. 220,779 crore (US$ 51 billion), the highest-ever for an Indian company and profit after tax of Rs. 7,499 crore (US$ 1.73 billion) for fiscal 2006-07. Indian Oil is also the highest ranked Indian company in the prestigious *Fortune* 'Global 500' listing, at the 153rd position. It is also the 21st largest petroleum company in the world.

Network beyond Compare

Indian Oil and its subsidiaries account for 47 per cent petroleum products market share in the industry, 40.4 per cent national refining capacity and 67 per cent downstream sector pipelines capacity. With a combined refining capacity of 60.2 million tonnes per annum (1.2 million barrels per day), the Indian Oil Group of companies owns and operates 10 of India's 19 refineries (total capacity of 149 million tonnes per annum). These include two refineries of subsidiary Chennai Petroleum Corporation Limited (CPCL) and one of Bongaigaon Refinery and Petrochemicals Limited (BRPL).

The Company's cross-country crude oil and product pipelines network, spanning over 9,200 km with capacity of over 61.7 million tonnes per annum, meets the vital energy needs of the country.

As the flagship national oil company in the downstream sector, Indian Oil, together with its IBP Division reaches precious petroleum products to millions of people everyday through a countrywide network of around 32,550 sales points. They are backed for supplies by 177 bulk storage terminals and depots, 97 aviation fuel stations and 90 Indane LPG bottling plants.

Indian Oil operates the largest and the widest network of petrol & diesel stations in the country, numbering over 16,450. It reaches Indane cooking gas to the doorsteps of over 46.4 million households in more than 2,700 markets through a network of 4,996 Indane distributors.

Indian Oil today, has the largest reach in the domestic market. In the year 2006-07, the Indian Oil group sold about 55 million tonnes of petroleum products in the country (out of the total consumption of 118.2 million tonnes).

Indian Oil's ISO-9002 certified Aviation Service commands a 63 per cent market share in aviation fuel business, meeting the fuel needs of domestic and international flag carriers, private airlines and the Indian Defence Services. Indian Oil also enjoys a dominant share of the bulk consumer business, i.e. of railways, state transport undertakings, industrial, agricultural and marine sectors.

Indian Oil's world class R&D Centre is perhaps Asia's finest. Besides conducting pioneering work in lubricants formulation, refinery processes, pipeline transportation and alternative fuels such as bio-diesel, the Centre is also the nodal agency of the Indian hydrocarbon sector for ushering in Hydrogen fuel in the country. Indian Oil joined the league of global technology providers in 2006-07 with its in-house developed Ind Max technology selected for the 4 MMTPA Fluidised Catalytic Cracking (FCC) unit at the Corporation's upcoming 15 MMTPA integrated refinery-cum-petrochemicals complex at Paradip in Orissa, as well as for the FCC unit coming up at BRPL.

Business Scoping

The 90s were a decade of cost cutting, re-engineering, downsizing as well as constant challenges to do more with lesser resources and yet faster. In the wake of liberalisation, the Indian economy was opening up and various sectors were being unshackled. In step with the market reforms process, the Indian petroleum industry was also witnessing a phased deregulation process.

Some of the significant events of that era that impacted Indian Oil's business outlook included permission to set up refineries in the private and joint sector in 1991, and deregulation of the lube oil market in 1993, which resulted in the entry of many multinational players. In the same year, marketing infrastructure and pipelines were opened to the private sector, and private players were permitted to market imported kerosene, Liquefied Petroleum Gas (LPG) and LSHS (Low Sulphur Heavy Stock). The year 1997 saw the historic announcement of phased dismantling of the Administered Price Mechanism (APM), which resulted in deregulation of all petroleum products except petrol, diesel, kerosene (for public distribution system) and LPG (for domestic use). In 1998, the refining sector was de-licensed, naphtha export was de-canalised and refiners in the private and joint sector were permitted to import crude. The year 1999 saw the Government deciding to disinvest its equity in the downstream oil sector and de-canalise export of petrol, diesel and ATF (Aviation Turbine Fuel). Foreign Direct Investment to the extent of 100 per cent equity was permitted by the Government in the historic Y2K. Successive years saw deregulation of all products.

All in all, the 90s proved to be very exciting and challenging times for the Indian hydrocarbon sector.

Indian Oil was born as a refining & marketing company. But with the economic liberalisation throwing up a plethora of opportunities, Indian Oil faced a whole new gamut of challenges. Way back in the 1990s, it was increasingly felt that being confined to the traditional business would not only restrict Indian Oil's growth but also increase risks. At that point in time, as a corporate, Indian Oil was threatened by the winds of liberalisation, faced the bleak prospect of complacence and was groping for answers. There was an imperative need to take stock—conduct a thorough SWOT analysis, capitalise on the strengths and harness new opportunities. Indian Oil felt a pressing need to develop strategies and plans to create positive relationships between people, practices, customer satisfaction and functional successes.

To quote *Frederick Slovak*, VP, Goodyear, who said, "*An organisation—no matter what it makes, no matter what its size; no matter how long it has or has not been around—needs to be reconfigurable on an annual, monthly, weekly, daily or even hourly basis. A system that cannot react to change is a dinosaur*".

A rigorous introspection, belief in its capabilities and the desire to reach the next level of growth, powered by the enhanced level of *Navratna* autonomy, resulted in a comprehensive business scoping exercise in the year 1999. Corporate Vision, Mission and strategies were formulated, internal controls were strengthened, and decision-making process was streamlined. This resulted in Indian Oil not only successfully countering the challenges of liberalization and globalisation, but also transforming itself into a suave market-oriented commercial entity.

Formulation of Indian Oil's Vision/Mission

In January 1999, we conducted what has gone down in the annals of Indian Oil's history as the '*Third Eye*' workshop. It was a massive HRD and business scoping exercise that drew people from all ranks to brainstorm the corporate vision—a shared dream, a picture of the future that Indian Oil People sought to create together. The statement so crystallized was to reflect the shared aspiration of the Indian Oil people.

The top management, including Chairman, Functional Directors, Heads of Units/Regions/Functions, a core group of Indian Oil Officers' Association as well as select young professionals, actively participated and contributed in the workshop, bringing out critical areas of concern across the Corporation, warranting immediate and sustained attention.

The exercise culminated in distilling the corporate Vision and Mission statements, which were ratified by the Navratna Board of Directors in its meeting held in July 1999. They are as follows:

Vision

A major diversified, transnational, integrated energy company, with national leadership and a strong environment conscience, playing a national role in oil security & public distribution.

Mission

- To achieve international standards of excellence in all aspects of energy and diversified business with focus on customer delight through value of products and services, and cost reduction.
- To maximize creation of wealth, value and satisfaction for the stakeholders.
- To attain leadership in developing, adopting and assimilating state-of—the-art technology for competitive advantage.
- To provide technology and services through sustained Research and Development.
- To foster a culture of participation and innovation for employee growth and contribution.
- To cultivate high standards of business ethics and Total Quality Management for a strong corporate identity and brand equity
- To help enrich the quality of life of the community and preserve ecological balance and heritage through a strong environment conscience.

Upon completion of the exercise, the then Chairman, Indian Oil, Mr. M.A. *Pathan*, addressed the Indian Oil People and said, "*I am confident that with your collective efforts, a common vision and specific goal-oriented missions, we will emerge as a stronger, integrated and diversified global entity."*

Strategies of the Navratna Indian Oil Board

World over, oil majors are vertically integrated. Since businesses are cyclic in nature, it is prudent to offset the downside of one vertical with the upside of another. Therefore, it was considered judicious for Indian Oil to widen its business portfolio and spread the enterprise risk. This would enable the Corporation to control the elements of supply chain, thereby rendering cost competitiveness. The issues of energy security, emergence of gas as the fuel of the future and opportunities for significant growth in petrochemicals became the key drivers in deciding upon the expansion of our business portfolio.

As stated earlier, the intensive business scoping exercise thoroughly examined the emerging challenges and resulted in re-orientation of our business strategies in response. It was decided to straddle the entire hydrocarbon value chain and the Corporate Vision & Mission were further drilled down into realizable rollout strategies to face the challenges that lay ahead. These strategies included:

- Integration,
- Diversification and
- Globalisation.

It was also decided to align people processes with business processes by rolling out a comprehensive Enterprise Resource Planning (ERP) model, code-named *Manthan,* uniting all Indian Oil locations in a common thread.

A snapshot of the essence of these initiatives spearheaded by the Indian Oil Management and how they shaped up over the last few years is given below:

1. ENTERPRISE RESOURCE PLANNING (PROJECT MANTHAN)

Indian Oil has implemented a major project of IT Re-engineering, simultaneously with Business Process Re-engineering (BPR), incorporating therein the best practices benchmarked to world standards. Project "Manthan" was aimed at achieving better, faster and cost-competitive business processes; simplifying and standardizing forms, procedures and workflows; facilitating automatic capturing of data duly verified at source, its transfer, processing and analysis; thereby realizing the goal of integrated business solutions.

A major component of the project was the implementation of the SAP R/3 software package of M/s SAP AG of Germany selected as ERP (Enterprise Resource Planning) solution.

Parallel to the implementation of the ERP package, Indian Oil has also customized eight additional or 'Add-On' software packages for implementation, covering core business areas like demand forecasting, transportation scheduling and distribution planning of crude oil and products, and for optimizing refinery operations and product mix solutions. These Add-On solutions are primarily aimed at forming part of the decision support system and working in tandem with the SAP R/3 solutions with an integrated approach towards optimization.

The total solution has been implemented over a robust hybrid Wide Area Network (WAN) and appropriate hardware. The Production Site, located at IIPM, Gurgaon, is the electronic hub of the project.

All units of the Corporation have been linked through an extensive and robust communication network using VSATs, leased lines, ISDN/PSTN dial-up lines, and the optical fibre cable communication system of Indian Oil's Pipelines Division. 224 VSAT links were installed at all strategic locations of Indian Oil in two phases. Most of the end-users have been connected to the central site through WAN.

Through this extensive project, Indian Oil has achieved the following objectives:

- Communication connectivity across the Corporation.
- Seamless integration of business processes and information flow.
- Uniform "look-feel" of software anywhere in the Corporation.
- Centralized control with decentralized customer response.
- Standard, accurate, real time data to support decision-making
- Extensive 'drill-down' reporting capabilities for trends analysis.
- High degree of reliability and security.

2. INTEGRATION

Indian Oil adopted the strategy of becoming a fully integrated player across the hydrocarbon value chain-backward as well as forward—to reduce the enterprise risks.

Backward Integration into Exploration & Production (E&P) of Crude Oil & Gas

Domestic Initiatives—Indian Oil made a foray into E&P sector in 1996. A humble beginning was made by securing two exploration blocks in consortium with ONGC, under the first round of the New Exploration Licensing Policy (NELP-1999) announced by the Government of India. In the first three rounds of NELP (1999-2002), Indian Oil bagged nine blocks in consortium with other corporates. Under the latest round of NELP-VI (2007), two blocks have been awarded to Indian Oil in consortium with GSPC, GAIL, HPCL and Petrogas. Indian Oil has also acquired participating interest in onshore blocks in Assam and Arunachal Pradesh.

Overseas Initiatives—Considering India's heavy dependence on oil imports, acquisition of equity oil abroad was considered as a focus area. Indian Oil's overseas initiatives include regular participation in the international bidding processes in target countries through the consortium approach. Indian Oil's overseas initiatives are as follows:

- *Iran*: Indian Oil has been a participant in the Farsi offshore exploration block in Iran since December 2002. This block was awarded by the National Iranian Oil Company (NIOC) under the Exploration Service Contract to the consortium of Indian Oil, ONGC Videsh Limited (operator), and Oil India Limited (OIL). Indian Oil has a 40 per cent participating interest in this block.
- *Libya*: The Indian Oil-OIL consortium has been awarded two onland blocks in Sirte Basin in Libya by the National Oil Corporation (NOC) under the first and second bidding round of the Exploration and Production Sharing Agreements (EPSA-IV) respectively. OIL is the operator and Indian Oil has a 50 per cent participating interest each in both the blocks.
- *Gabon*: Indian Oil-OIL consortium has been awarded one block in Gabon. Indian Oil has a 45 per cent participating interest and OIL is the operator.
- *Nigeria*: Indian Oil has a 17.5 per cent participating interest in a Nigerian block, with Summit Oil as the operator.
- *Yemen:* Indian Oil has two blocks in Yemen, with Medco as the operator. The Corporation has a 15 per cent participating interest in both the blocks.

The Government of India has also approved a fast dispensation mechanism for the Indian Oil-OIL consortium, through the Empowered Committee of Secretaries, as available to ONGC Videsh Limited The Consortium would form project-specific special purpose vehicles for acquisition of overseas E&P assets. This decision will significantly enhance Indian Oil's institutional capacity for taking such initiatives.

Coal Bed Methane (CBM)—Indian Oil, in consortium with ONGC, was awarded two CBM blocks—Bokaro and North Karanpura under CBM-1 in 2001. Indian Oil has a 20 per cent participating interest in both the blocks, which are currently in the second phase of exploration.

Acquisition of a mid-size overseas E&P company—The Indian Oil Board has accorded in-principle approval to pursue acquisition of a suitable overseas medium-sized E&P company to strengthen our E&P business. In this regard, we are considering several overseas companies with oil and gas assets/operations in Asia Pacific, Africa, South America and other countries.

Forward Integration into Petrochemicals

To straddle the entire hydrocarbon value chain, Indian Oil has envisaged entry into the petrochemicals vertical through utilisation of captive feedstock available from its own refineries. Indian Oil is currently implementing a petrochemicals master plan envisaging Rs. 30,000 crore (US$ 6.8 billion) investment by the year 2011-12. Two mega projects viz. LAB (Linear Alkyl Benzene) unit and PX/PTA (Para-Xylene/Purified Terephthalic Acid) unit have already been commissioned.

The world-scale LAB unit at Gujarat Refinery is designed to produce 1,20,000 TPA of Linear Alkyl Benzene for detergents manufacture using captive kerosene feedstock from the refinery. In its second year of operation, the Corporation has already captured 38 per cent market share and the product has been exported to Indonesia, Turkey, Thailand, Vietnam, Norway and Oman.

The integrated PX/PTA unit for polyester intermediates, with a world-class capacity of 5,53,000 tonnes, is located at Panipat Refinery and is based on captive naphtha stream from the refinery. Indian Oil recently touched a new milestone when the cumulative revenue from the PTA business crossed Rs. 1,000 crore in a short span of ten months since commencement of sales in September 2006. The sales revenue also includes substantial deemed exports of PTA valued at over Rs. 225 crore.

In keeping with our corporate plans to nurture world-scale petrochemical hubs, an olefin-based Naphtha Cracker with downstream polymer units at Panipat and an integrated grassroots refinery-cum-petrochemicals complex at Paradip, on the east coast, are under implementation. The Panipat Naphtha Cracker project is targeted to produce 8,00,000 TPA of ethylene based on utilisation of captive Naphtha along with downstream polymer units producing LLDPE (Linear Low Density Polyethylene), HDPE (High Density Polyethylene), PP (Polypropylene) & specialty chemical MEG (Mono Ethyl Glycol). The total project is expected to be commissioned by November 2009 at an approved cost of Rs.14,439 crore. The Rs. 25,646 crore Paradip complex is proposed to be completed by 2011-12.

With the above initiatives, we hope that Indian Oil will soon be operating across the entire petrochemical value chain, particularly for bulk/commodity products. Indian Oil has inked an MoU with the Haryana State Industrial & Infrastructure Development Corporation (HSIIDC) to launch a special purpose vehicle for the development of a petrochemicals hub in Panipat. We have also entered into an MoU with the Govt. of West Bengal to explore the possibility of creation of a Petroleum, Chemicals & Petrochemicals Investment Region (PCPIR) at Haldia.

3. DIVERSIFICATION

The 19th century was dominated by coal, 20th century was fuelled by oil and 21st century is envisaged to belong to gas. Fuel choices are changing and gas has already started replacing petroleum fuels in industries as well as in domestic and transport sectors because of its environment-friendliness and economics. Therefore, in order to minimise the risk of liquid fuel substitution, Indian Oil has diversified into the Gas vertical.

Indian Oil holds a 30 per cent stake in Petronet LNG Limited and currently markets regasified LNG (R-LNG) to customers on a long-term contract basis. Additionally, Indian Oil also markets R-LNG procured under short-term contracts. In natural gas business, Indian Oil is targeting sale of 2 million tonnes in 2007-08, up from 1.5 million tonnes in 2006-2007. Construction of an LNG import terminal and city gas distribution projects are in the pipeline in partnership with GAIL (India) and Great Eastern Energy Corporation Limited To augment its business in this sector, Indian Oil has signed an MoU with Iran for import of 1.75 million tonnes of LNG per annum from the year 2009 onwards.

Indian Oil is taking the following initiatives in gas-related projects in India and abroad:

- MoU with Petropars for developing an Integrated LNG project in the North Pars fields of Iran.
- A 2.5 MMTPA LNG terminal at Ennore, expandable to 5 MMTPA.
- Iran-Pakistan-India Gas Pipeline Project (IPI).
- City Gas Distribution Projects in Lucknow, Agra, Asansol, Durgapur and Raniganj.

4. GLOBALISATION

In accordance with the mandate of a *Navratna* company and to emerge as a transnational energy major, Indian Oil is spreading its wings outside the country.

Exporting Goods and Services

Indian Oil started by exporting petroleum products. Exports for the year 2006-07 were 3.1 MMT, up from 2 MMT in the previous year. 10 TMT of Group-I & II lube oil base stock was exported to Middle East and Pakistan in 2006-07. Finished lubes, including turbine oil, rolling oil & Agro Spray oil are being exported to Bangladesh, Zambia and Nepal.

In an effort to globalize its expertise in the downstream hydrocarbon sector, Indian Oil has been actively pursuing business opportunities related to export of project consultancy and services abroad. Some of the achievements are as follows:

- Indian Oil has conducted training programmes for personnel of Sudan's Greater Nile Petroleum Operating Company on operation and maintenance, inspection, telecom & tele-supervisory and quality control procedures of pipelines.
- The manpower secondment agreement and the technical services agreement with Emirates National Oil Company,

Dubai, were extended for the ninth and tenth successive years in 2006-07.

- Indian Oil has been conducting training programmes on Refinery O&M for officials of the Iraqi oil industry. Training programmes have also been conducted for the officials of the Oman Refinery Company on the Isomerisation unit at Mathura Refinery.
- Indian Oil has bagged a pipeline consultancy contract in Sudan.
- Indian Oil is acquiring 12.5 per cent shares in the Trans—Anatolian Pipeline Company (TAPCO—a company promoted by Eni of Italy and Calik Enerji of Turkey). TAPCO would lay and operate a 550 km long crude oil pipeline of 50 million tonnes per annum capacity connecting Samsun and Ceyhan in Turkey.

Overseas Ventures

In its endeavour towards becoming global oil major, Indian Oil has been steadily consolidating and strengthening its overseas businesses. Subsidiaries have been set up in Sri Lanka, Mauritius and UAE. The details are placed below:

- *Lanka IOC (LIOC)*—It was incorporated on 3rd December 2002, as a wholly-owned subsidiary of Indian Oil to carry out retail marketing of petroleum products, bulk supply to industrial consumers, building and operating storage facilities at the Trincomalee tank farm, etc., in Sri Lanka, thereby not only providing energy security and supply stability but also upgrading the overall standards of service, particularly in the retail sector, in the island nation.

  Lanka IOC is the largest private sector company in the island nation and currently markets approx. 35,000 KL of petroleum products per month. The present market share of LIOC in retail fuel and lubricants sales is approx. 20 per cent and 13 per cent, respectively. Branded fuels, viz. LankaMile Diesel and LankaPremium Petrol—have also been launched to good acceptance and have reflected robust conversion rates of 21.2 per cent and 28.6 per cent, respectively.

  LIOC is building an 18,000 tonnes per annum Lube Blending Plant at Trincomalee, Sri Lanka, with an investment of US$

5 Million, which is scheduled to be commissioned by July 2007. As a long-term measure, LIOC has evinced interest to the Government of Sri Lanka to put up a grassroots refinery at Trincomalee.

- *Indian Oil Mauritius Limited (IOML)*—IOML was formed in October 2001 and commenced its operations in February 2004. It is already a name to reckon with in the island nation of Mauritius. In 2006-07, IOML sold 1,63,000 Kilolitre (KL) of petroleum products and achieved an overall market share of 16 per cent as against 14 per cent in the previous year. A comprehensive petroleum laboratory for testing all fuels and lubricants is already commissioned in March 2007. The laboratory as the first full-fledge petroleum products' testing laboratory in Mauritius, has already gained international accreditations such as ISO 9001-2000, and is successfully participating in the ASTM inter-laboratory proficiency programme.

  IOML is expanding its storage capacity from the current 18,000 KL to 24,000 KL, with an investment of Rs. 50 million, expected to be commissioned by September 2007. It is also building a Jet Fuel storage terminal, in consortium with other players in the Mauritian oil sector, at a cost of USD 16 million IOML is planning to lay a pipeline for its bunkering services and increasing its number of retail outlets from 9 to 25 by December 2008. Using Mauritius as a bridge, Indian Oil is actively exploring marketing opportunities in Reunion and African regions.
- *IOC Middle East FZE (IOCME)*—IOCME was established in May 2006 in UAE for marketing *SERVO* lubricants in the Middle East region. It oversees expansion of business in the Middle East region and is engaged in blending and marketing of *SERVO* lubricants as well as marketing of petroleum products in the Middle East, Africa and CIS countries.

Score Card: Benefits of Navratna Status

The tables below present a comparison in physical and financial performance of Indian Oil in 1997-98 (pre-Navratna status) and 2006-07 (present):

a) Physical performance

Parameter	*Unit*	*1997-98*	*2006-07*	*CAGR (%)*
Refinery Thruput	MMTPA	27.5	44.0	5.4
Pipeline Thruput	MMTPA	31.03	51.7	5.8
Sales	MMT	43.41	54.9	2.6
Retail Network	No.	13335	25406	7.4

b) Financial performance

Key Indicators	*1997-98 (Rs. Cr.)*	*2006-07 (Rs. Cr.)*	*CAGR (%)*
Turnover	59176	220779	15.8
Gross Profit	4128	14622	15.1
Net Profit	1706	7499	17.9
Value Added	9652	24716	11.0
Contribution to Central Exchequer	10302	28432	11.9
Cumulative Dividend	1050	13853	33.2
Net Worth	10614	34857	14.1
Market Capitalization	7761	46680	22.1
Gross Fixed Assets	13313	54837	17.0
Debt Equity Ratio	0.43:1	0.78:1	—

It may also be mentioned here that during the period January 1999 (i.e. after reconstitution of the Indian Oil Board with enhanced powers) to March 2007, investments valued at over Rs. 70,000 crore were approved by the *Navratna* Board.

Capital Investments

In line with the vision of becoming 'a major diversified, transnational, integrated energy company…', Indian Oil has evolved the strategies as detailed above. It has also invested heavily towards achieving its vision. During the Tenth Five-Year Plan, Indian Oil had committed Rs. 24,400 crore towards capital expenditure. Of this, Rs.12,173 crore were committed for upgradation, quality improvement and other projects at refineries, and Rs. 7,397 crore towards diversification into Gas & Petrochemicals. The major projects planned during this period were the 15 million tonnes grassroots refinery at Paradip, augmentation of capacity at Panipat Refinery, Naphtha Cracker at Panipat and product upgradation facilities at various other refineries. Of the committed Rs. 24,400 crore, Indian Oil spent Rs. 17,929 crore, during the tenth plan.

For the Eleventh Five-Year Plan, Indian Oil has committed Rs.43,250 crore on various projects. Of this, Rs. 25,114 crore is committed towards revamping and upgrading the refining business and Rs. 11,870 crore to expanding the petrochemicals business. The major projects envisaged during eleventh five-year Plan are Paradip Refinery project, product upgradation at Gujarat and Barauni Refineries, and Naphtha Cracker project at Panipat.

Restructuring People Processes

Indian Oil is on a journey to evolve from a pure sectoral company with dominance in downstream in India to a vertically integrated, transnational energy organisation. In light of the evolving milieu of business, it is our 'People' who will render Indian Oil the competitive advantage by utilising the enhanced powers given to Indian Oil by the Government and will help it achieve the Corporate Vision. Therefore, there is a strong need to benchmark HR processes and ensure realignment of people capabilities with the Corporation's business priorities.

Indian Oil has restructured its people processes by focussing on:

a) *Performance, rewards and recognition*—The key aspect in strengthening and realignment of people capabilities is to develop a performance culture in the organisation by differentiating and rewarding different levels of individual performance. Indian Oil has designed and implemented an e-enabled system for efficient management of performance. In order to develop the scheme, the element of individual performance was introduced in the existing Productivity Incentive Scheme for Officers. A robust and objective Performance Management System being the pre-requisite for a successful individual performance-based reward system, we underwent a process to review and suggest essential changes in the existing Performance Management System for Officers, and proposed a revised Productivity Incentive Scheme comprising an element of individual performance along with the team performance. Effective appraisal year 2005-06 a new robust and more objective electronic Performance Management System (e-PMS) has been designed and implemented. This incorporates weightage for individual performance (20%) and team performance (80%) for incentive payouts.

E-PMS seeks to determine individual performance and potential through a system that is objective & transparent, robust, easy to use and aligned to business needs. This performance-linked individual-based incentive scheme fosters and rewards good performance and creates a strong correlation between performance and pay. This individual-based productivity incentive scheme has been designed after extensive study related to oil and gas industry both from global and Indian perspective, and has been successful in instilling a high performance culture along with enhanced employee engagement.

b) *Developing competencies*—In the light of re-orienting strategies to suit the dynamic business scenario, it was imperative to ensure alignment of skill sets of the employees for time-bound realisation of business objectives. Indian Oil re-visited its business priorities while going forward, and developed people capabilities aligned to and required for a deregulated environment. Accordingly, a review of the competencies of Pivotal Roles in the organisation, held by officers of the level of Deputy General Managers, General Managers and Executive Directors was considered necessary. Based on this, the Key Result Area(s) for each of the unique roles/positions and the competencies required in the current business context by this senior management group were also reframed.

c) *Effective HR Processes*—The HR Module in the ERP system of Indian Oil covers important sub-modules pertaining to various HR functions of Personnel, Management Services, Training, and Establishment section, which includes organogram, recruitment, maintaining employee master data, assignments, separation records, training & event management, leave management, etc.

   There are about 33,500 employee masters maintained in SAP including those of the newly formed IBP Division and subsidiaries like BRPL. The SAP HR Module meets the employee master data requirement of e-PMS. This is operational in the form of an automatic interface programme which runs daily in the background in SAP system and updates e-PMS employee master data on delta changes made in the employee masters in SAP.

Beyond Profits: Caring is sharing

It is the firm resolve of Indian Oil to move beyond business, touch every heart and fuel a billion dreams.

a) *Corporate Sustainability Programmes*—At Indian Oil, community development programmes have been the cornerstone of success right from its inception in the year 1964. The Corporation's objectives in this key performance area are enshrined in its Mission statement: "...to help enrich the quality of life of the community and preserve ecological balance and heritage through a strong environment conscience..."

   As a constructive partner in the communities in which it operates, Indian Oil has been taking concrete actions to realise its corporate social responsibility objectives, thereby building value for all its stakeholders. The Corporation respects human rights, values its employees, and invests in innovative technologies and solutions for sustainable energy flow and economic growth.

   In the past four decades, Indian Oil has supported innumerable social and community initiatives in India—touching the lives of millions of Indians positively, by supporting environmental and healthcare projects and social, cultural and educational programmes.

   Besides focusing primarily on the welfare of economically and socially deprived sections of the society, Indian Oil also aims at developing techno-economically viable and environment-friendly products & services for the benefit of millions of its consumers, while at the same time ensuring the highest standards of safety and environment protection in its operations. Every year, Indian Oil sets aside a fixed portion of its profits for spreading smiles in millions of lives across the country through a comprehensive community welfare and development programme. About one-fourth of the community development funds are spent on the welfare of Scheduled Caste and Scheduled Tribe beneficiaries. Indian Oil's concerted social responsibility programme partner communities in health, family welfare, education, environment protection, provision of potable water, sanitation, and empowerment of women and other marginalised groups.

Indian Oil has always been in the forefront in times of national emergencies. Indian OilPeople have time and again rallied to help victims of natural calamities, maintaining uninterrupted supply of petroleum products and contributing to relief and rehabilitation measures in cash and kind.

Indian Oil's community-focused initiatives include allotment of petrol/diesel station dealerships (retail outlets) and LPG distributorships to beneficiaries from among Scheduled Castes, Scheduled Tribes, physically handicapped, ex-servicemen, war widows, etc. The Corporation has also unveiled Kisan Seva Kendras as small-format retail outlets to reach quality products and services to people in the rural areas.

b) *Scholarships*—The Indian Oil Scholarship Scheme spreads the light of education in the lives of hundreds of meritorious and deserving students from economically and socially deprived sections of society. The scheme offers 450 scholarships every year to bright students selected on 'merit-cum-means' basis. Of these, 250 scholarships are for 10+/ITI students on a zonal basis, at Rs. 1,000 per month for two years, 100 scholarships for engineering students and 40 for medical students at Rs. 2,000 per month for four years. Sixty students of post-graduation in Business Management are entitled to a scholarship of Rs. 2,000 per month for a period of two years. The scheme gives special encouragement to girl students, physically challenged students and students from Jammu & Kashmir and the North-eastern States.

c) *Sports Scholarships*—To encourage promising and talented youngsters and to create a pool of top class sports persons, Indian Oil has been offering sports scholarships in seven categories for budding sports persons. Sports scholarships are offered to upcoming players in the age group of 15-18 years and potential/talented players below 15 years but above 14 years of age. In team games, it is given to State level players and in individual sports, based on national ranking in the respective category. The duration of the sports scholarships is of three years, subject to performance review every year. Apart from 'catching them young', Indian Oil pursues a policy of providing employment to national and international sports persons so that they are assured of financial security and are free to concentrate on earning laurels for the country.

d) Indian Oil has also set up 'The Indian Oil Foundation' as a non-profit trust to protect, preserve and promote national heritage monuments. With a corpus fund of Rs. 25 crore and a recurring annual contribution, work is underway in collaboration with Archaeological Survey of India (ASI) and National Culture Fund (NCF) of the Government of India to promote awareness, knowledge and involvement in our national heritage and culture. The sites adopted by the Foundation include Konark Sun Temple (Orissa), Khajuraho (Madhya Pradesh), Kanheri Caves (Maharashtra), and Hampi (Karnataka).

Pursuing a Green Agenda

As part of its environment-protection initiatives, Indian Oil is investing Rs. 12,000 crore in state-of-the-art technologies at its refineries for production of green fuels meeting global standards. To further reduce dependence on precious petroleum products and secure the nation's energy security, the Corporation is now in the process of commercializing various options in alternative fuels such as Ethanol-blended Petrol, Bio-diesel, and Hydrogen/Hydrogen-CNG mixture.

With safety, health and environment protection high on its corporate agenda, Indian Oil is committed to conducting business with a strong environment conscience, so as to ensure sustainable development, safe workplaces and enrichment of the quality of life of its employees, customers and the community. Indian Oil is also committed to the Global Compact Programme of the United Nations and endeavours to abide by the 10 principles of the programme, some of which are already part of the Corporation's Vision and Mission statements.

CONCLUSION

I wish to quote the world famous philosopher *Confucius*, who said,

> "Teach me, I forget
> Show me, I remember
> Involve me, I understand."

Indian Oil's experience with empowerment has been extremely encouraging. The Indian Oil story above justifiably highlights the role of enhanced autonomy in unleashing the latent potential of these repositories of national talent.

The PSEs have been ably guided by the positive policies of the Government; initially in the mid-80s by the performance-oriented MoU system and thereafter through structured reforms. These reforms addressed some of the long-pending issues of functional autonomy and operational freedom, besides achieving professionalization of the PSE Boards. The *Navratna* status accorded to select PSEs not only ensured increased autonomy, but also helped them to improve their overall performance considerably. Since authority and accountability go hand in hand, the *Navratnas* also demonstrated greater accountability both in performance and in delivering greater value to their various stakeholders.

While the recommendations of Arjun Sengupta Committee provided new impetus to the growth and performance of Central PSEs, the constitution of a Board for Reconstruction of Public Sector Enterprises (BRPSE) in December 2004 by the Government needs to be lauded. But several reforms are already in place or in the final stage of being rolled out. However, the "PSE Reform/Empowerment Process" is still an unfinished agenda, since it has to be a continuous process, as new changes continuously evolve in the marketplace. No company in the hydrocarbon sector today can ignore the fact that as the demand for the products rises, so do the risks associated with the advent of unrelenting volatility of the global oil & gas market due to economic and geopolitical factors.

For instance, in the evolving milieu of business, Indian Oil currently faces challenges due to increasing crude oil prices and a cap on domestic selling prices of the four major fuels, viz. petrol, diesel, kerosene (for PDS) and LPG (for domestic use). Although the Administered Price Mechanism (APM) was dismantled in 2002, the petroleum downstream marketing sector in India continues to operate in a semi-deregulated pricing regime, which results in substantial price under-realisation of petroleum products. In this scenario, it is indeed challenging to remain focused on retaining both mind share and market share amidst spiralling crude oil prices on the one hand, and the need to freeze retail prices due to socio-political compulsions, on the other.

In this age of communication and mass media awareness, customers shift their loyalties in a flash, on instant news of discounts and incentives. Showing signs of maturing, India's downstream petroleum sector too is moving dynamically. A simple "turn of the steering" lures business away from one Retail Outlet to another. Thus, there is pressing need to nurture brand value, and create a meaningful differentiation to ensure a memorable brand experience. This is a major challenge for Indian Oil, more so, when our customers are as diverse as kerosene users in a tiny village at one end, and sophisticated international airlines at major airports on the other.

The corporate sector in India is on a roll today like never before, aided by an overall robust performance of the Indian economy. The GDP grew by 7.5 per cent in 2004-05, 8.4 per cent in 2005-06, 9.4 per cent in 2006-07, and is projected to grow similarly this year too. The Indian economy has become more open, globally integrated and competitive. There is now no palpable distinction in terms of "deliverables" between a PSE and a non-PSE company. Companies are graded as either "performers" or "non-performers", and customers continuously demand quality products and services, irrespective of where the ownership of a company lies.

In such a situation, the long-term vision of the Government should be to provide complete and full autonomy to the PSEs—operational as well as financial—to enable them to measure up to the demands of the global marketplace. Empowerment of PSEs is the only way to make them vibrant and dynamic economic entities.

Corporate Governance: A Public Sector Perspective

*G. Ojha**

INTRODUCTION

Of late, the issue of Corporate Governance in Public Sector enterprises is being discussed widely. Up to 1980s, it was generally believed that the conflict of interest between the management and the owners of the company, which is key to the issue of Corporate Governance, did not operate with any degree of significance in Public Sector enterprises. Moreover, with 100 per cent of the ownership of PSEs with the Government, the issue of protecting the interest of minority shareholders did not arise. Besides these, it was the general perception that the conduct of PSEs would be near ideal at a higher level of Governance—where the focus is on issues such as ethics, values, and harmony with the larger constituency outside the periphery of corporate entity.

It is generally well accepted that the PSEs adhere to the law of the land, and are tax compliant, and other malpractices that may increase the residual income of shareholders at the cost of the economy/society, are much less in the PSEs. As such, Corporate Governance, which is the guiding mechanism for executive action towards stakeholders' expectations, works in a satisfactory way in the case of Public Sector enterprises. In this context, while there could be diverse views on the issue of returns on investment in these enterprises, there are hardly any doubts vis-à-vis 'transparency'. Various agencies such as C&AG, CVC and CBI, the Parliament and its Committees and other checks and balances created to oversee the functioning of these enterprises ensure that the PSEs conform to the objectives they are expected to fulfill.

---

* Director (Personnel), Steel Authority of India Limited.

CORPORATE GOVERNANCE AND PSEs

There are a few key issues that are germane to the governance in Public Sector enterprises. Some of these issues were important even in the pre-1991 era in India, that is before the listing of PSEs on the stock exchanges. Companies that government enlisted on the stock exchanges have to comply with the statutes of listing requirements under the SEBI guidelines. The listed PSEs, are required to comply with all the requirements of law and listing agreements like publication of quarterly financial results, filing of periodical information with Stock Exchanges and Registrar of Companies and disclosure of information to the shareholders etc. With the process of disinvestments of PSE shares in 1990s, moreover, some basic changes in the governance of PSEs have come. Other than the standard accounting statements, share price movement captures the market rating of PSE performance and future expectations.

THE ISSUE OF OVER-GOVERNANCE

In addition to compliance of all requirements under the SEBI guidelines, the PSEs are subject to review of accounts by the Comptroller and Auditor General of India and placing of annual report of the Company before the Parliament. Besides these, there are periodic reviews by the Parliamentary committees and discussions in the Parliament during question answer sessions.

The PSEs thus function on a regular basis under the watchful eyes of the Government auditors who are placed in their premises. Many of the key processes such as marketing and procurement come under detailed scrutiny. Furthermore, the PSEs do not have to be just and equitable only in practice, but also appear to be so.

COMPETITION VERSUS TRANSPARENCY

Competing in the market place today depends on providing optimal customer satisfaction. This in today's business environment calls for ensuring value for money, cultivating customer relationship and excelling in customer services. However, while ensuring each of the above factors, PSEs have to ensure the perspective of probity. In the real life situation, the issue of over governance hampers actions of the personnel on the ground as it is restrictive. As the market becomes competitive, each customer has to be given special treatment. Depending upon their size, sector, potential etc., the customers are extended special commercial terms, thereby making marketing decisions subjective. However, the differential pricing extended through various schemes, many at times become difficult to explain. As such, while the price and commercial terms are never known exactly for a private supplier, the public sector operations have to be transparent for the total transaction, affecting in the process the competitive power of PSEs. Many a times, the field personnel shy away from taking decisions, thus affecting the bottom line of the company while mitigating personal risk.

Material procurement is another area where the practice in private and public sectors significantly differ. Adherence to laid down processes—say a 'Purchase Process' many a times takes precedence over the ultimate objective of getting the right material at the best rates. Many a times, technology brings solution for introducing more competitive systems. Today, the IT platform is being used by some PSEs for reverse auction and for cutting inordinate delays and litigation of the traditional tendering process. However, the coverage of material on this platform is limited.

PREVALENCE OF COMMITTEE CULTURE

In absence of technology, the tendency in PSEs is to opt for decisions through committees, wherever the quantity of transaction is significant. However, decisions by committee may not always result in better decision making. Attendant delays and lack of individual responsibility makes members lax. In case of any anomaly, although the error could be at the individual level, the entire group is held accountable.

DELAY IN DISPUTE SETTLEMENT

Another area overburdening the systems in the PSEs, concerns commercial disputes. Commercial transactions in real life, many a times, end up in commercial disputes. The practice in private sector is to settle these across the table. In the public sector, however, the rules and regulations are such that they foreclose any scope for negotiations for resolving commercial disputes. Any decision to settle commercial dispute is open to criticism. The tendency, therefore, is to allow the legal process to take its course resulting in inordinate delays and consequent loss to the Company. The adverse effect is not only on the cost of litigation but also diversion of managerial time from business management to dispute resolution.

CHANGING CULTURAL MOORINGS AND ROLE OF GOVERNMENT

A primary goal of good corporate governance is, however, to foster a culture of creativity, innovation and entrepreneurship to augment the prospect of enterprise and thereby the shareholder value. Seen in this context, the challenge before the PSEs is how to keep employees motivated to take appropriate risk rather than be safe and passive and meet the norms laid out in the books.

The Administrative Ministry plays an executive role in overseeing the operation of the PSE, and assessing the performance of Top Management/CEO. In regard to many of the key issues such as monitoring investment decisions beyond certain value, appointment of CEO/Directors, reviewing the performance of the company on a quarterly basis, the Govt./Administrative ministry is discharging an executive function. The fiduciary role of the Government is carried out through its nominees on the Board of Directors as well as through review of the performance by the CAG, Parliamentary Committees etc.

There is a view that the PSEs should not be answerable directly to Parliamentary Committees, Parliament and other government agencies. That, however, would be unfair. Given the accountability associated with use of public funds, it is just and logical for elected representatives of the people to ask questions about performance of PSEs, and the Government as a fiduciary to the public money, has to be answerable to the Parliament. If the Govt. is to be accountable for the PSEs, the concept of control over the PSEs follows logically.

THE PSE BOARDS AND INDEPENDENT DIRECTORS

The problem of PSEs in terms of size and composition of the Board is however, peculiar. Some of the PSEs are very big in size, and have plants/units sufficiently large, requiring representation of their heads/ CEOs on the Board of the company. Chairman of the PSEs normally being the chief executive and having functional Directors on the Board, the size of the Board becomes very large, especially so, with the induction of equal number of independent Directors from outside. While the SEBI treats Institutional directors on the Board of the companies as independent Directors (whether the Institution is investing institution, or lending institution), the Government Nominee

Directors on the boards of PSEs, in the opinion of SEBI, are not treated as independent thereby enlarging the Board further to fulfill the requisite positions by independent Directors.

No doubt, induction of independent Directors on the Board provides strength and brings in the much needed outside perspective for supplementing the knowledge of the full time Directors, and thus enhances the contribution of the Board to the business. But, too large a board in size is not conducive in transact the business of the company in an effective manner.

It is broadly believed that independent Directors on the Board of PSEs will:

(a) improve/professionalize the Board by bringing in their varied experience and knowledge; and
(b) act as a check to protect the overall interest of the enterprise and the minority share holders.

It has, nevertheless, to be recognized that unlike the private sector, the PSE Board does not appraise the performance of top management. Appointment of full time Directors and nomination of independent persons on the Board is in the hands of the Government. Compensation is again not in the hands of the Compensation Committee of the Board. Although the Board has a delegation of power, higher than the CEO, some of the critical decisions go for approval of the Administrative Ministry.

POSSIBLE DIRECTIONS OF PSE REFORMS

How does one make Board functional in the real sense? There are three key issues that need addressing in the context namely

1. Redefining Government's Ownership and Executive Roles
2. Empowerment of the PSE Boards
3. Issues related to Audit of Accounts

REDEFINING GOVERNMENT'S OWNERSHIP AND EXECUTIVE ROLES

A few important changes in management of PSEs have taken place recently, which have lessened the need for executive control. Traditionally, budgetary support from Government—either through equity or by way of long term loan, were the main sources of financing the PSEs. Of late, Government has been keeping itself away from financing PSEs. As a result, PSEs are now at par with other public limited companies in the Private Sector as they are raising funds on their own from the market either through leveraging long term loans based on their equity, or raising resources directly from the capital market.

Given this background, the traditional executive role discharged by the Government needs to undergo a change. There is, moreover, a need to align two different lines of control that the PSE management are subjected to, namely, (a) the PSE Board, and (b) the Administrative Ministry.

To eliminate the conflict between executive and ownership roles, Government may delegate the executive power to the Board and an autonomous body that can act on its behalf. A separate autonomous body can be created to oversee the selection, appointment, performance evaluation and remuneration of the Directors. It will also induct the independent Directors on the Board. The body will oversee all the Central PSEs and the role of Government may be confined to that of policy making. The model will be similar to the practice being followed in countries such as New Zealand, Australia and South Africa.

EMPOWERMENT OF THE PSE BOARDS

If the Government is going to play the role of only owner or shareholder, then PSEs will be basically Board managed companies, and the Board will be accountable to shareholders and protect their interest in the management of the company. It will be responsible for formulating Company's plans—both long term and short term, oversee their implementation, and periodically monitor them.

Although the salary of the Board members will be determined based on the norms, decided by the Government of India/Department of Public Enterprises the Board should have the power to fix perquisites subject to a ceiling. The Board members may also be given the stock option as incentive. Further, the CEO of the Board should have the power to give additional charge to a Director against temporary vacancy as well as the power of rotation of Directors with the approval of the Board.

ISSUES RELATED TO AUDIT OF ACCOUNTS

As there is little gain to the management in hiding the material facts, it is generally observed that PSEs fully cooperate in auditing and are responsive to suggestions from the auditors. Moreover, besides review of accounts and audit of the statutory auditors nominated by the CAG, the system of Peer Review is already in place in PSEs. Nevertheless, given the competition PSEs have to operate in, there is a need to lessen such supervision at the operating level, by multiple agencies.

In conclusion, Corporate Governance in the PSEs, like that for any enterprise under any form of ownership, should promote an environment that should encourage innovation and risk taking with due accountability. At a macro level, Corporate Governance practice, which are appropriate for the private sector should hold good for the public sector.

Unshackling the Indian Public Sector

*V.K. Agarwal**

INTRODUCTION

In his address to the nation on the eve of Republic Day, 2001 Mr. K.R. Narayanan, the former President of India, observed, 'What we have done is to keep pace with world developments. While making necessary changes in our policies, it is important to recognize the contributions made by India in its earlier stage of development and that it is standing upon the shoulders of our earlier policies and their results that we are today liberalizing and globalizing our economy.'

Empowerment of public sector enterprises is an important part of this liberalization and globalization strategy that the nation is pursuing. Yet nobody expected autonomy to come to public sector enterprises easily. There were problems on many sides. The government did not want to unshackle the PSEs for various reasons—some justifiable and others not so. There was a reluctance to part with control over the PSEs as there was the apprehension that transferred power may not be used well even if not misused grossly.

PSEs were, moreover, seen as legitimate tools in the hands of the government for the furtherance of its social objectives. On the occasion of release of the monograph on the study "The Indian CEOs—Competencies for Success" jointly conducted by PESB, BPCL and Hay Group in 2005, the Hon'ble Prime Minister Dr. Manmohan Singh in 2005 observed; 'Our investment in the public sector is not an act of faith, nor a measure of social security. The public sector is meant to strengthen national capabilities so that our economy can grow and our Nation can be strengthened.'

The PSEs were, however, not fully ready to receive the autonomy in one go. The mindset was not that of a private company where the system of checks and balances operates differently, to say the least. It is no surprise

* Managing Director, RITES Limited.

therefore that after several years of liberalization of the (Indian) economy there are still a host of issues that are engaging our attention.

WHY PSE EMPOWERMENT? WHY GREATER AUTONOMY?

PSE empowerment is not an end in itself but the means to further national objectives. These objectives are:

- Accelerating the growth of the Indian economy.
- Investing in sectors and regions where private sector is unwilling to invest
- Increasing the competitiveness of PSEs

It is the public sector that enabled the development of indigenous capabilities in the early decades after independence. Arguably, the private sector would have achieved the same growth levels, but that would have led to foreign domination in many lines of production. Entities, such as public sector banks with rural orientation have been initiatives where the social focus is important and urgent. Public sector enterprises have, moreover, been established in sectors and regions where the private sector does not and sometimes cannot operate. And this is the *raison d'etre* for the existence of PSEs.

RITES LTD AS A CPSE

RITES was incorporated in the year 1974 under the Companies Act 1956 with the objective to enhance the technological image of the country and earn foreign exchange through export of consultancy and supply/operation/maintenance of railway rolling stock and transport related services and equipment. It has also been providing consultancy and other services to projects of national importance. A few examples of such consultancy project by RITES are:

- Key role in Design of Metro Systems
- Total Traffic System Study for India (for all major transportation modes)

RITES is a mini-ratna consultancy company and is a repository of experience and knowledge. RITES is ranked first in India and 64th in the world amongst the top 200 engineering consultants. (Source: Swedish International Survey) In terms of financial performance, it achieved an all time high turnover of 414 crores in 2005-06 with net profit of 101 crores (Annexure.1). As high as one-third of its turnover came from overseas business.

IMPEDIMENTS TO FURTHER GROWTH

With the explosive growth of industry in recent years the CPSEs are faced today with a variety of challenges. While some challenges could be tackled effectively, there are many others that need to be addressed at the earliest. A few of these impediments to growth of public sector enterprises are discussed below.

Wide Disparity in Emoluments between the Public and Private Sectors

Wide disparity in the emoluments between employees of CPSEs and of private corporate sector is leading to a serious drain of skills from the public sector. Competence and efficiency, however, do not vary directly with the size of the salary packet; it would therefore be naive to believe that if the employees of PSEs were paid salaries comparable to their peers, say, in Infosys or General Electric, they would transform the PSEs into dynamic institutions generating large profits. However, the truth is that while paying a higher salary may yield only limited results, the existence of significantly higher pay in the private sector is leading to brain drain from the public sector. One frequently, hears the argument that the low emoluments in PSEs are due to the fact that the chairman cannot get more than what the top civil servants get as their salaries and hence everyone down the line is poorly paid. The answer to this dilemma is that the civil servants also ought to be paid better.

In addition to high attrition rates in the public sector, there is this added problem of inability to attract the best talent to the public sector. Very few graduates from front ranking institutions are joining PSEs. The disparity in salaries is resulting in:

- Low morale
- Inadequate motivation
- Poaching by competitors

Poaching of employees is in regard especially to staff with considerable experience and knowledge. This is resulting in not-so-level playing field for the public sector. It is like competing with the world players with the hands tied behind the back. The urgency of this situation is especially felt in a consultancy organization like RITES. Experience of prior consulting is extremely important in this business. As such the loss is big if an experienced consultant of RITES joins a private sector competitor.

WHAT CAN BE DONE?

While various suggestions already exist on this issue, I have the following recommendations to make:

1. Employees Compensation

While ceilings on pay/salaries of employees may remain as before, these can still be raised in a big way from the current levels. The company boards may, accordingly, be mandated to come up with short and long-term plans. The pay of the employees can be restructured to include incentives such as:

- higher variable pay.
- stock options (particularly in consultancy organizations).
- profit-sharing
- merger of DA with 50 per cent of Basic pay (in IDA PSEs) etc.
- performance linked remuneration—performance linked bonus to be given to CEOs & Functional Directors up to 1 per cent of net profits.

The compensation package for the CEO and the senior management on the other hand should be in two parts of 'basic salary' and 'performance-linked remuneration'. In order to provide adequate incentive to the management in PSEs (as also to attract the best talent available in the industry), the performance linked portion of the remuneration should be sufficiently high. At the same time, the senior management should be prepared to take the flak if the performance is not up to the mark.

2. Foreign Business Travel

All travels by CEO/Directors should be within the competence of the Board of Directors (BOD) if it is in line with the company's business policy. It just does not make sense to restrict the movements and leave it in the hands of controlling ministries. Ministries should trust the BODs in this respect. A great deal has been already said in this context for reducing the interference by the ministers and the ministries. Our Prime Minister had this to say about it in January 2005;"... it is entirely possible that private sector companies are far better off and that public sector enterprises have to still contend with ministers and ministries. If so, we must change this and give greater functional autonomy to public sector CEOs." This functional autonomy is taking its time to come. Accelerating this is the need of the hour.

3. Joint Ventures/Capital Investment

In order to facilitate a faster growth path for the PSEs, they have to be encouraged to go in for inorganic growth. At the recent conference of Chief Executives of central public sector enterprises, the Prime Minister, Dr. Manmohan Singh, asked them *to learn from their private sector counterparts and seize opportunities for mergers, acquisitions, amalgamations, takeovers and creating new joint ventures.* Public-private partnerships are also an important means of improving the PSEs' ability to compete in an increasingly dynamic and challenging environment through quick access to technology, opening up new markets, providing means for synergy as also giving access to new resources.

4. Right-sizing of PSEs

PSE managers have to recognize that in the context of right-sizing and high employee turnover in PSEs, there is an increasing importance of knowledge management though IT. Both the numbers as well as the type of human resource require continuous review to ensure that the skill sets available are just right for meeting the changing needs of the organization. While inducting younger people, there is also the unpleasant need of getting rid of the dead wood so as to keep the organization healthy. This will require even the VRS schemes to be more attractive.

5. Independent Directors and BOD Meetings

While Independent Directors can be instrumental in improving the decision making processes in PSEs very significantly, there is a need for careful selection and ensuring that greater attention is paid to how we identify Independent Directors. A system of performance evaluation (or feedback) of Independent Directors may also be developed and applied. This will increase the sense of responsibility amongst the Independent Directors. A familiarization programme for Independent Directors may also be considered, especially in areas of financial appraisal and project evaluation etc.

The frequency and duration of Board meetings and the attendance record of the Directors (especially Independent Directors) should be also brought in the public domain. Participation in BODs by video conferencing should be encouraged/permitted. All joint ventures/capital investment, not only in India but also abroad, should be within the competence of the BOD, provided it is within specified limits and within the administrative ministry's policy.

CONCLUSION

In short, we would like the PSEs to be more autonomous and more determined players in the business arena. PSE empowerment must proceed apace so that they may become world class players by:

- Taking quick commercial decisions
- Compete in the world market albeit with some restraints
- Bridge the technology gap where it exists

The time of the Indian public sector has come. Let us seize it.

Annex 1

PROFIT AND LOSS ACCOUNT—RITES LTD.

(Rs. Lakhs)

PARTICULARS	2005-06	2004-05	2003-04	2002-03
(1) INCOME				
(A) SALES/OPERATING INCOME	41401	23690	27807	26283
(B) EXICE DUTY	1963	1494	1112	846
(C) NET SALES	39438	22196	26695	25437
(D) OTHER INCOME/RECEIPTS	3204	1834	1759	1440
(E) ACCRET10N/DEPLETION IN STOCKS	4629	60	-1506	1396
TOTAL	47271	24090	26948	28273
(2) EXPENDITURE				
(A) PURCHASE OF FINISHED GOOD CONSUMPTION OF RAW MATERIALS	10617	1130	1420	3467
(B) STORES & SPARES	174	117	294	307
(C) POWERS FUEL	163	157	111	86
(D) MANUFACTURING/DIRECT/ OPERATING EXP.	5888	0	0	1310
(E) SALARY, WAGES & BENEFITS/EMPLOYEE EXP.	8108	7548	7615	7671
(F) OTHER EXPENSES	5400	6602	7923	8,789
(G) PROVISIONS	2226	851	281	681
TOTAL	32576	16405	17644	22311
(3) PROFIT BEFORE DEP, INT, TAXES & EP (PBDITEP)	14695	7685	9304	5962
(4) DEPRECIATION	1207	521	557	397
(5) DRE/PERL EXP WRITTEN OFF	0	0	0	0
(6) PROFIT BEFORE INT., TAXES & EP (PBITEP)	13488	7164	8747	5565
(7) INTEREST				
(A) ON CENTRAL GOVERNMENT LOANS	0	0	0	0
(B) ON FOREIGN LOANS	0	0	0	0
(C) OTHERS	0	43	228	900
(D) LESS INTEREST CAPITALISED	0	0	0	0
(E) CHARGED TO P & L ACCOUNT	0	43	228	900
(8) PROFIT BEFORE TAX & EP (PBTEP)	13488	7121	8519	466^
(9) TAX PROVISIONS	3381	2640	2462	605
(10) NET PROFIT/LOSS(-) BEFORE EP	10107	4481	6057	4060
(11) NET EXTRA-ORD. ITEMS	191	361	1287	-5443
(12) NET PROFIT/LOSS (-)	9916	4120	4770	9503
(13) DIVIDEND DECLARED	2000	1200	1167	500
(14) DIVIDEND TAX	281	165	150	32
(15) RETAINED PROFIT	7635	2755	3453	8971

Central Public Sector Enterprises: Challenges Ahead

*R.C. Panda**

India opted for the mixed economy framework after Independence. This allowed for the role of both the public and the private sectors in the economic development of the country. Investments in the public sector enterprises have been the result of the plan provisions under the Five Year Plans. The Central Public Sector Enterprises (CPSEs) have been established largely in areas that are delineated under the Central and the Concurrent List of the Constitution of India. Public sector investments under the Plans moreover have generally been made to bridge the gap between the required investments in the economy and the investment forthcoming from the private sector.

Beginning with 5 CPSEs on the eve of the First Five Year Plan, there were 245 CPSEs as on 31st March, 2006 (Table 1). The Second Five Year Plan that coincided with the Industrial Policy Resolution of 1956, laid emphasis on the investment in the heavy engineering industries, and this continued to hold sway until the Fifth Five Year Plan. It was only during the Sixth Five Year Plan that the Government of India decided to set up CPSEs in the infrastructure sectors. The GDP growth rate in the Indian economy significantly improved consequent to the investment in infrastructure, especially so in the power sector. This only shows the close relationship between the investment in CPSEs and the growth of the economy.

Although the larger number of CPSEs belong to the category of 'Greenfield projects', CPSEs, such as, National Textile Corporation, Coal India Limited (and its subsidiaries), Iron and Steel Co. have been the results of nationalization/take over from the private sector as they faced 'closures' or else did not meet the minimum safety standards and working conditions. Recent years have witnessed disinvestment

* Secretary to Government of India, Ministry of Heavy Industries and Public Enterprises.

in enterprises like Indian Petrochemicals Corporation Ltd., Bharat Aluminum Company, and Maruti Udyog Limited leading to their privatization.

TABLE 1: FIVE YEAR PLANS AND INVESTMENT IN CPSEs

Particulars	*Total investment (Rs. in crore)*	*Enterprises (Nos)*
On the eve of the Ist Five Year Plan	29	5
On the eve of the 2nd Five Year Plan (1.4.1956)	81	21
On the eve of the 3rd Five Year Plan (1.4.1961)	948	47
At the end of 3rd Five Year Plan (31.3.1966)	2,410	73
On the eve of the 4th Five Year Plan (1.4.1969)	3,897	84
On the eve of the 5th Five Year Plan (1.4.1974)	6,237	122
At the end of 5th Five Year Plan (31.3.1979)	15,534	169
On the eve of the 6th Five Year Plan (1.4.1980)	18,150	179
On the eve of the 7th Five Year Plan (1.4.1985)	42,673	215
At the end of 7th Five Year Plan (31.3.1990)	99,329	244
On the eve of the 8th Five Year Plan (1.4.1992)	1,35,445	246
At the end of 8th Five Year Plan (31.3.1997)	2,13,610	242
At the end of 9th Five Year Plan (31.3.2002)	3,24,614	240
As on 31.03.2003	3,35,647	240
As on 31.03.2004	3,49,994	242
As on 31.03.2005	3,57,939	237
As on 31.03.2006	3,93,057	245

Source: Department of Public Enterprises (GoI), Public Enterprises Survey (2005-06)

The Industrial Policy Reforms (1991) of Government of India opened the whole of the manufacturing sector (barring few exceptions) for private sector investment. This was the beginning of the 1st generation of economic reforms and delicensing in many sectors. Subsequently trade liberalization, consequent to the WTO agreement, has also made things more competitive for the CPSEs. The monopoly regime of the Public sector got the jolt. Many of the CPSEs have, nevertheless, withstood 'competition' and are increasingly taking advantage of opportunities beyond the domestic market. This was the starting point for Navratnas and Miniratnas which were provided with more operational autonomy by the Government-owner to face the challenges from the private sector.

CONTRIBUTION OF CPSEs TO THE ECONOMY

The CPSEs are stated to be the bulwarks of the economy as they are into the technologically more advanced sectors of heavy engineering, steel, energy and transportation. While they have contributed to 'self-sufficiency of the economy', they have served the objectives of regional growth and creation of job opportunities for the people. These large corporations are into areas that are technologically complex. Their operations depended on association of a large number of skilled and highly qualified people (also called "techno-structure"), and is claimed to be changing the lives of the people.

The total turnover of CPSEs has been showing a continuous rise over the years. It thus went up from Rs. 2,76,002 crore in 1987-88 to Rs. 8,32,584 crore in 2005-06 (Table 2). Net worth (aggregate) of all CPSEs has also kept pace with the increase in turnover. Accordingly, the net worth of all CPSEs that was Rs. 1,34,443 crore in 1987-88 went up to Rs. 4,12,737 crore in 2005-06. Contribution to the shareholders, mainly the Government of India has been also showing a continuous rise over the years. The dividend payment of all CPSEs went up from Rs. 3609 crore in 1987-88 to Rs. 2,28,86 crore in 2005-06, contribution to the Government by way of taxes, interests and dividends put together have been also on the rise, which went up from Rs. 42,289 crore in 1987-88 to Rs. 1,25,384 crore in 2005-06.

TABLE 2: HIGHLIGHTS ON CPSEs, DURING 2005—06 (AS ON 31ST MARCH, 2006)

Total number of CPSEs		245
CPSEs under construction		20
CPSEs in operation		225
Profit making CPSEs		157
Loss making CPSEs		58
CPSEs not furnished information		10
		Growth over the previous year (%)
Total Investment in CPSEs	Rs. 3,93,057 cr	9.81%
Total Turnover	Rs. 8,32,584 cr	11.86%
Total Networth	Rs. 4,12,737 cr	20.83%
Total Net profit	Rs. 70,288 cr	8.20%
Total Dividend declared	Rs. 22,886 cr	10.46%
Total Contribution to Central Exchequer	Rs. 1,25,384 cr	13.36%
Total Foreign Exchange Earned	Rs. 46,403 cr	9.83%

ELEVENTH PLAN AND CPSEs

The target GDP growth rate during the 11th Five Year Plan has been kept at an average of around 9 per cent, with acceleration through the Plan period and ending with a rate of around 10 per cent in the final year. The GDP growth of 9 per cent calls for a 32.3 per cent of domestic savings and an investment of 35 per cent (as percentage of

GDP) during the 11th Plan period (Table 3). A perusal of savings rate assumed for the PSEs under these three scenario, shows that the share of PSEs in domestic savings declines to 2.8 per cent on a 9 per cent GDP growth scenario when compared to those assumed for 7 per cent (3.1%) and 8 per cent (3.1%) growth. This does not, however, imply that the desired savings **in** *absolute terms* will come down. In this context, the 11th Plan cautions, 'the savings of public sector enterprises would need to increase somewhat since PSE investment financed by Internal Resources and Extra-budgetary Resources (IEBR), would need to increase by 1.5 per cent of GDP'. Indeed, a good many commercial enterprises, companies (CPSEs, departmental enterprises and financial companies) have significant 'reserves and surplus' on their balance sheets and through either leveraging these surplus funds with debt funds or raising funds directly from the capital market they can mobilize much larger resources.

The alternative growth scenarios and the commensurate *savings and investments* required in the economy for achieving these growth rates are given below:

TABLE 3 SAVINGS AND INVESTMENTS, DURING 11TH PLAN

	Growth Scenarios (as % of GDP)		
	7%	8%	9%
I. Gross Domestic Savings, of which	27.1	29.6	32.3
(1.1) Household	20.1	20.5	21.0
(1.2) Corporate	5.0	5.5	6.1
(1.3) PSEs	3.1	3.1	2.8
(1.4) Government	-1.1	0.5	2.4
II. Investments of which,	29.1	32.0	35.1
(2.1) Public	8.4	9.8	11.2
(2.2) Private	20.7	22.2	23.9

Source: Planning Commission (GoI), Approach Paper to the 11th Plan.

The different Working Groups Reports prepared in the Planning Commission for the formulation of the Eleventh Plan, moreover, point towards the need for large scale investments in power, steel, coal, hydro-carbon and transportation sectors etc. The average level of public sector investment during the 10th Plan has been equal to 6.7 per cent of GDP. This will have to be raised to 11.2 per cent of GDP during the 11th Plan, *and that is a challenge before the public sector*. It is worthwhile mentioning that the figures on public investment mentioned above (for the 11th Plan) does not take into account the investments that may be forthcoming from the public-private-partnership (PPP) mode. The 11th Plan, in this regard, observes, 'PPP offers a distinct possibility for increasing total investment in certain key sectors by using limited amount of public resources to leverage a much larger amount of private investment'. Even when assuming that some measure of success in this direction will be achieved, *the public sector investment would have to increase from 6.7 per cent of GDP in the 10th Plan to 10.2 per cent of GDP for achieving the targeted 9 per cent growth of GDP.*

COMPETITION AND CPSEs

As already mentioned, the CPSEs do not operate any more under a closed economy model. With lower tariffs and sectors no more reserved exclusively for them, they are faced with competition in the market. Competitiveness, in turn, is a function of *efficiency, superior technology, marketing skills and customer satisfaction.* The CPSEs shall have to pay greater attention to all these aspects. Although 'globalization' of the Indian economy poses 'threats' of all kinds to the domestic industries, it also promises 'opportunities'. The CPSEs will have to employ all kind of planning and marketing strategies, such as, expansions to a critical size to reap economies of scale, modernization, university-industry research collaboration, takeovers, mergers and acquisition and forward contact (with both buyers and sellers).

The Government policy has been to remove all irritants for the healthy functioning of public enterprises. Government commitment towards a stronger and vibrant public sector is reflected in the *National Common Minimum Programme (NCMP)*, which calls for strengthening and empowering the PSEs with full managerial and financial autonomy. The *Memorandum of Understanding system* may have to be further strengthened for ensuring greater autonomy to public enterprises and for providing a more meaningful interface with the Government. During the current year, the Government has taken the bold initiative of bringing even the 'sick and loss making CPSEs' under the umbrella of the MoU system. Besides expanding the scope of the MoU system, various recommendations of the Ad-hoc Group of Experts (AGE) on Empowerment of CPSEs have been also implemented. Accordingly, greater financial and managerial autonomy has been granted to the *Navratna, Miniratna and profit making PSEs* with a view to facilitate timely investment and business decisions. 'Navratna' enterprises have been allowed to incur expenditure on purchase of new items or for replacement without any monetary ceiling. They can now enter into technology joint ventures or strategic alliances and obtain technology and know-how by purchase or other arrangements. Such enterprises can also effect organizational restructuring including establishment of profit centre's, opening of offices in India and abroad, creating new activity centres, etc. The Board of Directors of these enterprises can further delegate power relating to the Human Resource Management to below Board level executives or sub-committees. They can raise debt from both the domestic or international capital markets subject to the compliance of normal procedural conditions. The same applies in regard to decision relating to *'mergers and acquisitions'*.

Public Enterprises have to run as Board-led organizations, having the highest *concern for professionalism. Enlisting of more and more PSEs on the stock exchanges* has been observed to enhance professionalization of the Board of Directors through induction of Independent Directors. *Independent Directors on the boards of PSEs* will also ensure greater transparency and effectiveness in decision-making. It is important to keep ready a list of Independent Directors from among the experts and professionals with capability to guide the enterprise in the right manner. It is also important for the Independent Directors to fulfil the expectations from them. It goes without saying that their independence should be protected/guaranteed.

There is, moreover, a need for specified 'code of conduct and business ethics' for the Board and senior management. The Government, therefore, attaches utmost importance to the matters relating to *Corporate Governance*. The Department of Public Enterprises has recently formulated the guidelines on the various aspects of Corporate Governance, in consultation with the various stakeholders. In view of the Clause 49 of SEBI guidelines and for reasons of wider concerns, it is essential that the Central Public Enterprises introduce an effective Corporate Governance system.

Enterprises flourish where there is a premium on *entrepreneurship*. Entrepreneurship requires enabling and facilitative environment, along with considerable immunity to the Board of Directors and to the chief executive officer (Management) to facilitate quick decision-making. Too much regulation restricts entrepreneurial drive and makes the Management risk averse. There is a need to empower the Board suitably to speed up decision-making while at the same time good adhering to the code of corporate conduct.

A progressive and proactive approach is being adopted to set PSEs free on the road to becoming globally competitive entities. The PSE executives feel that the *remuneration* of the executives and senior management in PSEs is not commensurate with the duties and responsibilities that they undertake. The Government is making efforts to bridge the gap between such aspirations and the present emoluments, in order to give a sense of job satisfaction to the employees and the management of CPSEs. *Justice Jagannath Rao* is currently heading the *Second Pay Revision Committee* to address to all these issues.

WAY FORWARD

Public Enterprises also need to take measures on their own for empowerment and growth. The issues before CPSEs may be enumerated as follows:

- Mission and Vision,
- Modernization and expansion,
- Technology development,
- Market strategies,
- Corporate Social Responsibility.

- *Mission and Vision*: There is need for enhancing the profitability of CPSEs through increased volumes of output/turnover. CPSEs will do well to *unlock their value* through *superior utilization of assets* and increasing their market share. Today the product profile is changing very fast and the CPSEs have not been able to keep pace with the changing times. Stagnant/declining market share only shows complacency. CPSEs should inculcate an insatiable feeling for increasing their market share, and try to emerge in the long-run as leaders in their sectors. Size being essence of the growth in the modern world, public enterprises should do everything to achieve the critical minimum for reaping 'economies of scale' having *Global Vision with Local action*. Some CPSEs do figure in the list of 'Fortune 500' companies of the world. Major PSEs particularly, the Navratnas are global players.
- *Modernization and expansion* could also result in the improvement of productivity and ultimately profitability. They should look at mergers, acquisitions, amalgamations, takeovers, and de-mergers as an integral part of their business strategy. The modernization will create further value addition

through effective cost-controls, less expensive financing, higher productivity and improved man management, production processes and automation etc.

- *Technology development*, which was the citadel of public enterprises, can be a very important catalyst for the growth of public enterprises. The CPSEs should create conducive climate for innovations, change and registering intellectual property rights. These can be achieved by *strengthening the base for Research and Development*. The creativity and breakthrough in regard to *intellectual property rights will determine the growth and longevity of an enterprise*. PSEs need to be empowered for growth, both through policy orientation and making concerted efforts in building competencies and technical efficiencies. Investment in R & D should be an important commitment of the public sector as PSEs operate in a highly competitive environment and face competition from both domestic and foreign private sector companies.
- *Market strategies*: The CPSEs are observed to be weak in marketing. Their too much dependence on Government support has weakened the marketing competitiveness. Although the common man has a sense of faith in the public sector as a brand, PSEs are unable to utilize this trust for betterment. 'Globalization' has come to stay. India needs to benefit from 'globalizations'. Needless to say, the present condition of CPSEs leaves much to do in regard to '*Quality*' as an essential feature of goods and services provided by CPSEs. Quality improves competitiveness and there is greater appeal for products and services. *Customer satisfaction and complaint resolution also need to be paid equal attention.*
- Finally, the *corporate social responsibility* is an emerging societal issue for the CPSEs. The CPSEs have been ahead of others in this respect. They have served the national and social objectives of 'regional development' and 'self-sufficiency' very well. They should continue to do so and promote educational and health care facilities in the regions wherever they are located, improve the environmental conditions of the local people as part of nation building.

Public sector in India has come of age. Full managerial and commercial autonomy to profit making PSEs has been achieved to a large extent. Major PSEs particularly the Navratnas are global players. Although some PSEs have transformed themselves into sound commercial enterprises capable of competing with the best in the world, getting listed on the stock exchanges and enhancing professionalization of their Board of Directors will have to their primary tasks. They will also have to adopt good corporate governance vis-a-vis business ethics, probity and transparency.

Part III
Report of
Ad Hoc Group of Experts
on Empowerment of
Central Public Sector Enterprises

Report of Ad Hoc Group of Experts on Empowerment of Central Public Sector Enterprises

CHAPTER 1
INTRODUCTION

1.1 The last couple of decades have witnessed an accelerated pace of political and economic integration across the world and the increasing-interdependence between economies of different countries. This phenomenon, which is broadly called 'globalisation', has been reinforced in the last decade by an increasing impact of the multilateral trade regime ushered in by the formation of the World Trade Organization in 1994. Another phenomenon that has assumed tremendous significance is the technological revolution, including information technology that is sweeping the world forcefully in an all pervasive manner. Any failure to respond to this can only lead to obsolescence, in the total sense of the term. Technology, information and ideas are no longer confined within the boundaries of a sovereign state. All the above mentioned factors have also caused institutional changes, including modifications in the policy, industrial organization and administration of laws and regulations that govern the behaviour of economic agents.

1.2 The response of India to this changing world environment has resulted in far-reaching economic reforms initiated more comprehensively since the beginning of the 1990s. Fiscal and monetary policies, trade and export-import policies, industrial policies, etc. have all been aligned with the new reforms and initiatives.

1.3 With increasing competition from the domestic private sector as well as foreign companies in the wake of liberalization and globalisation, the need to empower Central Public Sector Enterprises (CPSEs) with greater financial and operational powers was realized in order to enable them to effectively face increasing levels of competition. To delegate these powers, the concept of Navratna and Miniratna was introduced in July and October 1997. The powers delegated were related to incurring Capital expenditure, formation of Joint Ventures/ Subsidiaries/strategic alliances, implementation of HRD policies including VRS etc. Later, certain powers for incurring Capital expenditure were also delegated to other profit making CPSEs. The professionalization of Boards of Directors was made a precondition to ensure that the enhanced powers were used prudently. Professionals were inducted in the Boards of Directors of these CPSEs and audit committees were also set up. These measures have helped in more objective and quicker decision-making by the Boards of Directors of CPSEs, with the independent Directors bringing in fresh thinking. The National Common Minimum Programme of the UPA Government has mandated devolution of full managerial and commercial autonomy to successful and profit making CPSEs operating in a competitive environment. Such measures are expected to motivate the Management and the employees of the Navratna and Miniratna CPSEs to perform better. These would also motivate other CPSEs to improve their performance in order to achieve the coveted status of being either a Navratna or Miniratna.

1.4 The first delegation of powers to Navratnas/Miniratnas in 1997 has certainly contributed to the improved performance of some of those Enterprises. But the fast changing world economic environment and the mandate of the National Common Minimum Programme now call for some bold and new thinking, and not mere incrementalism in empowerment. The last decade or so has witnessed perceptible performance improvements in a number of companies, whether it be GE or Motorola elsewhere in the world or Bajaj Auto, Infosys or Wipro at home. The managements of these companies did not believe in incrementalism of performance; and the quantum leaps in their performance have been the result of fully accountable but fully empowered management teams. Repeating/inducing such success in the CPSEs will require more than incremental empowerment. In a deregulated, fast changing and competitive economy, and with gradual dismantling of tariff barriers as envisaged in the non-agricultural market access negotiations in WTO, a company which is not adaptive and not growing fast enough will definitely cease to exist. The rigour of these new challenges is equally matched by unprecedented opportunities in the new world order which are such that a determined management can take its company to new levels of success much more quickly and effectively than in the past. Such opportunities can, however, be exploited fully by CPSEs only if certain specific areas are addressed in respect of autonomy accompanied by accountability. They are:

- Issues of ownership by the Government and delegation of administrative and financial powers to CPSEs
- Audit of Government companies
- Constitutional Issues
- Parliamentary Accountability
- Vigilance Issues

CHAPTER 2
OWNERSHIP ISSUES AND POWERS OF CPSES

2.1 The question of the autonomy of CPSEs essentially relates to the issues of ownership, control and management. Ownership is usually associated with the overall control of the enterprise for the long-term value creation of the company and achieving its medium and long-term objectives. The shareholders who are the owners seldom get involved in controlling the day-to-day operations of the company. For that, the companies have their Board of Directors, who are responsible for reviewing and overseeing the effectiveness of operations and management at periodic intervals. The Management, in turn, is in the charge of the Chief Executive of the company assisted by other functional Directors. In order to ensure effective governance of the company, it is necessary to properly design and implement the ownership functions, the powers and operational procedures of the Board of Directors and the responsibilities together with suitable checks and balances for exercising control over the Management.

2.2 For maintaining the overall control of the company, it is not necessary that the owner should own 100 per cent of the shares. A majority of shareholding is in most cases sufficient for all purposes and even a minority shareholding in a widely held company may often let the owners have basic control of the company operations, necessary to ensure the maintenance and improvement of the value of the assets of the company, as well as implementation of the programmes for realizing its basic objectives.

2.3 The National Common Minimum Programme (NCMP) of the UPA Government affirms commitment to a strong and effective public sector. To facilitate better commercial functioning of the successful and profit-making CPSEs which are operating in a competitive environment, the NCMP has pledged to devolve full managerial and commercial autonomy. It is also mentioned in the NCMP that generally profit-making CPSEs will not be privatized.

The Ad-hoc Group of Experts (AGE), therefore, felt that the Government, as the principal owner of the CPSEs, should have complete flexibility of owning or disinvesting its shares to obtain the maximum value for their assets through sale and purchase or disinvestment and reinvestment of the shares. The Group was of the view that this issue has to be dealt with differentially by dividing the CPSEs in two categories: Navratnas, Miniratnas and other consistently profit-making CPSEs (those CPSEs which have been making profits for the past three consecutive years and have a positive net worth) in Category I and the other CPSEs in Category II.

In keeping with the letter and spirit of the NCMP, the Group was of the view that a decision, if any, to privatize a Category I CPSE by reducing Government shareholding to a level less than 51 per cent in it should be taken only with the consent of the Parliament, as the ultimate representative of the people. However, in case of other CPSEs (Category II), the Government should have full flexibility of owning or disinvesting their shares. The Board of Directors of both categories of CPSEs should also have the power to raise equity capital from the market, so long as the Government's share of the overall equity remains above 51 per cent.

2.4 The Ministry in charge of the company should recognize the fact that they are not the owners of the company but are only exercising the functions of ownership as a custodian on behalf of the Government and the public at large. The Group felt that the current system of the Ministry being in overall charge of a CPSE, facilitating its functions and looking after its interests has been quite useful and should therefore be continued, subject to certain suggestions which have been made in the subsequent paragraphs. However, it must be ensured that the Ministry takes into account not only the interest of the Government as a whole but also of the non-governmental shareholders, who are equally interested in safeguarding the value of their asset. This is particularly important as many of the CPSEs are now listed in the stock markets, with their shares held by members of the public at large as well as financial/non-financial institutions. Furthermore, it also must be ensured that the Government in discharging the functions of ownership does not get involved in controlling the details of operations and the day-to-day management of the company. Finally, as far as the listed CPSEs are concerned, the Government should also facilitate the fulfilment of the provisions of Clause 49 of listing agreement, in conformity with the guidelines of the market regulator, SEBI.

2.5 The Group considered several models of ownership of companies and an arms-length relationship of government with the Board of Directors and the Management and came to the view that the governance of CPSEs, and especially the Navratnas and Miniratnas and other profit making companies should continue to be supervised by the three tier system, namely, the Ministry concerned representing the Government, the Board of Directors, and the Management, with the role, powers and functions of each of them clearly defined and codified. After studying the working of all the three tiers involved, the Group was strongly of the view that an institutional arrangement is required in order to ensure harmonious relations and interactions among the three tiers and to provide for the redressal of grievances of the stakeholders. To fulfil this requirement, the Group recommends the establishment of six overarching sectoral Supervisory Bodies, consisting of ten members each, with the following composition:

Permanent Members

- Minister of Finance,
- Minister in charge of DPE—Convener,
- Five independent distinguished experts of the relevant sector.

Agenda Specific Members

- Minister of Administrative Ministry of the concerned CPSE,
- Secretary of Administrative Ministry of the concerned CPSE,
- Chief Executive of the concerned CPSE.

The five independent expert members representing diverse, professional and non-political interests from the relevant sector should be nominated for a fixed term by the Prime Minister.

Separate Supervisory Bodies should be set up for the sectors indicated below. These six sectors have been suggested to ensure that these bodies are not ministry-specific but cover a broad and diverse group of CPSEs.

- Energy
- Manufacturing
- Infrastructure
- Trading & Services
- Food & Agriculture
- Social Sector

The Role of the Supervisory Body

2.6 The Supervisory Body will undertake the following responsibilities:

- To take an overview of the conformity of corporate strategy to the Vision and the Mission of the CPSE
- To periodically review interactions between the administrative Ministry and the CPSE
- To be the arbiter of ethics; in particular, to review all allegations against the members of the Board of Directors and make appropriate recommendation to the concerned authority.

- To recommend continuation/separation of Functional Directors in case of difference between recommendations of the Public Enterprises Selection Board (PESB) and the Ministry concerned.
- To monitor redressal of stakeholder grievances
- To consider any other issue to promote independent, efficient and cohesive functioning of the concerned Board of Directors

The Supervisory Body should not give any direct instructions to the CPSEs. It should give its views only on matters referred to it. The Supervisory Body would also provide a formal grievance redressal system for the Board Members of CPSEs.

2.7 There are some issues related to Vigilance. Details of the same along with the suggested role of Supervisory Body in the resolution of such issues are dealt with in Chapter-6 under the heading 'Vigilance Management in Public Sector Enterprises'.

2.8 In all other matters, whenever there is a difference of views between the Ministry and the Management, the advice of the Supervisory Body must be sought prior to deciding any course of action by the Government.

The Role of the Ministry

2.9 The Ministry should effectively perform the role of the shareholders and owners of the company. The Ministry should consult other ministries, including finance and other relevant departments and, where necessary, obtain the approval of the cabinet. It should facilitate the implementation of the projects of the company in conformity with overall Government policy.

2.10 The Ministry, in exercising the function of ownership, is responsible for the appointment of the Chief Executive as well as the Functional Directors of the company. It should follow the established guidelines with regard to these appointments, based on the recommendation of PESB. Although the Ministries have the power to recommend the termination of their services to the PESB, in the case of appointment and termination (except in case of Schedule 'C' & 'D' CPSEs where the Ministry concerned is competent for such approvals if the same are in line with the PESB recommendations), the decisions of the Ministry concerned must continue to be subject to the approval of the Appointments Committee of the Cabinet. In the case of adverse actions like reprimand, suspension, premature termination, denial of extension of tenure, superseding the recommendations of PESB, etc., the case should be referred to the new Supervisory Body and ACC should take its views into account before taking any decision. It is further suggested that considering the benefits of continuity in leadership positions, the appointments to the Board level positions in CPSEs may be made for the period up to superannuation instead of shorter fixed tenure. In any case, the current system has a provision for premature termination in case of non-performance.

2.11 The views of the Ministry should be communicated for consideration by the Board of Directors through the Government Directors, who would take up these matters at the meetings of the Board of Directors. The Ministry should not give instruction directly or indirectly to the management. That should be the prerogative of the Board of Directors.

2.12 The Government Director(s) should interact with the companies only as Members of the Board, where decisions in general should continue to be taken by a consensus or a majority. If the Government Director(s) feel that the Board of Directors has not appropriately taken into account the views of the Ministry on a given subject, they ought to refer the matter back to the Ministry, which after consulting the Supervisory Body, can instruct the Board of Directors and the Management to follow its directions. But such instructions must be given in the form of Presidential Directives. The issuance of such Presidential Directives should have the approval of the Cabinet.

2.13 The Ministry should not normally review the functioning of a CPSE more than twice a year. Such review should be based on reports of the Board of Directors and selected major performance indicators. These indicators, numbering not more than five, may be chosen from among the indicators agreed upon in the MoUs and considered appropriate by the Cabinet Secretariat and other agencies. The Ministry should be able to assess the performance of the company in terms of these indicators and also consider the fulfilment and non-fulfilment of the obligations of both the management of the company and of the Government departments concerned as spelt out in the MoUs. A special review may, however, take place in addition to the half-yearly session, if the concerned Ministry wishes to take stock of any issue of outstanding importance referred by it to a CPSE.

Since the profitability of CPSEs is influenced by several factors such as the administered price mechanism and fluctuations in international price of the commodities, the Group recommends that the Ministries concerned should develop CPSE-specific criteria to determine their overall performance, independent of profitability.

2.14 The Group felt that to increase the autonomy of the CPSEs the Government must accept the difference between ownership and management and ensure that CPSEs are run by the Boards of Directors and not by the owner. The procedures of governance suggested above should ensure such autonomy. However, in order to make the whole relationship clear and transparent, the Group recommends that there should be a negative list of areas which must be kept away from the intervention of the Government (except for respective jurisdiction of CAG and CVC). That list should, inter alia, include:

- Decisions relating to Pricing/Distribution policy
- Decisions on Exports/Imports
- Appointment of dealers and agents
- Appointment/promotion/transfer/suspension of below Board level employees
- Award of Contracts and procurement decisions
- Selection of Consultants and Joint Venture partners
- Issuance of directive or guideline restricting the authority of the Board of Directors [empowerment once provided to the Board of Directors should not be diluted without the approval of the authority which had originally sanctioned it].
- Insistence on CPSEs furnishing information considered commercially sensitive by the Board of Directors in answers to questions raised in the Parliament and its Committees.

- Issuance of instructions for intervening in any manner in the business or administrative decisions of the CPSEs.
- Withholding of implementation of recommendations of PESB in respect of tenure extensions of Board Members
- Non observance of SEBI stipulations for listed companies regarding appointment of non-official Directors.

2.15 In regard to the investments of the company and the ceilings that currently exist for Joint Ventures and other Capital expenditures for the Navratna and Miniratna companies, the Group is of the view that these decisions should be left entirely to the Board of Directors and owners should only review the implementation of these decisions in light of the MOU-related performance indictors mentioned above. In case, there is any difficulty in implementing this recommendation immediately, it is suggested that the same could be executed in two steps.

As the first step, the Group recommends the delegation of authority to the Board of Directors of the Navratna, Miniratna and other profit-making CPSEs be raised as mentioned hereunder:

A. *Investments for Capital Expenditure*

- *For Navratnas*: The Board of Directors to continue to enjoy the powers to approve investments in their own projects without any limits.
- *For Miniratnas-I*: The delegation may be increased from the existing Rs. 300 cr. to Rs. 500 cr. or an amount equivalent to their net worth, whichever is less.
- *For Miniratnas-II*: The delegation may be increased from the existing Rs. 150 cr. to Rs. 250 cr. or an amount equivalent to 50 per cent of their net worth, whichever is less.
- *For other Profit-making CPSEs*: The delegation may be increased to Rs. 150 cr. or an amount equivalent to 50 per cent of their net worth, whichever is less.

B. *Investments in Joint Ventures and Subsidiaries*

- *For Navratnas*: Keeping in view the increasingly large size of infrastructure projects and in order to achieve better economies of scale, Navratna delegation to invest equity in Joint Venture Companies/Subsidiaries needs to be enhanced from Rs. 200 crore (up to a maximum of 5 per cent of Net Worth) in one project to at least Rs.1000 crore or 15 per cent of Net Worth, whichever is less, in one Joint Venture/Subsidiary. Further, the present overall ceiling of equity investment up to 15 per cent of Networth in all Joint Ventures/Subsidiaries put together also needs to be increased to at least 30 per cent of the Net Worth.

- *For Miniratnas-I*: Miniratna-I delegation to invest equity in Joint Venture Companies/Subsidiaries needs to be enhanced to Rs. 500 crore or 15 per cent of Net Worth, whichever is less, in one Joint Venture/Subsidiary. Further, the overall ceiling of equity investment in all Joint Ventures/Subsidiaries put together also needs to be increased to at least 30 per cent of Net Worth.
- *For Miniratnas-II*: Miniratna-II delegation to invest equity in Joint Venture Companies/Subsidiaries needs to be enhanced to Rs. 250 crore or 15 per cent of Net Worth, whichever is less, in one Joint Venture/Subsidiary. Further, the overall ceiling of equity investment in all Joint Ventures/Subsidiaries put together also needs to be increased to at least 30 per cent of Net Worth.
- *For other Profit-making CPSEs*: These CPSEs may be delegated the powers to invest equity in Joint Venture Companies/Subsidiaries up to Rs. 100 crore or 15 per cent of Net Worth, whichever is less, in one Joint Venture/ Subsidiary. Further, the overall ceiling of equity investment in all Joint Ventures/Subsidiaries should be 30 per cent of Net Worth.

  However, if the Board of Directors feels it necessary to exceed the levels of investment limits recommended above in a given case, it may refer the matter to the Ministry for an appropriate decision in cases deserving of special consideration on individual merit.

C. *Creation and Disinvestment of Subsidiaries*: The Board of Directors may be empowered to create Subsidiaries for existing/new activities with equity investments within the overall limits specified for creating Subsidiaries. The Board of Directors may be further empowered to transfer assets to such subsidiaries from the parent company. The Board of Directors may also be empowered to float fresh equity and divest their shareholding in such Subsidiaries complying with SEBI guidelines. However, in case any existing fixed assets of the holding company have been transferred to a Subsidiary, then such subsidiary may not be allowed to transfer these assets to anyone other than the parent CPSE. Also, disinvestment in such a subsidiary company to an extent of more than 50 per cent , if proposed at a later date by the holding CPSE, would require the approval of the Government.

D. *Subsequent investments in Successful JVs*: The above mentioned limits may be applicable only for initial investments in these joint ventures. In case the JV Company is operating successfully for a defined period, say two years, any further investment in such successful and profitable Joint Ventures may not have any limitations prescribed.

E. *JVs between Navratnas*: While there is no restriction on Capital investment that a Navratna company can make in its own projects/ventures, there is a restriction on the amount of investment it can make when two or more Navratna CPSEs take up a project/venture together. It would therefore be in the fitness of things that Navratna CPSEs should have powers to make equity investments without any limit in Joint Ventures with other Navratna CPSE(s).

F. *Mergers and Acquisitions*: As per existing Delegation of Powers, Navratna and Miniratna companies can enter into Joint Venture arrangements within the parameters laid down in the respective circulars. However, for equity participation in existing companies or acquiring stake in existing/new companies or for deciding on mergers and acquisitions for promoting further business, prior approval of Government is required. The powers to decide on mergers, acquisitions and acquiring minority or majority stakes in existing or new companies should be delegated to the Boards of Directors of Navratna and Miniratna CPSEs where such decisions are necessary to facilitate business promotion within ceilings as proposed for Joint Ventures.

G. *Investment Approvals where Budgetary Support is involved*: At present the Navratnas, Miniratnas and other profit making CPSEs are not permitted to avail of Budgetary Support even for expansion, diversification or other developmental purposes without losing their Navratna/Miniratna status. The Group recommends that these restrictions may be relaxed so that Budgetary Support to implement planned developmental activities should not result in disqualifying the CPSEs from retaining their Navratna/Miniratna status.

H. *Investment Approval for Projects involving Government Guarantees*: The Boards of Directors of Navratna, Miniratna and other profit making CPSEs should be given powers to approve Capital expenditure without the requirement of seeking PIB/CCEA approvals even in case of projects involving government guarantees, as funding by multilateral agencies invariably involves government guarantee. However, this should be subject to ceilings, if any, prescribed for investment delegations.

I. *Appointment of Functional Directors in Subsidiaries and JVs by the Board of Directors of the Holding Company*: CPSEs have been entering new business fields to add value to their core business. Sometimes they choose to do so through a JV or a Subsidiary with the intention to bring in the required technological/managerial expertise as well as to protect the parent balance sheet from the business risks of the new venture. Such new ventures can succeed only when they work in a seamless manner with the parent organization to leverage the parent's strength. Also, complete accountability of the management of the Joint Venture/Subsidiary to the parent organization is absolutely essential for the new venture to progress and add value to the core business of the parent organization. Company law provides for the placement of Functional Directors in the subsidiaries by the holding company. However, Government of India (Transaction of Business) Rules,

1961 provide for the appointment of Functional Directors by the Government. The Group recommends that full-time Board level appointments in Joint Ventures/ Subsidiaries may be made by the Board of Directors of the holding Company in line with provisions of Section 255, 256 and 257 of the Companies Act for partly owned Government companies.

J. *Chief Executive to be Member in the Search Committee for Independent Directors*: The guidelines of DPE and SEBI require CPSEs to have some Independent Directors on their Board of Directors. With the market becoming more complicated, performance and survival of the CPSEs require the wise counsel and directions by eminent persons with good stature in the industry and the market. To identify and induct such eminent persons, there is a need to adhere strictly to the prescribed qualification requirements without any dilution. Also, Search Committees formed to identify Independent Directors should include the Chief Executive of the concerned CPSE as a Member.

The Group further recommends that the restrictions contained in the interim delegation by way of the first step towards autonomy of successful CPSEs as described above, should be removed as the next and final step within a period of three years from now, whereafter investment decisions should be entirely left to the Board of Directors.

2.16 The Board of Directors already have the full authority to raise short-term or long-term loans from the market without any prior approval from the Government, subject to existing rules and procedures laid down by regulatory authorities like the RBI or SEBI. In the same manner, the Board of Directors should have the power to raise equity capital from the market, so long as the Government's share of the overall equity remains above 51 per cent. Raising such equity may require enhancement of the authorized capital, for which Government permission would be necessary. It may be stipulated that such permission for expanding the authorized capital would be given in a time-bound manner provided the Government's shareholding does not fall below 51 per cent. At the time of granting such approval, the Government may decide to extinguish a part of its shareholding at the price which the company shares command in the market. If the Government does extinguish some shares in this manner it would amount to disinvestment in a transparent market-determined way. But if the Government does not extinguish any share, the proportion of the Government's shareholding would come down without giving up the ownership or control over the company.

2.17 Finally, there are certain issues like foreign travel of the Chief Executive and the Functional Directors, which are currently referred to the Ministry for approval. The Group felt that there should be detailed procedural guidelines including limits of financial expenditure in this regard formulated by the Board of Directors of the CPSE concerned, and accordingly recommends that no reference to the Government for approval should be necessary unless deviation from guidelines approved by the Board is intended.

The Role of the Board of Directors

2.18 The Board of Directors should be fully responsible for the control and supervision of the Management of the company. It should be responsible for placement and promotion of senior personnel, formulation of company's policy for creation/abolition/up-gradation of posts, rewards and incentives for meritorious performance and out-of-turn promotions, and on all matters relating to human resource development.

2.19 The Board of Directors, subject to statutory requirements, Government policy and regulatory guidelines issued by RBI, should have the powers to pursue new lines of business, make suitable acquisitions of companies, set up JVs/Subsidiaries and exit a line of business, and to make Capital expenditure up to levels as indicated in Para 2.15 without prior approval of the Government.

2.20 No more than two officers should be nominated as Board Members by the Government on the Board of Directors for Navratna, Miniratna or other profit-making CPSEs.

The performance of Government Directors on Board of Directors of CPSEs must be suitably reflected in their Confidential Reports. Furthermore, it is suggested that a suitable appraisal system for performance review of non-official Independent Directors may also be developed.

2.21 Existing DPE guideline for CPSEs permits 5 per cent of distributable profit to be allocated to employees as performance-linked bonus/incentive. Functional Directors of CPSEs serve on contract/covenant and their compensation is governed by the terms and conditions of the appointment. However, keeping in mind the significance of the role played by the leadership (the Chief Executive and the Functional Directors) in the success of the organization, the Group is of the view that the Chief Executive and the Functional Directors should also be entitled to performance linked bonus/incentive within the permissible limit of 5 per cent of distributable profit. The Group recommends that the Compensation Committee of the Board as constituted under the 'Listing Agreement' may decide the quantum of such performance linked incentives, on the basis of the individual's performance and contributions during the year under review. The Compensation Committee may also devise CPSE-specific norms for determination of such incentives. Such bonus/incentives would, however, be governed by the limits prescribed in the Companies Act.

The Role of the Management

2.22 The Chief Executive should be entirely responsible for the day-to-day management and operation of the company under the overall supervision of the Board of Directors. The appointment of the Chief Executive should be made strictly in accordance with the procedures laid down for this purpose.

2.23 The Management should be free to exercise all powers explicitly delegated by the Board of Directors. It should function under the supervision of the Chief Executive and Functional Directors on the Board.

2.24 It should be responsible for implementation of the decisions of the Board of Directors and compliance of all statutory requirements as well as policy guidelines.

CHAPTER 3
AUDIT OF GOVERNMENT COMPANIES

3.1 Pursuant to Section 19(1) of Comptroller and Auditor-General's (C&AG) Duties, Powers and Conditions of Service Act, 1971, audit of the accounts of Government companies is conducted by the Comptroller and Auditor-General in accordance with the provisions of the Companies Act, 1956. Under Section 619 of the Companies Act, 1956, the Auditor (Chartered Accountant) of a Government Company is appointed or re-appointed by C&AG. It is further stipulated that C&AG shall have the power to (a) direct the auditor to conduct the audit in a specified manner, (b) give instructions on any matter relating to the performance of his functions, (c) conduct himself a supplementary or test audit of the company's accounts and (d) comment upon or supplement the audit report in such manner as he (C&AG) thinks fit. The comments of C&AG are to be placed before AGM along with Auditor's Report.

3.2 As regards the present status of audit in CPSEs, C&AG appoints the statutory auditor of Government Company. The statutory auditor audits the account of the CPSEs in accordance with the provisions of Companies Act and other applicable statutes. C&AG has issued directions to statutory auditors of Government Companies requiring them to furnish to C&AG a detailed report covering various items specified in the questionnaire, in addition to the normal auditor's report under Companies Act, 1956, within three weeks from the date of signing their Auditors' Report. After the receipt of certified accounts and Auditor's Report, C&AG conducts supplementary or test audit based on which the comments of C&AG upon the report of Statutory Auditors or a supplementary report by him may be issued. These comments form part and parcel of Auditor's Report. C&AG also does a transaction/propriety audit in addition to supplementary/test audit. In some CPSEs there are resident audit parties who conduct concurrent audit. Under such audit, the propriety of the transaction is also subjected to scrutiny. The authority of such audit is not specified as far as Companies Act, 1956 is concerned.

3.3 *Concerns of CPSEs*

- *Test/Supplementary Audit*: The basic concern of CPSEs regarding test/supplementary audit of C&AG is that it leads to delay in finalization of audit of accounts resulting in non-compliance of directives of SEBI regarding publication of audited results and quarterly results.

Since statutory audit is conducted by statutory auditor appointed by the C&AG in the manner directed by him, it is felt that the test/supplementary audit is duplication of audit work already done by statutory auditor.

- *Transaction/Test Audit*: The main focus of such audit is to bring to light the mistakes made in the past. On account of the benefit of hindsight, circumstances/compulsions under which such business decisions were taken tend to get glossed over or ignored by the auditor.

Such audit highlights only isolated deficiencies of CPSEs, which damage their corporate image in the public to the detriment of their commercial interests.

Such audit also leads to a defensive attitude on the part of corporate executives leading to delay in decisions, which may not be in the best commercial interests of the Company.

3.4 The requirement of transaction audit is perhaps borrowed from the system of audit in government. CPSEs, being commercial entities, have their own system of internal audit, which requires compliance in conformity with standards laid down by the Institute of Chartered Accountants of India, disclosure guidelines of SEBI (for listed companies) and compliance to the observations of Audit Committees and Statutory Audit.

Keeping in view the above statutory requirements and concerns of CPSEs, the Group makes the following suggestions, which may be considered for implementation.

Test/Supplementary Audit

- C&AG may consider issuance of revised guidelines to statutory auditors and rely mainly on their report.
- Test/supplementary audit may be resorted to only in exceptional cases rather than as a routine exercise.
- Appointment of Statutory Auditors may be made at the earliest in the beginning of financial year.
- Appointment of Branch auditors may be dispensed with. Only those firms of Chartered Accountants which are capable of making Head Office as well as Branch Office audit may be considered for appointment.

- C&AG may also consider giving suitable directions for consultations with Statutory Auditors at appropriate levels to minimize the need for supplementary audit.
- C&AG may consider making its audit concurrent with the audit by statutory auditors so as to complete it along with the audit by the statutory auditors. Normally statutory auditors conduct their audit in two phases i.e. one up to December, which is completed before end of the year and next phase after year-end. C & AG may also like to adopt similar practice

Transaction/Test Audit

After considerable deliberation, the Group was of the view that only malafide intentional mistakes, frauds, gross negligence or wilful ignorance of advice/suggestions should form part of Audit Observation. However, bonafide errors of judgment may be mentioned by the audit only as suggestions for improvement of performance in future. Overall performance should be the guiding criterion rather than review of individual commercial decision. Otherwise the Executives will be apprehensive of making commercial judgements and decisions, which will be detrimental to the commercial interest of CPSEs.

CHAPTER 4
ARTCLE 12 OF THE CONSTITUTION AND CPSEs

4.1 Some judicial pronouncements have declared public enterprises to be an extension or arm of the State under Article 12 of the Constitution. Under Article 12, 'State', unless the context otherwise requires, includes the Government and Parliament of India and the Governments and Legislature of each of the States and all local or other authorities within the territory of India or under the control of the Government of India. Although Article 12, in so many words, does not provide that CPSEs fall within the definition of the 'State', they still are deemed as being included in the category 'other authorities' and therefore, covered under the definition of 'State' as pronounced by different Courts including the Apex Court.

4.2 In the competitive environment in the wake of liberalization/ globalization, this situation undermines the entrepreneurial and commercial functioning of public enterprises and puts them at a disadvantageous position vis-à-vis their private sector counterparts and competitors. This negation of the essential distinction between government per se and public enterprise—a distinction conceived by Parliament and embodied in the Industrial Policy Resolution of 1956—has led to a situation where any aggrieved employee or contractor can move the court against the Management of public enterprises calling in question individual actions or decisions in the same way as against the State. This would seem to imply that government enterprises can function only as government departments and in accordance with the modalities, procedures and styles similar to government administration. This impedes decision-making in CPSEs, particularly in the competitive environment in the wake of liberalization/globalization. Indeed, it is precisely because business cannot be run efficiently in the normal governmental style and in accordance with government procedures that public enterprises have been organized in the corporate form.

4.3 It was brought to the notice of the Group that the matter was considered by the Committee of Secretaries in 1987 and, based on its decision; the same was referred to the Ministry of Law suggesting that the possibility of inserting an explanation below the Article 12 may be examined. The suggested insertion was as under: "A statutory corporation, a company formed and registered under the Companies Act, 1956 or a society under the Societies Registration Act shall not be considered as 'State' for the purpose of this Article".

4.4 The Ministry of Law placed the issue before the Law Commission, which looked into various possibilities but could not find a solution. In its 145th Report submitted in 1992, the Law Commission concluded as follows:

Such an amendment would not be a proper or necessary measure to be adopted for dealing with the difficulties that may be experienced by public sector undertakings in the matter of award of contracts, rejection of tenders, service matters and the like arising out of the present applicability of Article 12 to such undertakings.

Having regard to the Preamble and total philosophy of the Constitution, even if such an amendment is made, some of the problems experienced by the public sector undertakings would still survive under the ordinary law.

In particular, judicial intervention in the form of injunctions issued under the ordinary law cannot be ruled out, even after the suggested amendment.

It is highly doubtful whether, in the light of the theory of non-amenability of the basic features of the Constitution as at present recognized, such an amendment will pass muster on the Constitution level.

4.5 While taking note of the deliberations on the subject in the past, one should still consider the dynamic changes that are taking place in the business and economic environment on account of globalization. Global competition is cutting into the margins and market shares of Indian corporates, including CPSEs, facilitated by crumbling tariff barriers. The far-reaching mandatory legal implications of Article 12 inhibit the functioning of CPSEs as commercial entities like similar companies in the private sector. In consideration of the foregoing position, the Group recommends that this issue could be revisited by the policy makers at an appropriate time in future.

CHAPTER 5
PARLIAMENTARY ACCOUNTABILITY

5.1 In India, Government Companies are governed by the provisions of Indian Companies Act 1956. Under Section 620 of the Act, the Central Government has a right to exempt partly or wholly the application of any provision of the Act to the government companies except Section 618, 619 (A). The audit and accountability to Parliament is prescribed under sections 619 and 619(A) of the Companies Act, which relate to audit and admission of annual report.

5.2 Public enterprises are accountable to the people through their elected representatives. Parliament exercises surveillance of a general nature over them and makes major legislative decisions about the policies relating to public enterprises. Parliament also authorizes budgetary allocations for investment and other needs of public enterprises where required. The property, assets, powers and functions of public enterprises emerge directly or indirectly from one or another legislation passed by the Parliament. Public enterprises, while enjoying autonomy in financial matters, are ultimately accountable to Parliament for investments made in them from the Consolidated Fund of India.

5.3 Currently, Parliament exercises control over the CPSEs in the following manner:

- ❖ Members of the Parliament can ask questions to the concerned Minister on the working of public enterprises under his charge.
- ❖ Members of Parliament can discuss the affair of the public enterprises when the House takes up demands for grants for discussion and vote.
- ❖ Parliament can examine the working of selected enterprises through its committees.
- ❖ Parliament receives every year a comprehensive appraisal of the working of selected public enterprises done by the Audit Board.
- ❖ Public enterprises are required to present to Parliament their annual report together with a copy of the audit report made by the C&AG of India.
- ❖ Oral Evidence of CPSEs before Parliamentary Committees is also required to be given from time to time.

5.4 The Chief Executives of Navratna CPSEs were given an opportunity to express their views before the Group. Their views are summarized below:

- ❖ Accountability to Parliament may be deemed as complied with through Annual Reports.
- ❖ Questions on sensitive operational matters need to be avoided in the interest of business confidentiality and competitiveness of CPSEs.
- ❖ Screening Committee may be set up for Parliament Questions so as to avoid submission of voluminous data and sensitive business information.
- ❖ Instead of various Parliamentary Committees, there should be only one Committee, which should cover all aspects.

- ❖ Obligations should be the same for public and private sector in the interest of level playing field.
- ❖ Independent body should be created to exercise all ownership rights of the Government.
- ❖ Parliament should focus mainly on the review of performance of CPSEs.

5.5 On the basis of the above cited presentations and discussions, the Group would suggest the following for the consideration of appropriate authorities:

- ❖ Day to day affairs of CPSEs may not be taken up in the Parliament
- ❖ Conduct of Chief Executive and Functional Directors may not be discussed in the Parliament as there are other fora available for this purpose.
- ❖ It is essential to distinguish between accountability to Parliament and involvement of the Government in day-to-day functioning, personnel related matters etc. of CPSEs.
- ❖ Control points and occasions could be few, effective and concerned with major aspects of public enterprise policy. Their focus should be on enabling the enterprises to fulfil the norms of accountability expected of them.
- ❖ Profitability and working could be tested from time to time by the Parliament in enterprises where production and expansion are taking place since it involves government expenditure.
- ❖ Appropriate competent authorities in the Government and the Parliament may therefore like to consider setting up of a screening committee to screen Parliament questions from the angle mentioned above as well as the need for confidentiality of business decisions.

CHAPTER 6
VIGILANCE MANAGEMENT IN PUBLIC SECTOR ENTERPRISES

6.1 The Central Vigilance Commission (CVC) was set up by the Government of India by its Resolution dated 11.2.1964 in pursuance.of the recommendations of the Santhanam Committee. The Commission acts as the apex body for exercising general superintendence and control over vigilance matters with a view to ensuring probity in public administration. It is vested with the authority of initiating investigations/enquiries into cases involving corruption, malpractices and lack of integrity. The CVC possesses statutory status by virtue of the Central Vigilance Commission Bill passed by the Parliament which received assent of the President on 11th September, 2003. The aim of the Act is to provide for the constitution of CVC to inquire into offences alleged to have been committed under the Prevention of Corruption Act, 1988 by certain categories of public servants including those of public enterprises.

6.2 Section 8(1)(h) of the Act provides that the Commission shall exercise superintendence over the administration of various Ministries of the Central Government or Corporations established by or under any Central Act, Government Companies, Societies and Local Authorities owned or controlled by the Government. Executives on the Board of Directors of CPSEs and two levels below the Board of Directors fall within the purview of CVC, as important decision making in most of the CPSEs is limited to two levels below the Board level. The Commission tenders appropriate advice to the concerned disciplinary authorities in all matters of corruption, malpractices, misconduct, lack of integrity etc.

6.3 *Special Chapter on Vigilance Management in CPSEs:* CVC in consultation with the Department of Personnel and Training (DoPT) and some other bodies had issued a Special Chapter on Vigilance Management in CPSEs and the role and functioning of CVC. It covers the entire gamut of vigilance principles and procedures to regulate vigilance management in CPSEs to deal with any complaints of corruption, gross negligence, misconduct, recklessness, lack of integrity or other kinds of malpractices on the part of public servants.

Present Vigilance Set Up in Cpses

6.4 A study was conducted by Department of AR & PG on vigilance set-up in respect of CPSEs. It prescribed a Model Vigilance Structure at different levels (Corporate/Unit/Regional) in CPSEs to deal with investigations, disciplinary proceedings, anti-corruption work and preventive vigilance with adequate personnel to carry out all necessary functions to prevent possibilities of corruption. Guidelines have been issued to the CPSEs for necessary compliance as per the size of the organization. Under Section 8(1)(h) of the Act Central Vigilance Commission has issued instructions to the CPSEs to encourage a culture of honesty, greater transparency in administration, speedy departmental inquiries, transparent decision-making on NITs etc.

6.5 *Appointment of Chief Vigilance Officers:* To provide for adequate vigilance apparatus in CPSEs, appointment of Chief Vigilance Officer (CVO) with concurrence of Central Vigilance Commission has to be made along with a number of vigilance officers with desired manpower requirements of skilled and trained vigilance personnel. The CVO acts as a link with the CVC and CPSEs. He functions as the principal vigilance aide to the Chief Executive and as the focal point in respect of the entire work relating to vigilance. The role of the Chief Vigilance Officer is both preventive and punitive.

6.6 CPSEs having full-time posts of CVOs fill up such posts as per the procedure prescribed for appointments under the Central Staffing Scheme. DoPT requests the Cadre Controlling Authority of various organized services to offer officers of proven integrity for these posts. The names so received are forwarded along with bio-data of the officers concerned and their ACR dossiers to the Commission for approval. The DoPT maintains a panel of names approved by the Commission, which are operative for a period of one year. The Commission then prepares a panel of names and recommends it to the administrative Ministry/Department concerned for making appointment.

In case of CPSEs, which do not have full-time posts of CVOs, one of the officers from a panel of three senior officers forwarded to CVC by the PSE is selected by the Commission as the CVO.

6.7 *Examinations/Investigations of Complaint against Board Level Appointees:* CVC has issued necessary instructions in the matter of dealing with complaints against the Board Level Appointees. If the CVO of an administrative Ministry asks for a factual report against a Board level appointee from the CVO of the PSE, the latter sends the same to the CVO of the Ministry, after endorsing a copy of the report to the CMD to keep him informed of the development. However, if the CMD himself is the subject matter of the investigation, the CVO of the PSE need not endorse a copy of the report to him. In such cases it is the responsibility of the CVO of the Ministry to obtain the version of CMD at the appropriate time. The CVO of the Ministry has to make a reference to the CVC after collecting all the relevant facts and following the prescribed procedure.

6.8 *Investigations by the CBI-Constitution of Central Advisory Board:* The special chapter on Vigilance Management issued by CVC provides as under:

- ❖ Considering the complexities involved in commercial decisions of the PSE, the CBI may find it worthwhile to obtain the benefit of expert advice from various disciplines before registration of PE/RC. A Central Advisory Board may be constituted to assist CBI for this purpose. Appointments on the Board may be made from the panel of names approved by the CVC. The Board should give its considered opinion within one month from the date of reference before registration of PE/RC, failing which the CBI would be competent to decide the matter without advice. Advice of the Board should not be binding on the CBI.

6.9 *Strengthening of Vigilance Machinery in CPSEs:* CVC has been issuing necessary instructions to strengthen vigilance set-up in the CPSEs. The CVOs of the level of Joint Secretaries to the Govt. of India and above in the Schedule 'A' and 'B' Companies have been given status equivalent to that of a Functional Director with other facilities and perquisites available to the Functional Directors in these companies. CVC has also recommended creation of the post of CVO at the level of Functional Director in Schedule 'A' companies, which has hitherto been acted upon only in the Navratna CPSEs.

Concerns/Suggestions of Chief Executives of CPSEs

6.10 The current business environment calls for speedy decision making amid a welter of factors and changes induced by globalization, liberalization, technology changes and continuously increasing competition. Public Sector Enterprises are being evaluated as commercial entities and are expected to take business decisions in a dynamic scenario. There is need to empower these CPSEs by providing mechanisms which would enable speedier decision making in a changing business environment with all the inherent risks.

6.11 During the discussions with Chief Executives of some of the Navratna central public sector enterprises, certain points relating to vigilance administration in CPSEs were brought to the notice of the Ad-hoc Expert Group. Views were expressed to the effect that the role of CBI/CVC should be restricted and CPSE executives may be protected against misconceived and unnecessary vigilance action based on lack of full appreciation of business related decisions. It was suggested that necessary measures may be recommended in this regard so that executives in CPSEs do not shy away from taking business decisions on account of fear of vigilance action. This is particularly significant for improving the commercial functioning of CPSEs in the competitive environment in the wake of liberalization/globalization.

6.12 CVC had constituted a Committee under the Chairmanship of Mr. Arvind Pande, ex-Chairman, SAIL to study the vigilance administration in the Public Sector Enterprises and to recommend measures to strengthen it. The Committee has since submitted its report to the Commission and the recommendations made therein are under consideration of the Commission in consultation with concerned Ministries/ Departments for a final decision on the report. Some of the recommendations of Arvind Pande Committee are relevant to the issues raised by the Chief Executives of some Navratna CPSEs before the Expert Group. Keeping the committees recommendations in mind, the Group recommends the following:

- The CVC and the CPSEs need to adopt an approach of capacity building that can integrate better with the modern day requirements of risk management, security management, and financial controls and compliance. This effort will add discernible value to the competitiveness of the enterprise apart from promoting probity, and integrity amongst public officials and supporting, synergizing and fostering corporate governance

- The coverage of CVC's jurisdiction should be restricted to executives of E-8, E-9 levels and Functional Directors (including the Chief Executive) of all companies. This ensures parity going by the pay scales of Schedule-D companies' directors and the E-8. However, the CVC may consider making specific exemptions in the case of select *Navratnas,* which have in place internal systems, controls, and procedures that would demonstrably meet the preset standards evolved by the CVC. In case of such exceptions, the CVC's jurisdiction could be limited to the Director level only. However, it is recommended that this empowerment should be earned by the respective organizations by meeting quality standards and subject to withdrawal of the privilege should their systems fall short of the standards in future.
- Anonymous and pseudonymous complaints forwarded by Hon'ble MPs or MLAs should be verified by the concerned CVOs or official. Where the complainant is identifiable, it could be suggested to the MP or MLA concerned to obtain the complainant's signature and name, failing which the case may be proceeded with as if the Hon'ble MP or MLA is the complainant.
- The CVC may consider issuing guidelines specifically allowing CPSEs to initiate proceedings under the relevant sections of the IPC and the CrPC in all cases wherein complaints have delayed strategic decisions and are ultimately found to be unfounded, malicious and false.
- The process of vigilance clearance may be simplified in the case of PSE officials aspiring for Board appointments. The CVO concerned should be empowered to verify the records, make enquiries, and furnish the assessment without countrywide scrutiny through various CBI offices. It is also recommended that a period of 5 years should be the periodicity of re-verification, unless there is good reason to do so at a shorter interval.
- Prior approval of the Government in the concerned Ministry is required for launching criminal prosecution against officers above a designated rank working with the

Ministry. The employees of PSEs who are equivalent in rank to that level should be treated on par with the latter as CPSEs are treated as Government and its employees as public servants.

- Furthermore, the vigilance cases against Board members of CPSEs need to be referred to the 'Advisory Board' of CVC (similar to the one constituted for the Banking sector) as envisaged in para 3.3.29 of Pande Committee Report to determine whether a given decision was bona fide or malafide. The decision of the Advisory Board should be binding on the investigating agency.
- If as a result of the inquiry it is proposed to launch prosecution, then the sanctions/permissions for initiating prosecution or suspension of the Board level incumbents should be granted after fully consulting the Supervisory Body. The recommendation of the Supervisory Body should normally be accepted by the prosecuting agencies, unless there are strong reasons for a contrary view.
- The CVOs should be trained more frequently and intensively, and should be adequately equipped with knowledge of management audit, decision making processes, domain issues of particular industries, financial analysis and transaction, risk management, control systems, coordination abilities etc.
- The vigilance set up of Subsidiaries of CPSEs should be under the vigilance administration of the holding company and need not have direct interface with the CVC.
- Decision on suspension of Board level officials by the Ministry must be taken after obtaining the concurrence of the Supervisory Body. In case of other officials below Board-level concurrence of the sub-committee of the Board must be obtained.

No. 18(24)/2003-GM
Government of India
Ministry of Heavy Industries & Public Enterprises
Department of Public Enterprises
....

Block No.14, CGO Complex,
Lodhi Road, New Delhi 110003.

Dated the 11th November, 2004

Subject: Constitution of an Ad-hoc Group of experts to consider issues relating to autonomy, delegation of financial powers, etc. of Central Public Sector Undertakings.

It has been decided to set up an Ad-hoc Group of experts to consider issues like autonomy, greater delegation of financial powers, corporate governance, R&D, technological upgradation, effective functioning in a competitive environment, etc. related to the Central Public Sector Undertakings in the context of the mandate under the National Common Minimum Programme.

2. The composition of the Group is as under:-

(i)	Dr. Arjun Sengupta	Chairman
(ii)	Shri Anwarul Hoda, Member, Planning Commission	
(iii)	Dr. Adarsh Kishore, Secretary to Government, Department of Public Enterprises	Convenor
(iv)	Dr. Nitish Sengupta	
(v)	Shri Moosa Raza	
(vi)	Shri Prabir Sengupta	
(vii)	Shri Subir Raha, CMD, ONGC Ltd.	
(viii)	Shri C.P. Jain, CMD, NTPC Ltd. and Chairman, SCOPE	
(ix)	Shri A.K. Rath, Joint Secretary, DPE	

3. Detailed Terms of Reference of the Group shall be notified separately.

4. The Ad-hoc Group will submit its recommendations to the Government within one month's time.

(G.S. Bothyal)
Director
Tel.24360218

To

Members of the Group

Copy to PS to Secretary (PE)

Appendices

Appendix 1

List of Central Public Sector Enterprises in Different States/Union Territories as Per Their Registered Offices as on 31-3-2006

S. No.	*NAME OF PSU*
ANDHRA PRADESH	
1.	BHARAT DYNAMICS LTD.
2.	BHARAT HEAVY PLATE & VESSELS LTD.
3.	ELECTRONICS CORPN. OF INDIA LTD.
4.	HINDUSTAN FLUOROCARBONS LIMITED
5.	HMT BEARINGS LTD.
6.	MISHRA DHATU NIGAM LTD.
7.	NATIONAL MINERAL DEVELOPMENT CORPN. LTD.
8.	PRAGA TOOLS LTD.
9.	RASHTRIYA ISPAT NIGAM LTD.
10.	SPONGE IRON INDIA LTD.
ARUNACHAL PRADESH	
11.	DONYI POLO ASHOK HOTEL LTD.
ASSAM	
12.	ASSAM ASHOK HOTEL CORPN. LTD.
13.	BONGAIGAON REFINERY & PETROCHEMICALS LTD.
14.	BRAHMAPUTRA VALLEY FERTILIZER CORPN. LTD.
15.	NORTH EASTERN REGIONAL AGRI. MARKETING CORP.LTD.
16.	NUMALIGARH REFINARY LTD.
17.	OIL INDIA LTD.
BIHAR	
18.	BHARAT WAGON & ENGG. CO. LTD.
19.	BIHAR DRUGS & ORGANIC CHEMICALS LTD.
20.	PYRITES, PHOSPHATES & CHEMICALS LTD.
CHHATTISGARH	
21.	FERRO SCRAP NIGAM LTD.
22.	SOUTH EASTERN COALFIELDS LTD.

S. No.	*NAME OF PSU*
DELHI	
23.	AIR INDIA AIR TRANSPORT SERVICES LTD.
24.	AIRLINE ALLIED SERVICES LTD.
25.	AIRPORTS AUTHORITY OF INDIA LTD.
26.	AKALTARA POWER LTD.
27.	BHARAT HEAVY ELECTRICALS LTD.
28.	BHARAT SANCHAR NIGAM LTD.
29.	CEMENT CORPN. OF INDIA LTD.
30.	CENTRAL COTTAGE INDUSTRIES CORPN. OF INDIA LTD.
31.	CENTRAL ELECTRONICS LTD.
32.	CENTRAL WAREHOUSING CORPN.
33.	CERTIFICATION ENGINEERS INTERNATIONAL LTD.
34.	COASTAL GUJRAT POWER LTD.
35.	COASTAL KARNATAKA POWER LTD.
36.	COASTAL MAHARASHTRA MEGA POWER LTD.
37.	CONTAINER CORPORATION OF INDIA LTD.
38.	DREDGING CORPN.OF INDIA LTD.
39.	EDUCATIONAL CONSULTANTS (INDIA) LTD.
40.	ENGINEERS INDIA LTD.
41.	FERTILIZER CORPN. OF INDIA LTD.
42.	FOOD CORPN. OF INDIA
43.	FRESH & HEALTHY ENTERPRISES LTD.
44.	GAIL (INDIA) LTD.
45.	HANDICRAFTS & HANDLOOM EXPORTS CORP. OF INDIA LTD.
46.	HINDUSTAN FERTILIZER CORPN. LTD.
47.	HINDUSTAN INSECTICIDES LTD.
48.	HINDUSTAN PAPER CORPORATION LTD.
49.	HINDUSTAN PREFAB LTD.
50.	HINDUSTAN SHIPYARD LTD.
51.	HINDUSTAN VEGETABLE OILS CORPN. LTD.
52.	HOUSING & URBAN DEV. CORPN. LTD.
53.	HSCC (INDIA) LTD.
54.	INDIA TOURISM DEV. CORPN.LTD.
55.	INDIA TRADE PROMOTION ORGANISATION
56.	INDIAN AIRLINES LTD.
57.	INDIAN OIL TECHNOLOGIES LTD.
58.	INDIAN RAILWAY CATERING AND TOURISM CORPN. LTD.

S. No.	NAME OF PSU
59.	INDIAN RAILWAY FINANCE CORPORATION LTD.
60.	INDIAN RENEWABLE ENERGY DEVT.AGENCY LTD.
61.	INDIAN STRATEGIC PETROLEUM RESERVES LTD.
62.	IRCON INTERNATIONAL LTD.
63.	KONKAN RAILWAY CORPORATION LTD.
64.	KUMARAKUPPA FRONTIER HOTELS LTD.
65.	M M T C LTD.
66.	MAHANAGAR TELEPHONE NIGAM LTD.
67.	NATIONAL BACKWARD CLASSES FINANCE & DEVELOPMENT CORP.
68.	NATIONAL BLDG. CONSTN. CORPN. LTD.
69.	NATIONAL FERTILIZERS LTD.
70.	NATIONAL HANDICAPPED FINANCE & DEVPT. CORPN.
71.	NATIONAL HYDROELECTRIC POWER CORPN.LTD.
72.	NATIONAL INFORMATICS CENTRE SERVICES INCORPORATED
73.	NATIONAL MINORITIES DEVP. & FINANCE CORPN.
74.	NATIONAL PROJECTS CONSTRUCTION CORPN. LTD.
75.	NATIONAL RESEARCH DEVP. CORPN.
76.	NATIONAL SAFAI KARAMCHARIS' FINANCE & DEVPT. CORPN.
77.	NATIONAL SCHEDULED CASTES FINANCE & DEVP. CORPN.
78.	NATIONAL SCHEDULED TRIBES FINANCE & DEVP. CORPN.
79.	NATIONAL SEEDS CORPN. LTD.
80.	NATIONAL SMALL INDUSTRIES CORPN. LTD.
81.	NATIONAL TEXTILE CORPN. (Holding Co.) LTD.
82.	NTC(DELHI,PUNJAB & RAJASTHAN) LTD.
83.	NTPC ELECTRIC SUPPLY COMPANY LTD.
84.	NTPC HYDRO LTD.
85.	NTPC LTD.
86.	NTPC VIDYUT VYAPAR NIGAM LTD.
87.	NUCLEAR POWER CORPN. OF INDIA LTD.
88.	OIL & NATURAL GAS CORPORATION LTD.
89.	ONGC VIDESH LTD.
90.	P E C LTD.
91.	PARBATI KOLDAM TRANSMISSION COMPANY
92.	PAWAN HANS HELICOPTERS LTD.
93.	PIPAVAV POWER DEVP. COMPANY LTD.
94.	POWER FINANCE CORPORATION
95.	POWER GRID CORPORATION OF INDIA LTD

S. No.	*NAME OF PSU*
96.	RAIL VIKAS NIGAM LTD.
97.	RAILTEL CORPORATION INDIA LTD.
98.	RITES LTD.
99.	RURAL ELECTRIFICATION CORPN. LTD.
100.	SASAN POWER LTD.
101.	SECURITY PRINTING & MINING CORPN. INDIA LTD.
102.	STATE FARMS CORPORATION OF INDIA LTD.
103.	STATE TRADING CORPN. OF INDIA LTD.
104.	STEEL AUTHORITY OF INDIA LTD.
105.	TEHRI HYDRO DEVELOPMENT CORP. LTD..
106.	TELECOMMUNICATIONS CONSULTANTS (INDIA) LTD.
107.	WATER & POWER CONSULTANCY SERVICES(INDIA) LTD.
GOA	
108.	GOA SHIPYARD LTD.
GUJRAT	
109.	NTC(GUJARAT)LTD.
HARYANA	
110.	INDIAN DRUGS & PHARMACEUTICALS LTD.
HIMACHAL PRADESH	
111.	SATLUJ JAL VIDYUT NIGAM LTD.
JAMMU & KASHMIR	
112.	HMT CHINAR WATCHES LTD.
113.	J & K MINERAL DEVELOPMENT CORPN. LTD.
JHARKHAND	
114.	BHARAT COKING COAL LTD.
115.	BHARAT REFRACTORIES LTD.
116.	CENTRAL COALFIELDS LTD.
117.	CENTRAL MINE PLANNING & DESIGN INSTITUTE LTD.
118.	ENGINEERING PROJECTS (INDIA) LTD.
119.	HEAVY ENGINEERING CORPN. LTD.
120.	MECON LTD.
121.	PROJECTS & DEVELOPMENT INDIA LTD.

S. No.	*NAME OF PSU*
122.	RANCHI ASHOK BIHAR HOTEL CORPN. LTD.
123.	URANIUM CORPORATION OF INDIA LTD.
KARNATAKA	
124.	ANTRIX CORPORATION LTD.
125.	BHARAT EARTH MOVERS LTD.
126.	BHARAT ELECTRONICS LTD.
127.	HINDUSTAN AERONAUTICS LTD.
128.	HMT (INTERNATIONAL) LTD.
129.	HMT LTD.
130.	HMT MACHINE TOOLS LTD.
131.	HMT WATCHES LTD.
132.	I T I LTD.
133.	KARNATAKA ANTIBIOTICS & PHARMACEUTICALS LTD.
134.	KARNATAKA TRADE PROMOTION ORGANISATION
135.	KUDREMUKH IRON ORE CO.LTD
136.	MANGALORE REFINARY & PETROCHEMICALS LTD.
137.	NTC(A.PRADESH, KARNATAKA, KERALA & MAHE)LTD.
138.	STCL LTD.
139.	TUNGABHADRA STEEL PRODUCTS LTD.
140.	VIGNYAN INDUSTRIES LTD.
KERALA	
141.	COCHIN SHIPYARD LTD.
142.	FERTILIZERS & CHEMICALS (TRAVANCORE) LTD.
143.	HINDUSTAN LATEX LTD.
144.	HINDUSTAN NEWSPRINT LTD.
145.	INSTRUMENTATION CONTROL VALVES LTD.
MADHYA PRADESH	
146.	MADHYA PRADESH ASHOK HOTEL CORPN. LTD.
147.	NARMADA HYDROELECTRIC DEVELOPMENT CORPN. LTD.
148.	NEPA LTD.
149.	NORTHERN COALFIELDS LTD.
150.	NTC(MADHYA PRADESH)LTD.
MAHARAHASHTRA	
151.	AIR INDIA CHARTERS LTD.

S. No.	NAME OF PSU
152.	AIR INDIA LTD.
153.	BEL OPTRONICS LTD.
154.	BHARAT PETROLEUM CORPN. LTD.
155.	COTTON CORPN. OF INDIA LTD.
156.	EXPORT CREDIT GUARANTEE CORPN.OF INDIA LTD.
157.	HINDUSTAN ANTIBIOTICS LTD.
158.	HINDUSTAN ORGANIC CHEMICALS LTD.
159.	HINDUSTAN PETROLEUM CORPN. LTD.
160.	HOTEL CORPN. OF INDIA LTD.
161.	INDIAN OIL CORPORATION LTD.
162.	INDIAN RARE EARTHS LTD.
163.	MAHARASHTRA ELEKTROSMELT LTD.
164.	MANGANESE ORE(INDIA) LTD.
165.	MAZAGON DOCK LTD.
166.	MILLENNIUM TELECOM LTD.
167.	MINERAL EXPLORATION CORPN. LTD.
168.	MUMBAI RAILWAY VIKAS CORPORATION LTD.
169.	NATIONAL FILM DEV. CORPN. LTD.
170.	NTC(MAHARASHTRA NORTH)LTD.
171.	NTC(SOUTH MAHARASHTRA)LTD.
172.	RASHTRIYA CHEMICALS AND FERTILIZERS LTD.
173.	RICHARDSON & CRUDDAS(1972) LTD.
174.	SHIPPING CORPORATION OF INDIA LTD.
175.	WESTERN COALFIELDS LTD.
MEGHALAYA	
176.	NORTH EASTERN HANDICRAFTS & HANDLOOM DEV.CORPN. LTD.
177.	NORTH EASTERN ELECTRIC POWER CORPORATION LTD.
NAGALAND	
178.	NAGALAND PULP & PAPER COMPANY LTD.
ORISSA	
179.	MAHANADI COALFIELDLS LTD.
180.	NATIONAL ALUMINIUM COMPANY LTD.
181.	ORISSA DRUGS & CHEMICALS LTD.
182.	UTKAL ASHOK HOTEL CORPN. LTD.

S. No.	*NAME OF PSU*
PUNJAB	
183.	GURU GOBIND SINGH REFINARIES LTD.
184.	SEMI-CONDUCTOR COMPLEX LTD.
RAJASTHAN	
185.	FCI ARAVALI GYPSUM & MINERALS (INDIA) LTD.
186.	HINDUSTAN SALTS LTD.
187.	IL POWER ELECTRONICS LTD.
188.	INSTRUMENTATION DIGITAL CONTROL LTD.
189.	INSTRUMENTATION LTD.
190.	RAJASTHAN DRUGS & PHARMACEUTICALS LTD.
191.	RAJASTHAN ELECTRONICS AND INSTRUMENTS LTD.
192.	SAMBHAR SALTS LTD.
TAMILNADU	
193.	BHARATIYA NABHIKIYA VIDYUT NIGAM LTD.
194.	CHENNAI PETROLEUM CORPORATION LTD.
195.	ENNORE PORT LTD.
196.	HINDUSTAN PHOTO FILMS MANUFACTURING CO. LTD.
197.	IDPL (TAMILNADU) LTD.
198.	MADRAS FERTILIZERS LTD.
199.	NEYVELI LIGNITE CORPN. LTD.
200.	NTC(TAMILNADU & PONDICHERRY) LTD.
201.	SETHUSAMUDRAM CORPN. LTD.
202.	TAMIL NADU TRADE PROMOTION ORGANISATION
UTTAR PRADESH	
203.	ARTIFICIAL LIMBS MFG. CORPN. OF INDIA
204.	BHARAT IMMUNOLOGICALS & BIOLOGICALS CORP. LTD.
205.	BHARAT PUMPS & COMPRESSORS LTD.
206.	BHARAT YANTRA NIGAM LTD.
207.	BRITISH INDIA CORPORATION LTD.
208.	BROADCAST ENGG.CONSULTANTS INDIA LTD.
209.	BRUSHWARE LTD.
210.	NATIONAL HANDLOOM DEVELOPMENT CORPORATION LTD.
211.	NTC(UTTAR PRADESH)LTD.
212.	SCOOTERS INDIA LTD.
213.	TRIVENI STRUCTURALS LTD.

S. No.	NAME OF PSU

UTTARANCHAL

214. INDIAN MEDICINES & PHARMACEUTICAL CORPN. LTD.

WEST BENGAL

215. ANDREW YULE & COMPANY LTD.
216. BALMER LAWRIE & CO. LTD.
217. BALMER LAWRIE INVESTMENTS LTD.
218. BBJ CONSTRUCTION COMPANY LTD.
219. BENGAL CHEMICALS & PHARMACEUTICALS LTD.
220. BHARAT BHARI UDYOG NIGAM LTD.
221. BHARAT OPHTHALMIC GLASS LTD.
222. BIECCO LAWRIE LTD.
223. BIRDS JUTE & EXPORTS LTD.
224. BRAITHWAITE & CO. LTD.
225. BRIDGE & ROOF CO.(INDIA) LTD.
226. BURN STANDARD COMPANY LTD.
227. CENTRAL INLAND WATER TRANSPORT CORPN. LTD.
228. COAL INDIA LTD.
229. EASTERN COALFIELDS LTD.
230. GARDEN REACH SHIPBUILDERS & ENGINEERS LTD.
231. HINDUSTAN CABLES LTD.
232. HINDUSTAN COPPER LTD.
233. HINDUSTAN STEEL WORKS COSTN. LTD.
234. HOOGHLY DOCK AND PORT ENGINEERS LTD.
235. HOOGHLY PRINTING COMPANY LTD.
236. I.B.P. CO. LTD.
237. JUTE CORPN. OF INDIA LTD.
238. M S T C LTD.
239. NATIONAL INSTRUMENTS LTD.
240. NATIONAL JUTE MANUFACTURERS CORPORATION LTD.
241. NTC(WEST BENGAL,ASSAM,BIHAR & ORISSA)LTD.
242. TYRE CORPORATION OF INDIA LTD.

ANDAMAN & NICOBAR ISLANDS

243. ANDAMAN & NICOBAR ISL. FOREST & PLANT.DEV.CORP.LTD

S. No.	*NAME OF PSU*
CHANDIGARH	
244.	PUNJAB ASHOK HOTEL COMPANY LTD.
PONDICHERRY	
245.	PONDICHERRY ASHOK HOTEL CORPN. LTD.

Appendix 2

State-wise Central PSEs Thin Gross Block & Employment during 2004-05 and 2005-06

(*Gross Block in Rs. Lakhs and Employment in Nos.*)

S. No.	NAME OF PSU	2005-2006		2004-2005	
		Gross Block	Employment	Gross Block	Employment
ANDHRA PRADESH					
1.	INDIAN DRUGS & PHARMACEUTICALS LTD.	6423	11	6423	11
2.	INDIAN AIRLINES LTD.	17345	1479	17345	1479
3.	INDIAN OIL CORPORATION LTD.	120224	776	120224	776
4.	AIR INDIA LTD.	132	42	132	42
5.	AIRLINE ALLIED SERVICES LTD.	0	23	0	23
6.	AIRPORTS AUTHORITY OF INDIA LTD.	42408	653	40260	668
7.	BALMER LAWRIE & CO. LTD.	132	13	128	11
8.	BBJ CONSTRUCTION COMPANY LTD.	0	0	1	0
9.	BENGAL CHEMICALS & PHARMACEUTICALS LTD.	1	6	1	6
10.	BHARAT DYNAMICS LTD.	34189	2814	33333	2909
11.	BHARAT EARTH MOVERS LTD.	153	99	98	111
12.	BHARAT ELECTRONICS LTD.	8476	846	8476	858
13.	BHARAT HEAVY ELECTRICALS LTD.	67361	6444	59221	6530
14.	BHARAT HEAVY PLATE & VESSELS LTD.	7858	1442	7823	1508
15.	BHARAT PETROLEUM CORPN. LTD.	52144	329	45264	338
16.	BHARAT SANCHAR NIGAM LTD.	927327	34308	892005	35640

S. No.	NAME OF PSU	2005-2006		2004-2005	
		Gross Block	Employment	Gross Block	Employment
17.	BRIDGE & ROOF CO.(INDIA) LTD.	606	19	778	24
18.	CEMENT CORPN. OF INDIA LTD.	24275	448	24270	422
19.	CENTRAL COTTAGE INDUSTRIES CORPN. OF INDIA LT	161	3	161	2
20.	CENTRAL WAREHOUSING CORPN.	9142	811	9132	868
21.	COAL INDIA LTD.	1	7	1	8
22.	CONTAINER CORPORATION OF INDIA LTD.	2876	48	2713	42
23.	COTTON CORPN. OF INDIA LTD.	190	185	182	180
24.	DREDGING CORPN.OF INDIA LTD.	87150	752	84557	806
25.	ELECTRONICS CORPN. OF INDIA LTD.	19686	4368	18511	4536
26.	ENGINEERING PROJECTS (INDIA) LTD.	8	19	490	14
27.	ENGINEERS INDIA LTD.	0	37	0	26
28.	EXPORT CREDIT GUARANTEE CORPN.OF INDIA LTD.	143	18	78	15
29.	FERRO SCRAP NIGAM LTD.	1996	199	1722	200
30.	FERTILIZER CORPN. OF INDIA LTD.	27308	8	27308	9
31.	FERTILIZERS & CHEMICALS (TRAVANCORE) LTD.	20	45	21	49
32.	FOOD CORPN. OF INDIA	15707	4148	15585	4263
33.	GAIL (INDIA) LTD.	102370	153	96288	135
34.	HINDUSTAN AERONAUTICS LTD.	42563	2319	22795	2486
35.	HINDUSTAN ANTIBIOTICS LTD.	3	18	3	16
36.	HINDUSTAN CABLES LTD.	16500	1110	16500	1110
37.	HINDUSTAN FLUOROCARBONS LIMITED	5317	207	5348	213
38.	HINDUSTAN INSECTICIDES LTD.	1	13	6	13
39.	HINDUSTAN LATEX LTD.	40	11	0	13
40.	HINDUSTAN PAPER CORPORATION LTD.	1	3	1	3
41.	HINDUSTAN PETROLEUM CORPN. LTD.	503082	1697	379662	1702
42.	HINDUSTAN PHOTO FILMS MANUFACTURING CO. LTD.	3	3	3	2

S. No.	NAME OF PSU	2005-2006 Gross Block	2005-2006 Employment	2004-2005 Gross Block	2004-2005 Employment
43.	HINDUSTAN SHIPYARD LTD.	16981	3519	16810	3575
44.	HINDUSTAN STEEL WORKS COSTN. LTD.	519	116	538	118
45.	HMT BEARINGS LTD.	2930	326	2879	340
46.	HMT LTD.	1058	79	750	80
47.	HMT MACHINE TOOLS LTD.	3822	949	3827	923
48.	HOUSING & URBAN DEV. CORPN. LTD.	196	38	195	38
49.	I T I LTD.	24	32	24	31
50.	I.B.P. CO. LTD.	8614	42	5604	34
51.	INDIA TOURISM DEV. CORPN.LTD.	3	3	2	3
52.	INDIAN RAILWAY CATERING AND TOURISM CORPN. LT	37	629	22	631
53.	INDIAN RENEWABLE ENERGY DEVT.AGENCY LTD.	0	0	0	1
54.	INSTRUMENTATION LTD.	7	6	7	6
55.	IRCON INTERNATIONAL LTD.	17	1	17	7
56.	JUTE CORPN. OF INDIA LTD.	3	52	3	58
57.	KARNATAKA ANTIBIOTICS & PHARMACEUTICALS LTD.	0	32	0	27
58.	M M T C LTD.	512	97	534	98
59.	M S T C LTD.	30	19	29	19
60.	MADRAS FERTILIZERS LTD.	48	52	48	68
61.	MANGALORE REFINARY & PETROCHEMICALS LTD.	342	0	0	0
62.	MANGANESE ORE(INDIA) LTD.	0	2	0	1
63.	MECON LTD.	35	23	34	28
64.	MISHRA DHATU NIGAM LTD.	13291	1319	13184	1321
65.	NATIONAL ALUMINIUM COMPANY LTD.	8044	60	7804	59
66.	NATIONAL BACKWARD CLASSES FINANCE & DEVELOPME	1	0	1	0
67.	NATIONAL BLDG. CONSTN. CORPN. LTD.	101	50	99	43
68.	NATIONAL FILM DEV. CORPN. LTD.	2	3	1	3

S. No.	NAME OF PSU	2005-2006 Gross Block	2005-2006 Employment	2004-2005 Gross Block	2004-2005 Employment
69.	NATIONAL HANDLOOM DEVELOPMENT CORPORATION LTD	15	14	15	14
70.	NATIONAL MINERAL DEVELOPMENT CORPN. LTD.	9856	417	9936	465
71.	NATIONAL SCHEDULED TRIBES FINANCE & DEVP. COR	1	2	1	3
72.	NATIONAL SEEDS CORPN. LTD.	472	65	460	69
73.	NATIONAL SMALL INDUSTRIES CORPN. LTD.	384	33	362	37
74.	NEYVELI LIGNITE CORPN. LTD.	0	1	3	1
75.	NTC(A.PRADESH, KARNATAKA, KERALA & MAHE)LTD.	1139	227	1222	421
76.	NTPC LTD.	719579	2395	716431	2416
77.	NTPC VIDYUT VYAPAR NIGAM LTD.	0	2	0	0
78.	OIL & NATURAL GAS CORPORATION LTD.	310347	1495	446250	1521
79.	P E C LTD.	6	10	6	9
80.	POWER FINANCE CORPORATION	28000	0	28000	0
81.	POWER GRID CORPORATION OF INDIA LTD	420194	497	381074	488
82.	PRAGA TOOLS LTD.	3476	542	3614	542
83.	RAIL VIKAS NIGAM LTD.	0	9	0	0
84.	RASHTRIYA CHEMICALS AND FERTILIZERS LTD.	45	35	45	37
85.	RASHTRIYA ISPAT NIGAM LTD.	894818	16324	876106	16366
86.	RITES LTD.	83	42	83	53
87.	RURAL ELECTRIFICATION CORPN. LTD.	18	47	18	46
88.	SCOOTERS INDIA LTD.	0	3	0	0
89.	SEMI-CONDUCTOR COMPLEX LTD.	0	0	0	3
90.	SPONGE IRON INDIA LTD.	5771	309	5745	314
91.	STATE FARMS CORPORATION OF INDIA LTD.	0	8	0	6
92.	STATE TRADING CORPN. OF INDIA LTD.	523	40	524	40
93.	STEEL AUTHORITY OF INDIA LTD.	6550	240	6442	250
94.	TEHRI HYDRO DEVELOPMENT CORP. LTD..	0	11	0	10

S. No.	NAME OF PSU	2005-2006 Gross Block	2005-2006 Employment	2004-2005 Gross Block	2004-2005 Employment
95.	TELECOMMUNICATIONS CONSULTANTS (INDIA) LTD.	0	4	0	11
96.	URANIUM CORPORATION OF INDIA LTD.	403	8	0	0
97.	WATER & POWER CONSULTANCY SERVICES(INDIA) LTD	5	6	5	13
	TOTAL	4601624	96169	4465603	98714
ARUNACHAL PRADESH					
1.	HINDUSTAN PREFAB LTD.	0	11	0	0
2.	INDIAN OIL CORPORATION LTD.	2796	31	2796	31
3.	AIRPORTS AUTHORITY OF INDIA LTD.	18	3	12	3
4.	DONYI POLO ASHOK HOTEL LTD.	151	43	148	43
5.	ENGINEERING PROJECTS (INDIA) LTD.	0	0	0	2
6.	HOUSING & URBAN DEV. CORPN. LTD.	0	3	0	2
7.	NATIONAL BLDG. CONSTN. CORPN. LTD.	0	29	0	28
8.	NATIONAL HYDROELECTRIC POWER CORPN.LTD.	143107	741	108758	864
9.	NATIONAL SMALL INDUSTRIES CORPN. LTD.	0	1	0	0
10.	NORTH EASTERN ELECTRIC POWER CORPORATION LTD.	188646	1089	174611	924
11.	OIL INDIA LTD.	1319	145	1737	140
12.	POWER GRID CORPORATION OF INDIA LTD	8580	105	8052	102
13.	RITES LTD.	0	4	0	1
14.	TELECOMMUNICATIONS CONSULTANTS (INDIA) LTD.	0	3	0	2
15.	WATER & POWER CONSULTANCY SERVICES(INDIA) LTD	0	1	0	0
	TOTAL	344617	2209	296114	2142
ASSAM					
1.	INDIAN OIL CORPORATION LTD.	319872	3758	319872	3758

S. No.	NAME OF PSU	2005-2006		2004-2005	
		Gross Block	Employment	Gross Block	Employment
2.	AIR INDIA LTD.	15	1	15	1
3.	AIRLINE ALLIED SERVICES LTD.	1	0	1	0
4.	AIRPORTS AUTHORITY OF INDIA LTD.	37804	600	37395	588
5.	ANDREW YULE & COMPANY LTD.	10433	7920	10212	7917
6.	ARTIFICIAL LIMBS MFG. CORPN. OF INDIA	2	2	0	2
7.	ASSAM ASHOK HOTEL CORPN. LTD.	415	84	393	84
8.	BBJ CONSTRUCTION COMPANY LTD.	0	0	2	0
9.	BENGAL CHEMICALS & PHARMACEUTICALS LTD.	1	7	1	6
10.	BHARAT EARTH MOVERS LTD.	9	15	12	10
11.	BHARAT PETROLEUM CORPN. LTD.	330	9	256	11
12.	BHARAT PUMPS & COMPRESSORS LTD.	1	3	1	3
13.	BHARAT SANCHAR NIGAM LTD.	164714	6182	147952	6278
14.	BONGAIGAON REFINERY & PETROCHEMICALS LTD.	95315	1679	96760	1693
15.	BRAHMAPUTRA VALLEY FERTILIZER CORPN. LTD.	99078	1499	92250	1604
16.	BRIDGE & ROOF CO.(INDIA) LTD.	26	2	0	0
17.	CEMENT CORPN. OF INDIA LTD.	4719	381	4664	400
18.	CENTRAL INLAND WATER TRANSPORT CORPN. LTD.	18	74	20	76
19.	CENTRAL WAREHOUSING CORPN.	963	86	955	75
20.	COAL INDIA LTD.	11781	3391	11942	3489
21.	CONTAINER CORPORATION OF INDIA LTD.	163	5	162	6
22.	ENGINEERING PROJECTS (INDIA) LTD.	0	2	0	1
23.	ENGINEERS INDIA LTD.	0	1	0	2
24.	EXPORT CREDIT GUARANTEE CORPN.OF INDIA LTD.	0	2	0	2
25.	FOOD CORPN. OF INDIA	1947	2347	1703	2348
26.	GAIL (INDIA) LTD.	24596	119	24694	126
27.	HINDUSTAN LATEX LTD.	0	3	0	6

S. No.	NAME OF PSU	2005-2006		2004-2005	
		Gross Block	Employment	Gross Block	Employment
28.	HINDUSTAN PAPER CORPORATION LTD.	86426	2579	81273	2635
29.	HINDUSTAN PETROLEUM CORPN. LTD.	3395	27	2219	20
30.	HINDUSTAN PHOTO FILMS MANUFACTURING CO. LTD.	1	2	1	2
31.	HMT LTD.	180	0	180	0
32.	HOUSING & URBAN DEV. CORPN. LTD.	128	30	130	31
33.	I.B.P. CO. LTD.	278	3	268	3
34.	INDIA TOURISM DEV. CORPN.LTD.	5	4	5	4
35.	INDIAN RAILWAY CATERING AND TOURISM CORPN. LT	0	70	0	0
36.	JUTE CORPN. OF INDIA LTD.	4	167	5	175
37.	M M T C LTD.	0	3	0	3
38.	NATIONAL BLDG. CONSTN. CORPN. LTD.	8	98	36	85
39.	NATIONAL FILM DEV. CORPN. LTD.	1	1	1	1
40.	NATIONAL HANDLOOM DEVELOPMENT CORPORATION LTD	0	4	0	4
41.	NATIONAL HYDROELECTRIC POWER CORPN.LTD.	0	385	0	380
42.	NATIONAL SCHEDULED CASTES FINANCE & DEVP. COR	0	2	0	3
43.	NATIONAL SCHEDULED TRIBES FINANCE & DEVP. COR	1	1	1	1
44.	NATIONAL SEEDS CORPN. LTD.	44	10	44	9
45.	NATIONAL SMALL INDUSTRIES CORPN. LTD.	167	21	196	28
46.	NORTH EASTERN HANDICRAFTS & HANDLOOM DEV.COR	136	86	131	103
47.	NORTH EASTERN ELECTRIC POWER CORPORATION LTD.	199787	1089	197959	1093
48.	NORTH EASTERN REGIONAL AGRI. MARKETING CORP.L	178	25	178	25
49.	NTC(WEST BENGAL,ASSAM,BIHAR & ORISSA)LTD.	186	182	186	185
50.	NUMALIGARH REFINARY LTD.	266641	684	277621	673
51.	OIL & NATURAL GAS CORPORATION LTD.	1853111	7796	857321	8231
52.	OIL INDIA LTD.	580547	8743	516778	7930
53.	P E C LTD.	0	2	0	2

S. No.	*NAME OF PSU*	*2005-2006*		*2004-2005*	
		Gross Block	*Employment*	*Gross Block*	*Employment*
54.	POWER GRID CORPORATION OF INDIA LTD	133036	323	132338	320
55.	RASHTRIYA ISPAT NIGAM LTD.	6	0	6	0
56.	RITES LTD.	0	6	0	3
57.	RURAL ELECTRIFICATION CORPN. LTD.	2	12	2	12
58.	SCOOTERS INDIA LTD.	0	3	0	1
59.	STEEL AUTHORITY OF INDIA LTD.	314	28	496	35
60.	TEHRI HYDRO DEVELOPMENT CORP. LTD..	0	1	0	2
61.	TELECOMMUNICATIONS CONSULTANTS (INDIA) LTD.	1	0	0	7
62.	WATER & POWER CONSULTANCY SERVICES(INDIA) LTD	2	1	2	1
	TOTAL	**3896788**	**50560**	**2816639**	**50493**
BIHAR					
1.	NATIONAL JUTE MANUFACTURERS CORPORATION LTD.	1158	1252	1158	1252
2.	INDIAN OIL CORPORATION LTD.	312699	1926	312699	1926
3.	AIR INDIA LTD.	4	1	4	1
4.	AIRPORTS AUTHORITY OF INDIA LTD.	19401	249	18691	243
5.	BBJ CONSTRUCTION COMPANY LTD.	0	95	0	1
6.	BENGAL CHEMICALS & PHARMACEUTICALS LTD.	1	7	1	9
7.	BHARAT EARTH MOVERS LTD.	0	0	235	91
8.	BHARAT PETROLEUM CORPN. LTD.	14605	88	13151	85
9.	BHARAT SANCHAR NIGAM LTD.	306622	7490	292276	8002
10.	BHARAT WAGON & ENGG. CO. LTD.	1664	942	1664	953
11.	BIHAR DRUGS & ORGANIC CHEMICALS LTD.	2276	204	2276	204
12.	BONGAIGAON REFINERY & PETROCHEMICALS LTD.	391	1	390	2
13.	BRIDGE & ROOF CO.(INDIA) LTD.	0	0	20	10
14.	CENTRAL WAREHOUSING CORPN.	891	126	889	144

S. No.	NAME OF PSU	2005-2006		2004-2005	
		Gross Block	Employment	Gross Block	Employment
15.	COAL INDIA LTD.	4	25	4	26
16.	CONTAINER CORPORATION OF INDIA LTD.	413	3	411	3
17.	ENGINEERING PROJECTS (INDIA) LTD.	0	0	110	0
18.	ENGINEERS INDIA LTD.	0	1	0	3
19.	FOOD CORPN. OF INDIA	2888	1812	2785	1890
20.	HINDUSTAN ANTIBIOTICS LTD.	3	46	3	49
21.	HINDUSTAN FERTILIZER CORPN. LTD.	17923	7	18012	6
22.	HINDUSTAN LATEX LTD.	0	6	0	8
23.	HINDUSTAN PAPER CORPORATION LTD.	3	3	3	3
24.	HINDUSTAN PETROLEUM CORPN. LTD.	10784	69	10453	67
25.	HINDUSTAN PHOTO FILMS MANUFACTURING CO. LTD.	2	4	2	4
26.	HINDUSTAN STEEL WORKS COSTN. LTD.	433	35	384	40
27.	HMT MACHINE TOOLS LTD.	0	0	1	2
28.	HOUSING & URBAN DEV. CORPN. LTD.	168	13	165	12
29.	I.B.P. CO. LTD.	2760	26	2060	26
30.	INDIA TOURISM DEV. CORPN.LTD.	255	56	248	88
31.	INDIAN RAILWAY CATERING AND TOURISM CORPN. LT	667	157	661	4
32.	INSTRUMENTATION LTD.	0	1	0	1
33.	IRCON INTERNATIONAL LTD.	221	90	169	82
34.	JUTE CORPN. OF INDIA LTD.	5	135	6	151
35.	KARNATAKA ANTIBIOTICS & PHARMACEUTICALS LTD.	0	22	0	18
36.	M M T C LTD.	1143	1	1143	0
37.	NATIONAL BLDG. CONSTN. CORPN. LTD.	123	117	87	83
38.	NATIONAL HANDLOOM DEVELOPMENT CORPORATION LTD	0	1	0	1
39.	NATIONAL HYDROELECTRIC POWER CORPN.LTD.	88	123	58	120
40.	NATIONAL SCHEDULED CASTES FINANCE & DEVP. COR	1	2	0	2
41.	NATIONAL SEEDS CORPN. LTD.	64	48	57	52

S. No.	NAME OF PSU	2005-2006		2004-2005	
		Gross Block	Employment	Gross Block	Employment
42.	NATIONAL SMALL INDUSTRIES CORPN. LTD.	0	6	18	19
43.	NTC(WEST BENGAL,ASSAM,BIHAR & ORISSA)LTD.	280	560	280	582
44.	NTPC LTD.	558396	1515	385556	1324
45.	OIL & NATURAL GAS CORPORATION LTD.	0	0	5561	0
46.	OIL INDIA LTD.	2416	22	2667	20
47.	POWER GRID CORPORATION OF INDIA LTD	190385	484	127602	470
48.	PYRITES, PHOSPHATES & CHEMICALS LTD.	3365	16	3365	16
49.	RASHTRIYA CHEMICALS AND FERTILIZERS LTD.	6	2	6	3
50.	RASHTRIYA ISPAT NIGAM LTD.	17	4	1	4
51.	RITES LTD.	0	36	0	25
52.	RURAL ELECTRIFICATION CORPN. LTD.	7	28	7	25
53.	SCOOTERS INDIA LTD.	0	3	0	2
54.	STEEL AUTHORITY OF INDIA LTD.	128	218	146	230
55.	TEHRI HYDRO DEVELOPMENT CORP. LTD..	0	60	0	60
56.	TELECOMMUNICATIONS CONSULTANTS (INDIA) LTD.	0	5	0	8
57.	WATER & POWER CONSULTANCY SERVICES(INDIA) LTD	0	1	1	4
	TOTAL	**1452660**	**18144**	**1205486**	**18456**
CHHATTISGARH					
1.	AIRPORTS AUTHORITY OF INDIA LTD.	1411	69	1250	66
2.	BHARAT EARTH MOVERS LTD.	0	12	0	51
3.	BHARAT PETROLEUM CORPN. LTD.	4197	43	3145	18
4.	BHARAT REFRACTORIES LTD.	6968	675	6762	680
5.	BHARAT SANCHAR NIGAM LTD.	109913	2599	103758	2835
6.	BRIDGE & ROOF CO.(INDIA) LTD.	132	9	385	26

S. No.	NAME OF PSU	2005-2006		2004-2005	
		Gross Block	*Employment*	*Gross Block*	*Employment*
7.	CEMENT CORPN. OF INDIA LTD.	6633	116	6632	124
8.	CENTRAL MINE PLANNING & DESIGN INSTITUTE LTD.	1020	463	1863	387
9.	CENTRAL WAREHOUSING CORPN.	0	91	0	92
10.	CONTAINER CORPORATION OF INDIA LTD.	479	4	479	3
11.	ENGINEERING PROJECTS (INDIA) LTD.	1	4	1	1
12.	FERRO SCRAP NIGAM LTD.	3260	257	2369	241
13.	FERTILIZER CORPN. OF INDIA LTD.	1165	3	0	0
14.	FOOD CORPN. OF INDIA	3102	847	3006	855
15.	GAIL (INDIA) LTD.	0	1	0	0
16.	HINDUSTAN LATEX LTD.	0	0	0	3
17.	HINDUSTAN PETROLEUM CORPN. LTD.	11749	64	9897	69
18.	HINDUSTAN STEEL WORKS COSTN. LTD.	1443	478	1403	487
19.	HOUSING & URBAN DEV. CORPN. LTD.	89	13	89	14
20.	HSCC (INDIA) LTD.	0	1	0	1
21.	I.B.P. CO. LTD.	584	6	584	6
22.	INDIA TOURISM DEV. CORPN.LTD.	0	2	7	2
23.	INDIAN RAILWAY CATERING AND TOURISM CORPN. LT	0	45	0	0
24.	INSTRUMENTATION LTD.	17	13	18	15
25.	IRCON INTERNATIONAL LTD.	15	1	1	5
26.	KARNATAKA ANTIBIOTICS & PHARMACEUTICALS LTD.	0	4	0	5
27.	M M T C LTD.	0	2	0	0
28.	MAHARASHTRA ELEKTROSMELT LTD.	0	3	0	3
29.	MECON LTD.	74	28	72	37
30.	NATIONAL BLDG. CONSTN. CORPN. LTD.	132	31	29	24
31.	NATIONAL HANDLOOM DEVELOPMENT CORPORATION LTD	0	1	0	1
32.	NATIONAL HYDROELECTRIC POWER CORPN.LTD.	0	3	0	0

S. No.	*NAME OF PSU*	*2005-2006*		*2004-2005*	
		Gross Block	*Employment*	*Gross Block*	*Employment*
33.	NATIONAL MINERAL DEVELOPMENT CORPN. LTD.	95458	3595	94993	3420
34.	NATIONAL SEEDS CORPN. LTD.	0	1	0	1
35.	NATIONAL SMALL INDUSTRIES CORPN. LTD.	0	2	0	0
36.	NTC(MADHYA PRADESH)LTD.	3	3	3	4
37.	NTPC ELECTRIC SUPPLY COMPANY LTD.	0	0	0	3
38.	NTPC LTD.	589728	296	350641	218
39.	POWER GRID CORPORATION OF INDIA LTD	97923	106	73441	104
40.	RAIL VIKAS NIGAM LTD.	0	4	0	0
41.	RASHTRIYA CHEMICALS AND FERTILIZERS LTD.	0	4	0	4
42.	RITES LTD.	11	168	9	114
43.	SCOOTERS INDIA LTD.	0	0	0	1
44.	SOUTH EASTERN COALFIELDS LTD.	336134	52767	316843	53552
45.	STEEL AUTHORITY OF INDIA LTD.	653319	35633	630738	36442
46.	TELECOMMUNICATIONS CONSULTANTS (INDIA) LTD.	26	18	0	9
	TOTAL	**1924986**	**98485**	**1608418**	**99923**
GUJARAT					
1.	INDIAN OIL CORPORATION LTD.	1024402	3783	866499	3783
2.	AIR INDIA LTD.	104	40	104	40
3.	AIRPORTS AUTHORITY OF INDIA LTD.	39210	658	38440	664
4.	BALMER LAWRIE & CO. LTD.	69	4	68	4
5.	BHARAT EARTH MOVERS LTD.	23	16	22	41
6.	BHARAT HEAVY PLATE & VESSELS LTD.	5	1	5	2
7.	BHARAT PETROLEUM CORPN. LTD.	44693	344	39061	372

S. No.	NAME OF PSU	2005-2006		2004-2005	
		Gross Block	Employment	Gross Block	Employment
8.	BHARAT PUMPS & COMPRESSORS LTD.	1	5	1	5
9.	BHARAT SANCHAR NIGAM LTD.	723407	25839	700026	26962
10.	BRIDGE & ROOF CO.(INDIA) LTD.	1795	98	1726	125
11.	CENTRAL WAREHOUSING CORPN.	10073	305	7936	296
12.	CERTIFICATION ENGINEERS INTERNATIONAL LTD.	1	0	1	0
13.	COAL INDIA LTD.	3	12	2	12
14.	CONTAINER CORPORATION OF INDIA LTD.	5941	45	5508	47
15.	COTTON CORPN. OF INDIA LTD.	356	142	350	138
16.	DREDGING CORPN.OF INDIA LTD.	5	6	5	10
17.	ELECTRONICS CORPN. OF INDIA LTD.	2	9	2	9
18.	ENGINEERING PROJECTS (INDIA) LTD.	2	14	2	14
19.	ENGINEERS INDIA LTD.	356	105	186	90
20.	EXPORT CREDIT GUARANTEE CORPN.OF INDIA LTD.	227	22	178	17
21.	FERTILIZERS & CHEMICALS (TRAVANCORE) LTD.	0	0	0	2
22.	FOOD CORPN. OF INDIA	496	905	5096	953
23.	GAIL (INDIA) LTD.	200678	507	271604	521
24.	GURU GOBIND SINGH REFINARIES LTD.	3626	1	3331	2
25.	HINDUSTAN ANTIBIOTICS LTD.	2	12	2	12
26.	HINDUSTAN INSECTICIDES LTD.	2	7	2	7
27.	HINDUSTAN LATEX LTD.	0	6	0	5
28.	HINDUSTAN PAPER CORPORATION LTD.	3	4	3	4
29.	HINDUSTAN PETROLEUM CORPN. LTD.	47959	422	40973	333
30.	HINDUSTAN PHOTO FILMS MANUFACTURING CO. LTD.	0	0	2	0
31.	HINDUSTAN SALTS LTD.	409	38	389	54
32.	HMT MACHINE TOOLS LTD.	4	7	5	7
33.	HOUSING & URBAN DEV. CORPN. LTD.	63	27	61	29

S. No.	NAME OF PSU	2005-2006		2004-2005	
		Gross Block	Employment	Gross Block	Employment
34.	I T I LTD.	37	268	30	29
35.	I.B.P. CO. LTD.	5718	55	3218	55
36.	INDIA TOURISM DEV. CORPN.LTD.	13	3	12	3
37.	INDIAN RAILWAY CATERING AND TOURISM CORPN. LT	0	79	0	17
38.	INSTRUMENTATION LTD.	9	13	9	10
39.	IRCON INTERNATIONAL LTD.	114	38	126	87
40.	KARNATAKA ANTIBIOTICS & PHARMACEUTICALS LTD.	0	16	0	11
41.	M M T C LTD.	184	48	100	50
42.	M S T C LTD.	35	14	33	14
43.	MANGALORE REFINARY & PETROCHEMICALS LTD.	9	0	9	0
44.	MECON LTD.	0	2	1	1
45.	NATIONAL BLDG. CONSTN. CORPN. LTD.	22	215	15	186
46.	NATIONAL HANDLOOM DEVELOPMENT CORPORATION LTD	0	1	0	1
47.	NATIONAL SEEDS CORPN. LTD.	36	23	25	25
48.	NATIONAL SMALL INDUSTRIES CORPN. LTD.	385	35	385	37
49.	NTC(GUJARAT)LTD.	887	281	810	1395
50.	NTPC LTD.	400926	529	400308	494
51.	NUCLEAR POWER CORPN. OF INDIA LTD.	236366	1103	143284	1117
52.	OIL & NATURAL GAS CORPORATION LTD.	2411750	11036	1658444	11620
53.	OIL INDIA LTD.	50	9	42	8
54.	P E C LTD.	6	14	6	17
55.	POWER GRID CORPORATION OF INDIA LTD	42712	82	42249	74
56.	PROJECTS & DEVELOPMENT INDIA LTD.	332	96	409	105
57.	RAJASTHAN ELECTRONICS AND INSTRUMENTS LTD.	0	14	0	0
58.	RASHTRIYA CHEMICALS AND FERTILIZERS LTD.	8	11	9	13
59.	RASHTRIYA ISPAT NIGAM LTD.	322	11	301	11

S. No.	NAME OF PSU	2005-2006		2004-2005	
		Gross Block	Employment	Gross Block	Employment
60.	RITES LTD.	0	11	0	11
61.	RURAL ELECTRIFICATION CORPN. LTD.	4	14	4	14
62.	SCOOTERS INDIA LTD.	0	2	0	1
63.	STATE TRADING CORPN. OF INDIA LTD.	36	44	36	45
64.	STEEL AUTHORITY OF INDIA LTD.	1830	60	1827	70
65.	TEHRI HYDRO DEVELOPMENT CORP. LTD..	0	1	0	1
66.	TELECOMMUNICATIONS CONSULTANTS (INDIA) LTD.	1	8	0	4
67.	WATER & POWER CONSULTANCY SERVICES(INDIA) LTD	99	38	51	39
	TOTAL	**5205808**	**47558**	**4233333**	**50125**
HARYANA					
1.	INDIAN DRUGS & PHARMACEUTICALS LTD.	1142	133	1142	133
2.	HINDUSTAN PREFAB LTD.	0	1	0	1
3.	INDIAN OIL CORPORATION LTD.	1152986	2107	995083	2107
4.	AIR INDIA LTD.	20	3	20	3
5.	AIRPORTS AUTHORITY OF INDIA LTD.	5	1	4	1
6.	BALMER LAWRIE & CO. LTD.	516	7	482	5
7.	BHARAT ELECTRONICS LTD.	6945	635	6393	645
8.	BHARAT PETROLEUM CORPN. LTD.	32944	298	22367	290
9.	BHARAT SANCHAR NIGAM LTD.	291825	5981	272744	6364
10.	BRIDGE & ROOF CO.(INDIA) LTD.	139	14	1590	142
11.	CEMENT CORPN. OF INDIA LTD.	1010	29	1010	31
12.	CENTRAL WAREHOUSING CORPN.	5800	221	5766	218
13.	CONTAINER CORPORATION OF INDIA LTD.	1026	7	848	7
14.	COTTON CORPN. OF INDIA LTD.	49	45	45	45
15.	ENGINEERS INDIA LTD.	2655	214	2190	304

S. No.	NAME OF PSU	2005-2006		2004-2005	
		Gross Block	Employment	Gross Block	Employment
16.	EXPORT CREDIT GUARANTEE CORPN.OF INDIA LTD.	55	8	32	6
17.	FOOD CORPN. OF INDIA	6589	1877	5390	1971
18.	GAIL (INDIA) LTD.	68	10	11772	8
19.	GURU GOBIND SINGH REFINARIES LTD.	36	1	0	0
20.	HINDUSTAN INSECTICIDES LTD.	263	24	251	27
21.	HINDUSTAN LATEX LTD.	0	2	0	1
22.	HINDUSTAN PETROLEUM CORPN. LTD.	28396	128	23286	119
23.	HINDUSTAN STEEL WORKS COSTN. LTD.	1	3	0	0
24.	HMT BEARINGS LTD.	0	1	0	0
25.	HMT LTD.	9115	2123	8678	2172
26.	HMT MACHINE TOOLS LTD.	3063	708	3047	750
27.	I.B.P. CO. LTD.	4530	49	3530	50
28.	INDIAN OIL TECHNOLOGIES LTD.	0	5	0	5
29.	INSTRUMENTATION LTD.	1	5	1	5
30.	IRCON INTERNATIONAL LTD.	429	3	429	43
31.	KARNATAKA ANTIBIOTICS & PHARMACEUTICALS LTD.	0	3	0	3
32.	M M T C LTD.	0	9	0	10
33.	NATIONAL BLDG. CONSTN. CORPN. LTD.	1	36	4	111
34.	NATIONAL FERTILIZERS LTD.	42327	891	42145	905
35.	NATIONAL HANDICAPPED FINANCE & DEVPT. CORPN.	66	19	63	20
36.	NATIONAL HANDLOOM DEVELOPMENT CORPORATION LTD	0	7	0	8
37.	NATIONAL HYDROELECTRIC POWER CORPN.LTD.	20409	1644	17874	1700
38.	NATIONAL SEEDS CORPN. LTD.	0	18	0	18
39.	NATIONAL SMALL INDUSTRIES CORPN. LTD.	0	14	0	0
40.	NTC(DELHI,PUNJAB & RAJASTHAN) LTD.	0	7	0	8
41.	NTPC ELECTRIC SUPPLY COMPANY LTD.	0	0	0	6

S. No.	NAME OF PSU	2005-2006		2004-2005	
		Gross Block	Employment	Gross Block	Employment
42.	NTPC LTD.	94919	150	95249	158
43.	POWER GRID CORPORATION OF INDIA LTD	146959	836	123604	823
44.	RASHTRIYA CHEMICALS AND FERTILIZERS LTD.	10	2	0	3
45.	RASHTRIYA ISPAT NIGAM LTD.	185	10	174	10
46.	RITES LTD.	9726	1382	9467	1263
47.	RURAL ELECTRIFICATION CORPN. LTD.	3	30	0	29
48.	STATE FARMS CORPORATION OF INDIA LTD.	425	351	444	365
49.	STEEL AUTHORITY OF INDIA LTD.	2084	65	2081	75
50.	TEHRI HYDRO DEVELOPMENT CORP. LTD..	0	17	0	18
51.	TELECOMMUNICATIONS CONSULTANTS (INDIA) LTD.	0	0	14	1
52.	WATER & POWER CONSULTANCY SERVICES(INDIA) LTD	939	0	904	0
	TOTAL	**1867661**	**20134**	**1658123**	**20987**
HIMACHAL PRADESH					
1.	INDIAN OIL CORPORATION LTD.	15655	98	15655	98
2.	AIRPORTS AUTHORITY OF INDIA LTD.	15430	85	15840	77
3.	BHARAT PETROLEUM CORPN. LTD.	20	108	21	15
4.	BHARAT SANCHAR NIGAM LTD.	161966	3765	146495	3788
5.	CEMENT CORPN. OF INDIA LTD.	3112	343	3110	328
6.	CENTRAL WAREHOUSING CORPN.	68	10	68	9
7.	CONTAINER CORPORATION OF INDIA LTD.	0	1	0	0
8.	FOOD CORPN. OF INDIA	1800	198	409	167
9.	HINDUSTAN PETROLEUM CORPN. LTD.	2344	3	2313	5
10.	HINDUSTAN SALTS LTD.	125	34	71	46
11.	HOUSING & URBAN DEV. CORPN. LTD.	0	3	0	3

S. No.	NAME OF PSU	2005-2006 Gross Block	2005-2006 Employment	2004-2005 Gross Block	2004-2005 Employment
12.	HSCC (INDIA) LTD.	0	2	0	2
13.	I.B.P. CO. LTD.	176	2	176	2
14.	J & K MINERAL DEVELOPMENT CORPN. LTD.	495	7	0	0
15.	KARNATAKA ANTIBIOTICS & PHARMACEUTICALS LTD.	0	1	0	1
16.	NATIONAL HYDROELECTRIC POWER CORPN.LTD.	602280	3206	549909	3361
17.	NATIONAL MINERAL DEVELOPMENT CORPN. LTD.	17	1	17	2
18.	NATIONAL SEEDS CORPN. LTD.	0	5	0	5
19.	NTC(DELHI,PUNJAB & RAJASTHAN) LTD.	0	2	0	2
20.	NTPC LTD.	136418	195	106846	208
21.	OIL & NATURAL GAS CORPORATION LTD.	0	0	16223	0
22.	POWER GRID CORPORATION OF INDIA LTD	77731	78	76473	74
23.	RURAL ELECTRIFICATION CORPN. LTD.	1	8	3	8
24.	SATLUJ JAL VIDYUT NIGAM LTD.	809324	0	805611	1715
25.	TEHRI HYDRO DEVELOPMENT CORP. LTD..	0	6	0	6
26.	WATER & POWER CONSULTANCY SERVICES(INDIA) LTD	0	1	0	0
	TOTAL	**1826962**	**8162**	**1739240**	**9922**
JAMMU & KASHMIR					
1.	INDIAN OIL CORPORATION LTD.	13388	94	13388	94
2.	AIRPORTS AUTHORITY OF INDIA LTD.	4582	123	4412	129
3.	BHARAT EARTH MOVERS LTD.	5	8	5	6
4.	BHARAT PETROLEUM CORPN. LTD.	4924	16	2603	15
5.	BHARAT SANCHAR NIGAM LTD.	105872	2928	88761	2972
6.	FOOD CORPN. OF INDIA	2766	418	2599	389
7.	HANDICRAFTS & HANDLOOM EXPORTS CORP. OF INDIA	0	1	0	1
8.	HINDUSTAN PETROLEUM CORPN. LTD.	16784	69	14650	69

S. No.	NAME OF PSU	2005-2006		2004-2005	
		Gross Block	Employment	Gross Block	Employment
9.	HMT CHINAR WATCHES LTD.	1074	556	1052	621
10.	HOTEL CORPN. OF INDIA LTD.	2008	395	2008	403
11.	HOUSING & URBAN DEV. CORPN. LTD.	175	12	90	12
12.	I T I LTD.	811	205	418	186
13.	I.B.P. CO. LTD.	74	2	74	2
14.	INDIA TOURISM DEV. CORPN.LTD.	166	40	162	56
15.	INDIAN RAILWAY CATERING AND TOURISM CORPN. LT	0	20	0	0
16.	IRCON INTERNATIONAL LTD.	46	265	44	216
17.	J & K MINERAL DEVELOPMENT CORPN. LTD.	0	0	496	8
18.	KARNATAKA ANTIBIOTICS & PHARMACEUTICALS LTD.	0	1	0	1
19.	KONKAN RAILWAY CORPORATION LTD.	204	32	1	32
20.	M M T C LTD.	0	2	0	2
21.	NATIONAL BLDG. CONSTN. CORPN. LTD.	0	8	0	0
22.	NATIONAL HYDROELECTRIC POWER CORPN.LTD.	971589	3369	929064	3333
23.	NATIONAL MINERAL DEVELOPMENT CORPN. LTD.	0	1	0	1
24.	NATIONAL SEEDS CORPN. LTD.	0	3	0	3
25.	NATIONAL SMALL INDUSTRIES CORPN. LTD.	0	2	0	2
26.	NTC(DELHI,PUNJAB & RAJASTHAN) LTD.	0	5	0	7
27.	OIL & NATURAL GAS CORPORATION LTD.	378	0	6984	0
28.	POWER GRID CORPORATION OF INDIA LTD	116018	362	110238	344
29.	RITES LTD.	0	11	0	0
30.	RURAL ELECTRIFICATION CORPN. LTD.	2	10	1	11
31.	STEEL AUTHORITY OF INDIA LTD.	325	18	338	22
32.	TEHRI HYDRO DEVELOPMENT CORP. LTD..	0	5	0	5
33.	TELECOMMUNICATIONS CONSULTANTS (INDIA) LTD.	0	18	0	9
	TOTAL	**1241191**	**8999**	**1177388**	**8951**

S. No.	NAME OF PSU	2005-2006		2004-2005	
		Gross Block	Employment	Gross Block	Employment
JHARKHAND					
1.	INDIAN OIL CORPORATION LTD.	26190	208	26190	208
2.	INDIAN IRON & STEEL CO. LTD.	0	0	21377	4561
3.	AIRPORTS AUTHORITY OF INDIA LTD.	2509	100	2506	106
4.	BALMER LAWRIE & CO. LTD.	0	1	0	0
5.	BHARAT COKING COAL LTD.	360098	84430	341302	89065
6.	BHARAT EARTH MOVERS LTD.	237	138	0	142
7.	BHARAT PETROLEUM CORPN. LTD.	5259	77	3998	76
8.	BHARAT REFRACTORIES LTD.	5257	1001	5101	1009
9.	BHARAT SANCHAR NIGAM LTD.	156934	3714	145376	3781
10.	BRIDGE & ROOF CO.(INDIA) LTD.	251	26	0	0
11.	BURN STANDARD COMPANY LTD.	167	0	167	0
12.	CENTRAL COALFIELDS LTD.	430798	64042	424670	66702
13.	CENTRAL MINE PLANNING & DESIGN INSTITUTE LTD.	9623	1560	8421	1916
14.	CENTRAL WAREHOUSING CORPN.	0	32	0	23
15.	COAL INDIA LTD.	0	4	0	0
16.	CONTAINER CORPORATION OF INDIA LTD.	642	3	647	3
17.	EASTERN COALFIELDS LTD.	168832	14368	168256	15024
18.	ENGINEERING PROJECTS (INDIA) LTD.	110	38	0	30
19.	ENGINEERS INDIA LTD.	0	11	0	0
20.	FERRO SCRAP NIGAM LTD.	2619	161	2470	168
21.	FERTILIZER CORPN. OF INDIA LTD.	45867	15	46930	16
22.	FOOD CORPN. OF INDIA	483	458	469	480
23.	GARDEN REACH SHIPBUILDERS & ENGINEERS LTD.	1636	329	1625	356
24.	HEAVY ENGINEERING CORPN. LTD.	32587	3436	32651	3589
25.	HINDUSTAN COPPER LTD.	16445	1197	18292	1222

S. No.	NAME OF PSU	2005-2006		2004-2005	
		Gross Block	Employment	Gross Block	Employment
26.	HINDUSTAN LATEX LTD.	0	2	0	0
27.	HINDUSTAN PETROLEUM CORPN. LTD.	6826	72	5820	70
28.	HINDUSTAN STEEL WORKS COSTN. LTD.	1860	920	1942	920
29.	HOUSING & URBAN DEV. CORPN. LTD.	20	13	18	14
30.	I.B.P. CO. LTD.	1173	10	963	10
31.	INDIA TOURISM DEV. CORPN.LTD.	7	0	0	0
32.	INDIAN RAILWAY CATERING AND TOURISM CORPN. LT	0	51	0	0
33.	INSTRUMENTATION LTD.	20	0	20	0
34.	IRCON INTERNATIONAL LTD.	0	0	1	0
35.	KARNATAKA ANTIBIOTICS & PHARMACEUTICALS LTD.	0	7	0	9
36.	KONKAN RAILWAY CORPORATION LTD.	644	11	5	11
37.	M M T C LTD.	0	241	0	233
38.	MAHARASHTRA ELEKTROSMELT LTD.	0	1	0	1
39.	MECON LTD.	4006	1080	4205	1070
40.	NATIONAL BLDG. CONSTN. CORPN. LTD.	51	71	0	54
41.	NATIONAL HYDROELECTRIC POWER CORPN.LTD.	251	8	7991	48
42.	NATIONAL SEEDS CORPN. LTD.	0	3	0	3
43.	NATIONAL SMALL INDUSTRIES CORPN. LTD.	11	0	0	0
44.	NTPC LTD.	4893	28	0	0
45.	OIL & NATURAL GAS CORPORATION LTD.	2123	0	758	0
46.	POWER GRID CORPORATION OF INDIA LTD	26766	62	19214	52
47.	PROJECTS & DEVELOPMENT INDIA LTD.	3636	77	3639	142
48.	RANCHI ASHOK BIHAR HOTEL CORPN. LTD.	221	48	217	49
49.	RASHTRIYA CHEMICALS AND FERTILIZERS LTD.	0	1	0	1
50.	RITES LTD.	0	37	0	34
51.	RURAL ELECTRIFICATION CORPN. LTD.	2	4	0	4

S. No.	NAME OF PSU	2005-2006 Gross Block	2005-2006 Employment	2004-2005 Gross Block	2004-2005 Employment
52.	SCOOTERS INDIA LTD.	0	2	0	1
53.	STEEL AUTHORITY OF INDIA LTD.	757467	33649	706495	35411
54.	TEHRI HYDRO DEVELOPMENT CORP. LTD..	0	12	0	10
55.	TELECOMMUNICATIONS CONSULTANTS (INDIA) LTD.	0	4	0	0
56.	TRIVENI STRUCTURALS LTD.	0	0	0	8
57.	URANIUM CORPORATION OF INDIA LTD.	84621	4101	64058	4044
58.	WATER & POWER CONSULTANCY SERVICES(INDIA) LTD	3	0	0	0
	TOTAL	**2161145**	**215864**	**2065794**	**230676**
KARNATAKA					
1.	KUMARAKUPPA FRONTIER HOTELS LTD.	707	0	1007	0
2.	KARNATAKA TRADE PROMOTION ORGANISATION	1769	4	17	12
3.	INDIAN OIL CORPORATION LTD.	89467	638	89467	638
4.	TUNGABHADRA STEEL PRODUCTS LTD.	2122	342	2167	348
5.	AIR INDIA LTD.	715	57	715	57
6.	AIRLINE ALLIED SERVICES LTD.	0	1	0	1
7.	AIRPORTS AUTHORITY OF INDIA LTD.	5100	413	5012	394
8.	ANTRIX CORPORATION LTD.	91	14	86	16
9.	ARTIFICIAL LIMBS MFG. CORPN. OF INDIA	353	21	364	21
10.	BALMER LAWRIE & CO. LTD.	336	18	323	17
11.	BHARAT EARTH MOVERS LTD.	55748	11085	52836	11261
12.	BHARAT ELECTRONICS LTD.	76414	6495	72870	6567
13.	BHARAT HEAVY ELECTRICALS LTD.	22304	2911	20416	2976
14.	BHARAT PETROLEUM CORPN. LTD.	41983	322	37355	334
15.	BHARAT SANCHAR NIGAM LTD.	827019	23472	794145	24368

S. No.	NAME OF PSU	2005-2006		2004-2005	
		Gross Block	Employment	Gross Block	Employment
16.	BRIDGE & ROOF CO.(INDIA) LTD.	1426	105	275	14
17.	CEMENT CORPN. OF INDIA LTD.	1742	12	1744	10
18.	CENTRAL COTTAGE INDUSTRIES CORPN. OF INDIA LT	86	14	85	14
19.	CENTRAL WAREHOUSING CORPN.	5262	203	4749	205
20.	COAL INDIA LTD.	3	10	3	10
21.	CONTAINER CORPORATION OF INDIA LTD.	3563	41	3339	36
22.	COTTON CORPN. OF INDIA LTD.	31	62	27	57
23.	DREDGING CORPN.OF INDIA LTD.	18	12	18	19
24.	EDUCATIONAL CONSULTANTS (INDIA) LTD.	0	0	2	1
25.	ELECTRONICS CORPN. OF INDIA LTD.	49	62	36	56
26.	ENGINEERING PROJECTS (INDIA) LTD.	3	20	3	18
27.	ENGINEERS INDIA LTD.	0	8	0	11
28.	EXPORT CREDIT GUARANTEE CORPN.OF INDIA LTD.	334	23	244	22
29.	FERTILIZERS & CHEMICALS (TRAVANCORE) LTD.	33	47	33	43
30.	FOOD CORPN. OF INDIA	7284	817	7212	817
31.	GAIL (INDIA) LTD.	51	5	591	13
32.	HINDUSTAN AERONAUTICS LTD.	127170	12434	83668	12136
33.	HINDUSTAN COPPER LTD.	34	7	34	9
34.	HINDUSTAN LATEX LTD.	3028	363	2627	362
35.	HINDUSTAN PAPER CORPORATION LTD.	3	4	3	4
36.	HINDUSTAN PETROLEUM CORPN. LTD.	83843	469	76539	445
37.	HINDUSTAN PHOTO FILMS MANUFACTURING CO. LTD.	3	6	3	5
38.	HINDUSTAN STEEL WORKS COSTN. LTD.	6	18	174	33
39.	HINDUSTAN VEGETABLE OILS CORPN. LTD.	94	0	96	0
40.	HMT (INTERNATIONAL) LTD.	760	66	2234	73
41.	HMT CHINAR WATCHES LTD.	1	13	1	12

S. No.	NAME OF PSU	2005-2006 Gross Block	2005-2006 Employment	2004-2005 Gross Block	2004-2005 Employment
42.	HMT LTD.	1098	137	1429	148
43.	HMT MACHINE TOOLS LTD.	8527	1301	8758	1359
44.	HMT WATCHES LTD.	11443	1583	11443	1583
45.	HOUSING & URBAN DEV. CORPN. LTD.	500	37	498	43
46.	HSCC (INDIA) LTD.	20	1	20	1
47.	I T I LTD.	218841	3405	35593	3863
48.	I.B.P. CO. LTD.	4484	32	3899	32
49.	INDIA TOURISM DEV. CORPN.LTD.	270	59	263	77
50.	INDIA TRADE PROMOTION ORGANISATION	11	8	7	8
51.	INDIAN RAILWAY CATERING AND TOURISM CORPN. LT	0	93	0	0
52.	INSTRUMENTATION LTD.	0	2	0	3
53.	IRCON INTERNATIONAL LTD.	315	45	146	21
54.	KARNATAKA ANTIBIOTICS & PHARMACEUTICALS LTD.	2573	309	1641	314
55.	KONKAN RAILWAY CORPORATION LTD.	177876	796	177876	794
56.	KUDREMUKH IRON ORE CO.LTD	119182	1871	115874	1924
57.	M M T C LTD.	613	134	579	147
58.	M S T C LTD.	33	21	31	20
59.	MADRAS FERTILIZERS LTD.	51	57	51	70
60.	MANGALORE REFINARY & PETROCHEMICALS LTD.	717246	912	680672	919
61.	MAZAGON DOCK LTD.	0	1	1130	1
62.	MECON LTD.	3297	182	3313	187
63.	NATIONAL ALUMINIUM COMPANY LTD.	0	6	0	6
64.	NATIONAL BLDG. CONSTN. CORPN. LTD.	28	25	30	37
65.	NATIONAL FILM DEV. CORPN. LTD.	4	5	2	4
66.	NATIONAL HANDLOOM DEVELOPMENT CORPORATION LTD	0	3	0	3
67.	NATIONAL HYDROELECTRIC POWER CORPN.LTD.	512	18	632	45

S. No.	NAME OF PSU	2005-2006		2004-2005	
		Gross Block	Employment	Gross Block	Employment
68.	NATIONAL MINERAL DEVELOPMENT CORPN. LTD.	18373	1222	13184	1234
69.	NATIONAL RESEARCH DEVP. CORPN.	7	4	7	4
70.	NATIONAL SCHEDULED CASTES FINANCE & DEVP. COR	1	3	1	3
71.	NATIONAL SEEDS CORPN. LTD.	343	53	331	55
72.	NATIONAL SMALL INDUSTRIES CORPN. LTD.	54	26	59	14
73.	NEYVELI LIGNITE CORPN. LTD.	0	4	0	4
74.	NORTH EASTERN HANDICRAFTS & HANDLOOM DEV.COR	2	12	2	9
75.	NTC(A.PRADESH, KARNATAKA, KERALA & MAHE)LTD.	2425	528	2545	1413
76.	NTPC LTD.	386	18	386	21
77.	NUCLEAR POWER CORPN. OF INDIA LTD.	317583	1482	375444	1436
78.	OIL & NATURAL GAS CORPORATION LTD.	726	0	617	0
79.	P E C LTD.	2	5	2	6
80.	POWER GRID CORPORATION OF INDIA LTD	133708	362	132031	342
81.	PRAGA TOOLS LTD.	1	2	1	2
82.	RAJASTHAN ELECTRONICS AND INSTRUMENTS LTD.	0	13	0	0
83.	RASHTRIYA CHEMICALS AND FERTILIZERS LTD.	40	37	38	38
84.	RASHTRIYA ISPAT NIGAM LTD.	325	13	309	12
85.	RITES LTD.	62	57	32	52
86.	RURAL ELECTRIFICATION CORPN. LTD.	2	18	2	16
87.	SCOOTERS INDIA LTD.	0	1	0	1
88.	SEMI-CONDUCTOR COMPLEX LTD.	0	0	0	3
89.	STATE FARMS CORPORATION OF INDIA LTD.	224	129	228	131
90.	STATE TRADING CORPN. OF INDIA LTD.	72	15	75	19
91.	STCL LTD.	58	25	44	18
92.	STEEL AUTHORITY OF INDIA LTD.	29239	2635	28432	2726
93.	TEHRI HYDRO DEVELOPMENT CORP. LTD..	0	3	0	3

S. No.	*NAME OF PSU*	*2005-2006*		*2004-2005*	
		Gross Block	*Employment*	*Gross Block*	*Employment*
94.	TELECOMMUNICATIONS CONSULTANTS (INDIA) LTD.	0	3	0	5
95.	VIGNYAN INDUSTRIES LTD.	613	226	601	227
96.	WATER & POWER CONSULTANCY SERVICES(INDIA) LTD	3	6	3	0
	TOTAL	**3130128**	**78559**	**2858781**	**80838**
KERALA					
1.	INDIAN OIL CORPORATION LTD.	79412	438	79412	438
2.	KOCHI REFINERIES LTD.	0	0	257481	1908
3.	AIR INDIA LTD.	3560	300	3560	300
4.	AIRPORTS AUTHORITY OF INDIA LTD.	15090	891	15036	898
5.	BALMER LAWRIE & CO. LTD.	96	6	101	6
6.	BHARAT EARTH MOVERS LTD.	22	1	22	0
7.	BHARAT PETROLEUM CORPN. LTD.	300564	2149	34469	286
8.	BHARAT SANCHAR NIGAM LTD.	886727	20336	814523	21361
9.	BRIDGE & ROOF CO.(INDIA) LTD.	35	5	150	12
10.	CENTRAL WAREHOUSING CORPN.	2341	80	2341	89
11.	COCHIN SHIPYARD LTD.	21408	2075	20584	2109
12.	CONTAINER CORPORATION OF INDIA LTD.	175	5	175	7
13.	DREDGING CORPN.OF INDIA LTD.	5	2	5	5
14.	ENGINEERING PROJECTS (INDIA) LTD.	0	1	0	5
15.	ENGINEERS INDIA LTD.	0	7	0	11
16.	EXPORT CREDIT GUARANTEE CORPN.OF INDIA LTD.	212	13	155	13
17.	FERTILIZERS & CHEMICALS (TRAVANCORE) LTD.	145901	3873	145675	3982
18.	FOOD CORPN. OF INDIA	7400	1230	6974	1271
19.	GAIL (INDIA) LTD.	0	9	230	1

S. No.	NAME OF PSU	2005-2006		2004-2005	
		Gross Block	Employment	Gross Block	Employment
20.	HINDUSTAN ANTIBIOTICS LTD.	3	19	3	18
21.	HINDUSTAN INSECTICIDES LTD.	5428	448	5008	492
22.	HINDUSTAN LATEX LTD.	7672	1317	7559	1346
23.	HINDUSTAN NEWSPRINT LTD.	39282	1039	38165	1086
24.	HINDUSTAN ORGANIC CHEMICALS LTD.	25658	442	25658	442
25.	HINDUSTAN PAPER CORPORATION LTD.	2	2	2	3
26.	HINDUSTAN PETROLEUM CORPN. LTD.	27830	220	25638	206
27.	HINDUSTAN PHOTO FILMS MANUFACTURING CO. LTD.	3	7	3	7
28.	HINDUSTAN STEEL WORKS COSTN. LTD.	0	1	2	13
29.	HMT MACHINE TOOLS LTD.	3866	763	3866	831
30.	HOUSING & URBAN DEV. CORPN. LTD.	583	36	584	36
31.	I T I LTD.	17693	706	9685	707
32.	I.B.P. CO. LTD.	884	5	784	5
33.	INDIA TOURISM DEV. CORPN.LTD.	7	16	18	18
34.	INDIAN RAILWAY CATERING AND TOURISM CORPN. LT	8	387	0	0
35.	INDIAN RARE EARTHS LTD.	18070	1034	14738	1042
36.	INSTRUMENTATION LTD.	1583	336	1576	342
37.	KARNATAKA ANTIBIOTICS & PHARMACEUTICALS LTD.	0	12	0	11
38.	M M T C LTD.	0	12	0	12
39.	MADRAS FERTILIZERS LTD.	0	10	0	10
40.	MANGALORE REFINARY & PETROCHEMICALS LTD.	10	0	10	0
41.	MECON LTD.	0	3	0	3
42.	NATIONAL BLDG. CONSTN. CORPN. LTD.	1	17	0	10
43.	NATIONAL FILM DEV. CORPN. LTD.	2	3	1	3
44.	NATIONAL HANDLOOM DEVELOPMENT CORPORATION LTD	0	0	0	8
45.	NATIONAL MINERAL DEVELOPMENT CORPN. LTD.	5256	486	0	0

S. No.	*NAME OF PSU*	*2005-2006*		*2004-2005*	
		Gross Block	*Employment*	*Gross Block*	*Employment*
46.	NATIONAL SEEDS CORPN. LTD.	0	7	0	8
47.	NATIONAL SMALL INDUSTRIES CORPN. LTD.	0	12	0	0
48.	NTC(A.PRADESH, KARNATAKA, KERALA & MAHE)LTD.	4335	2551	4325	2645
49.	NTPC LTD.	114659	149	120227	161
50.	OIL & NATURAL GAS CORPORATION LTD.	0	0	165	0
51.	P E C LTD.	4	4	4	4
52.	POWER GRID CORPORATION OF INDIA LTD	48103	109	47252	105
53.	RAJASTHAN ELECTRONICS AND INSTRUMENTS LTD.	0	1	0	0
54.	RASHTRIYA ISPAT NIGAM LTD.	140	10	139	10
55.	RITES LTD.	0	9	0	16
56.	RURAL ELECTRIFICATION CORPN. LTD.	3	13	2	14
57.	SCOOTERS INDIA LTD.	0	1	0	1
58.	STATE FARMS CORPORATION OF INDIA LTD.	0	5	0	0
59.	STATE TRADING CORPN. OF INDIA LTD.	0	26	0	28
60.	STCL LTD.	6	10	5	10
61.	STEEL AUTHORITY OF INDIA LTD.	799	18	916	20
62.	TEHRI HYDRO DEVELOPMENT CORP. LTD..	0	8	0	9
63.	TELECOMMUNICATIONS CONSULTANTS (INDIA) LTD.	0	1	0	3
64.	WATER & POWER CONSULTANCY SERVICES(INDIA) LTD	0	0	6	8
	TOTAL	**1784838**	**41676**	**1687234**	**42395**
MADHYA PRADESH					
1.	INDIAN OIL CORPORATION LTD.	77536	502	77536	502
2.	AIR INDIA LTD.	12	3	12	3
3.	AIRPORTS AUTHORITY OF INDIA LTD.	4500	372	4095	337

S. No.	NAME OF PSU	2005-2006		2004-2005	
		Gross Block	Employment	Gross Block	Employment
4.	ARTIFICIAL LIMBS MFG. CORPN. OF INDIA	301	29	239	31
5.	BENGAL CHEMICALS & PHARMACEUTICALS LTD.	1	5	0	5
6.	BHARAT EARTH MOVERS LTD.	625	167	620	30
7.	BHARAT HEAVY ELECTRICALS LTD.	54282	7987	51483	8024
8.	BHARAT PETROLEUM CORPN. LTD.	29354	247	24512	263
9.	BHARAT SANCHAR NIGAM LTD.	433784	12630	412661	13979
10.	BRIDGE & ROOF CO.(INDIA) LTD.	600	75	375	31
11.	BURN STANDARD COMPANY LTD.	208	0	208	0
12.	CEMENT CORPN. OF INDIA LTD.	23336	67	19950	70
13.	CENTRAL MINE PLANNING & DESIGN INSTITUTE LTD.	625	174	0	140
14.	CENTRAL WAREHOUSING CORPN.	5584	353	5365	374
15.	CONTAINER CORPORATION OF INDIA LTD.	1633	20	1478	24
16.	COTTON CORPN. OF INDIA LTD.	162	58	159	58
17.	ELECTRONICS CORPN. OF INDIA LTD.	1	3	1	3
18.	ENGINEERS INDIA LTD.	0	0	0	3
19.	EXPORT CREDIT GUARANTEE CORPN.OF INDIA LTD.	19	5	6	5
20.	FERTILIZER CORPN. OF INDIA LTD.	0	0	1166	3
21.	FOOD CORPN. OF INDIA	2686	1409	2613	1469
22.	GAIL (INDIA) LTD.	417069	493	376214	516
23.	HINDUSTAN ANTIBIOTICS LTD.	2	26	2	26
24.	HINDUSTAN COPPER LTD.	15941	1054	32365	1070
25.	HINDUSTAN LATEX LTD.	0	8	0	7
26.	HINDUSTAN PAPER CORPORATION LTD.	2	2	2	2
27.	HINDUSTAN PETROLEUM CORPN. LTD.	32467	246	29271	196
28.	HINDUSTAN PHOTO FILMS MANUFACTURING CO. LTD.	2	4	2	4
29.	HINDUSTAN STEEL WORKS COSTN. LTD.	124	11	292	14

S. No.	NAME OF PSU	2005-2006 Gross Block	2005-2006 Employment	2004-2005 Gross Block	2004-2005 Employment
30.	HMT BEARINGS LTD.	0	1	0	0
31.	HMT MACHINE TOOLS LTD.	6	10	7	10
32.	HOUSING & URBAN DEV. CORPN. LTD.	260	26	261	26
33.	I T I LTD.	13	212	13	23
34.	I.B.P. CO. LTD.	15914	317	15889	319
35.	INDIAN RAILWAY CATERING AND TOURISM CORPN. LT	0	11	0	0
36.	INSTRUMENTATION LTD.	2	1	2	1
37.	IRCON INTERNATIONAL LTD.	38	38	15	15
38.	KARNATAKA ANTIBIOTICS & PHARMACEUTICALS LTD.	0	18	0	15
39.	M M T C LTD.	0	1	0	7
40.	M S T C LTD.	0	3	0	3
41.	MADHYA PRADESH ASHOK HOTEL CORPN. LTD.	411	63	409	67
42.	MANGANESE ORE(INDIA) LTD.	7287	3613	6095	3733
43.	NARMADA HYDROELECTRIC DEVELOPMENT CORPN. LTD.	528250	684	449640	507
44.	NATIONAL BLDG. CONSTN. CORPN. LTD.	116	19	48	40
45.	NATIONAL FERTILIZERS LTD.	157666	844	155233	873
46.	NATIONAL HANDLOOM DEVELOPMENT CORPORATION LTD	0	10	0	10
47.	NATIONAL HYDROELECTRIC POWER CORPN.LTD.	0	303	0	318
48.	NATIONAL MINERAL DEVELOPMENT CORPN. LTD.	0	6	0	435
49.	NATIONAL SCHEDULED TRIBES FINANCE & DEVP. COR	1	3	1	3
50.	NATIONAL SEEDS CORPN. LTD.	88	30	73	30
51.	NATIONAL SMALL INDUSTRIES CORPN. LTD.	62	10	62	16
52.	NEPA LTD.	11298	1195	11328	1204
53.	NORTHERN COALFIELDS LTD.	318432	9987	314815	10134
54.	NTC(MADHYA PRADESH)LTD.	891	993	1311	1085
55.	NTPC ELECTRIC SUPPLY COMPANY LTD.	0	0	0	17

S. No.	NAME OF PSU	2005-2006		2004-2005	
		Gross Block	Employment	Gross Block	Employment
56.	NTPC LTD.	683249	3627	569363	3537
57.	OIL & NATURAL GAS CORPORATION LTD.	0	0	9669	0
58.	P E C LTD.	3	0	3	2
59.	POWER GRID CORPORATION OF INDIA LTD	276343	264	211454	266
60.	PRAGA TOOLS LTD.	0	2	0	2
61.	RAJASTHAN ELECTRONICS AND INSTRUMENTS LTD.	0	1	0	0
62.	RASHTRIYA CHEMICALS AND FERTILIZERS LTD.	15	7	15	9
63.	RASHTRIYA ISPAT NIGAM LTD.	95	9	86	7
64.	RITES LTD.	0	79	0	81
65.	RURAL ELECTRIFICATION CORPN. LTD.	2	16	2	16
66.	SCOOTERS INDIA LTD.	0	3	0	2
67.	SOUTH EASTERN COALFIELDS LTD.	125526	33024	121004	33954
68.	STATE TRADING CORPN. OF INDIA LTD.	0	1	0	1
69.	STEEL AUTHORITY OF INDIA LTD.	4639	40	2954	48
70.	TEHRI HYDRO DEVELOPMENT CORP. LTD..	0	15	0	14
71.	TELECOMMUNICATIONS CONSULTANTS (INDIA) LTD.	18	46	2	11
72.	WATER & POWER CONSULTANCY SERVICES(INDIA) LTD	0	2	0	0
73.	WESTERN COALFIELDS LTD.	77832	24248	74793	25065
	TOTAL	**3309313**	**105732**	**2985174**	**109095**
MAHARAHASHTRA					
1.	INDIAN AIRLINES LTD.	13380	4489	13380	4489
2.	AIR INDIA AIR TRANSPORT SERVICES LTD.	1	159	1	159
3.	INDIAN OIL CORPORATION LTD.	115265	2537	115265	2537
4.	INDIAN OIL BLENDING LTD.	0	0	5361	254

S. No.	NAME OF PSU	2005-2006 Gross Block	2005-2006 Employment	2004-2005 Gross Block	2004-2005 Employment
5.	KOCHI REFINERIES LTD.	0	0	26	3
6.	AIR INDIA CHARTERS LTD.	10	30	10	30
7.	AIR INDIA LTD.	632085	12435	632085	12435
8.	AIRLINE ALLIED SERVICES LTD.	11	107	11	131
9.	AIRPORTS AUTHORITY OF INDIA LTD.	104270	3878	104169	3864
10.	ANDREW YULE & COMPANY LTD.	11	7	11	7
11.	ARTIFICIAL LIMBS MFG. CORPN. OF INDIA	3	3	0	3
12.	BALMER LAWRIE & CO. LTD.	10708	304	10368	297
13.	BBJ CONSTRUCTION COMPANY LTD.	5	0	5	1
14.	BEL OPTRONICS LTD.	4805	134	4538	129
15.	BENGAL CHEMICALS & PHARMACEUTICALS LTD.	1240	16	1156	23
16.	BHARAT EARTH MOVERS LTD.	227	110	238	100
17.	BHARAT ELECTRONICS LTD.	5777	827	5609	823
18.	BHARAT HEAVY ELECTRICALS LTD.	348	97	345	106
19.	BHARAT HEAVY PLATE & VESSELS LTD.	35	4	34	3
20.	BHARAT PETROLEUM CORPN. LTD.	982057	5938	904290	5877
21.	BHARAT PUMPS & COMPRESSORS LTD.	19	7	19	7
22.	BHARAT SANCHAR NIGAM LTD.	1193051	30184	1171400	32184
23.	BHARATIYA NABHIKIYA VIDYUT NIGAM LTD.	0	0	0	1
24.	BIECCO LAWRIE LTD.	8	2	8	4
25.	BONGAIGAON REFINERY & PETROCHEMICALS LTD.	58	6	53	6
26.	BRIDGE & ROOF CO.(INDIA) LTD.	470	89	590	89
27.	CEMENT CORPN. OF INDIA LTD.	0	0	0	24
28.	CENTRAL COTTAGE INDUSTRIES CORPN. OF INDIA LT	33	58	33	62
29.	CENTRAL MINE PLANNING & DESIGN INSTITUTE LTD.	845	396	980	311
30.	CENTRAL WAREHOUSING CORPN.	26393	799	24715	838

S. No.	NAME OF PSU	2005-2006		2004-2005	
		Gross Block	Employment	Gross Block	Employment
31.	CERTIFICATION ENGINEERS INTERNATIONAL LTD.	36	24	33	16
32.	COAL INDIA LTD.	21	12	18	13
33.	CONTAINER CORPORATION OF INDIA LTD.	16505	144	14724	141
34.	COTTON CORPN. OF INDIA LTD.	6091	367	6085	346
35.	DREDGING CORPN.OF INDIA LTD.	28	11	28	12
36.	ELECTRONICS CORPN. OF INDIA LTD.	253	141	225	137
37.	ENGINEERING PROJECTS (INDIA) LTD.	85	29	87	33
38.	ENGINEERS INDIA LTD.	701	90	1665	130
39.	EXPORT CREDIT GUARANTEE CORPN.OF INDIA LTD.	3929	281	4803	298
40.	FERRO SCRAP NIGAM LTD.	1658	102	1588	99
41.	FERTILIZERS & CHEMICALS (TRAVANCORE) LTD.	24	2	26	4
42.	FOOD CORPN. OF INDIA	6602	1811	6513	1924
43.	GAIL (INDIA) LTD.	44575	228	44388	206
44.	GOA SHIPYARD LTD.	0	6	0	6
45.	HANDICRAFTS & HANDLOOM EXPORTS CORP. OF INDIA	16	7	16	6
46.	HINDUSTAN AERONAUTICS LTD.	60600	5606	75875	5704
47.	HINDUSTAN ANTIBIOTICS LTD.	19995	1533	19833	1598
48.	HINDUSTAN COPPER LTD.	3390	135	3361	139
49.	HINDUSTAN INSECTICIDES LTD.	3910	743	4207	743
50.	HINDUSTAN LATEX LTD.	6	19	4	21
51.	HINDUSTAN ORGANIC CHEMICALS LTD.	44400	1071	44321	1084
52.	HINDUSTAN PAPER CORPORATION LTD.	9	11	9	12
53.	HINDUSTAN PETROLEUM CORPN. LTD.	535062	4874	453462	4675
54.	HINDUSTAN PHOTO FILMS MANUFACTURING CO. LTD.	2	4	2	4
55.	HINDUSTAN SHIPYARD LTD.	0	1	0	1
56.	HINDUSTAN STEEL WORKS COSTN. LTD.	3	5	0	2

S. No.	NAME OF PSU	2005-2006 Gross Block	2005-2006 Employment	2004-2005 Gross Block	2004-2005 Employment
57.	HINDUSTAN VEGETABLE OILS CORPN. LTD.	1290	0	1290	0
58.	HMT (INTERNATIONAL) LTD.	0	1	0	1
59.	HMT BEARINGS LTD.	0	2	0	4
60.	HMT LTD.	502	90	502	89
61.	HMT MACHINE TOOLS LTD.	22	28	26	31
62.	HOTEL CORPN. OF INDIA LTD.	817	475	789	437
63.	HOUSING & URBAN DEV. CORPN. LTD.	878	32	855	34
64.	HSCC (INDIA) LTD.	0	1	0	0
65.	I T I LTD.	245	355	118	49
66.	I.B.P. CO. LTD.	36023	661	36265	676
67.	INDIA TOURISM DEV. CORPN.LTD.	207	28	196	32
68.	INDIA TRADE PROMOTION ORGANISATION	31	37	32	39
69.	INDIAN RAILWAY CATERING AND TOURISM CORPN. LT	96	1265	66	535
70.	INDIAN RARE EARTHS LTD.	559	122	530	122
71.	INSTRUMENTATION LTD.	99	13	98	14
72.	IRCON INTERNATIONAL LTD.	697	42	346	23
73.	KARNATAKA ANTIBIOTICS & PHARMACEUTICALS LTD.	0	20	0	21
74.	KONKAN RAILWAY CORPORATION LTD.	186675	1895	186675	1890
75.	M M T C LTD.	1668	156	1686	156
76.	M S T C LTD.	203	27	199	29
77.	MAHANAGAR TELEPHONE NIGAM LTD.	777477	25710	760207	28241
78.	MAHARASHTRA ELEKTROSMELT LTD.	6105	798	5968	808
79.	MANGALORE REFINARY & PETROCHEMICALS LTD.	110	42	94	38
80.	MANGANESE ORE(INDIA) LTD.	7860	3381	6633	3430
81.	MAZAGON DOCK LTD.	23534	8089	23273	7788
82.	MECON LTD.	394	15	834	19

S. No.	NAME OF PSU	2005-2006 Gross Block	2005-2006 Employment	2004-2005 Gross Block	2004-2005 Employment
83.	MILLENNIUM TELECOM LTD.	33	0	35	9
84.	MINERAL EXPLORATION CORPN. LTD.	10270	2213	9970	2277
85.	MUMBAI RAILWAY VIKAS CORPORATION LTD.	170	133	157	115
86.	NATIONAL ALUMINIUM COMPANY LTD.	59	11	62	11
87.	NATIONAL BACKWARD CLASSES FINANCE & DEVELOPME	58	1	58	1
88.	NATIONAL BLDG. CONSTN. CORPN. LTD.	77	184	110	180
89.	NATIONAL FILM DEV. CORPN. LTD.	2445	127	2421	136
90.	NATIONAL HANDLOOM DEVELOPMENT CORPORATION LTD	81	12	81	11
91.	NATIONAL HYDROELECTRIC POWER CORPN.LTD.	1347	31	1181	40
92.	NATIONAL MINERAL DEVELOPMENT CORPN. LTD.	0	0	0	6
93.	NATIONAL SCHEDULED CASTES FINANCE & DEVP. COR	48	3	48	3
94.	NATIONAL SEEDS CORPN. LTD.	195	44	188	47
95.	NATIONAL SMALL INDUSTRIES CORPN. LTD.	129	51	145	46
96.	NEPA LTD.	0	2	0	4
97.	NEYVELI LIGNITE CORPN. LTD.	9	4	9	4
98.	NTC(MAHARASHTRA NORTH)LTD.	6091	4328	6176	5337
99.	NTC(SOUTH MAHARASHTRA)LTD.	4547	4778	5335	5220
100.	NTPC ELECTRIC SUPPLY COMPANY LTD.	0	0	0	7
101.	NTPC LTD.	4123	155	4080	128
102.	NUCLEAR POWER CORPN. OF INDIA LTD.	861460	4020	917964	4047
103.	NUMALIGARH REFINARY LTD.	0	1	0	0
104.	OIL & NATURAL GAS CORPORATION LTD.	5547097	6624	5464361	6718
105.	OIL INDIA LTD.	0	1	0	0
106.	P E C LTD.	24	10	24	9
107.	PAWAN HANS HELICOPTERS LTD.	35352	349	2500	367
108.	POWER FINANCE CORPORATION	546	2	546	2

S. No.	NAME OF PSU	2005-2006		2004-2005	
		Gross Block	Employment	Gross Block	Employment
109.	POWER GRID CORPORATION OF INDIA LTD	178559	354	153728	331
110.	PRAGA TOOLS LTD.	4	2	4	2
111.	PROJECTS & DEVELOPMENT INDIA LTD.	10	10	9	10
112.	RAIL VIKAS NIGAM LTD.	0	7	0	0
113.	RAJASTHAN ELECTRONICS AND INSTRUMENTS LTD.	0	3	0	0
114.	RASHTRIYA CHEMICALS AND FERTILIZERS LTD.	245421	4028	246946	4133
115.	RASHTRIYA ISPAT NIGAM LTD.	1456	37	1370	34
116.	RICHARDSON & CRUDDAS(1972) LTD.	3122	74	3319	77
117.	RITES LTD.	388	172	378	163
118.	RURAL ELECTRIFICATION CORPN. LTD.	6	22	3	17
119.	SCOOTERS INDIA LTD.	0	9	0	7
120.	SHIPPING CORPORATION OF INDIA LTD.	478248	797	464003	807
121.	STATE TRADING CORPN. OF INDIA LTD.	744	110	723	114
122.	STEEL AUTHORITY OF INDIA LTD.	5750	319	6237	325
123.	TEHRI HYDRO DEVELOPMENT CORP. LTD..	0	3	0	3
124.	TELECOMMUNICATIONS CONSULTANTS (INDIA) LTD.	28	14	28	12
125.	TRIVENI STRUCTURALS LTD.	0	1	0	1
126.	WATER & POWER CONSULTANCY SERVICES(INDIA) LTD	17	7	8	5
127.	WESTERN COALFIELDS LTD.	291757	43130	280096	43873
	TOTAL	**12564179**	**195341**	**12274958**	**201296**
MANIPUR					
1.	INDIAN OIL CORPORATION LTD.	1093	27	1093	27
2.	AIRPORTS AUTHORITY OF INDIA LTD.	2601	89	2503	83
3.	HINDUSTAN PETROLEUM CORPN. LTD.	0	0	1	0

S. No.	NAME OF PSU	2005-2006 Gross Block	2005-2006 Employment	2004-2005 Gross Block	2004-2005 Employment
4.	HOUSING & URBAN DEV. CORPN. LTD.	1	4	0	4
5.	NATIONAL BLDG. CONSTN. CORPN. LTD.	0	51	2	42
6.	NATIONAL HANDLOOM DEVELOPMENT CORPORATION LTD	0	1	0	1
7.	NATIONAL HYDROELECTRIC POWER CORPN.LTD.	17427	766	17397	896
8.	NATIONAL SMALL INDUSTRIES CORPN. LTD.	0	3	0	0
9.	NORTH EASTERN ELECTRIC POWER CORPORATION LTD.	159	59	146	0
10.	POWER GRID CORPORATION OF INDIA LTD	5123	117	5006	114
11.	TELECOMMUNICATIONS CONSULTANTS (INDIA) LTD.	0	1	0	1
	TOTAL	**26404**	**1118**	**26148**	**1168**
MEGHALAYA					
1.	INDIAN OIL CORPORATION LTD.	1029	3	1029	3
2.	AIRPORTS AUTHORITY OF INDIA LTD.	608	18	604	22
3.	ENGINEERING PROJECTS (INDIA) LTD.	10	15	10	13
4.	FOOD CORPN. OF INDIA	1561	163	1469	168
5.	HINDUSTAN PETROLEUM CORPN. LTD.	16	0	201	0
6.	HOUSING & URBAN DEV. CORPN. LTD.	5	4	0	5
7.	HSCC (INDIA) LTD.	4	5	4	9
8.	IRCON INTERNATIONAL LTD.	0	0	5	6
9.	JUTE CORPN. OF INDIA LTD.	1	5	1	4
10.	NATIONAL BLDG. CONSTN. CORPN. LTD.	0	14	0	7
11.	NATIONAL SMALL INDUSTRIES CORPN. LTD.	0	1	0	0
12.	NORTH EASTERN HANDICRAFTS & HANDLOOM DEV.COR	2	10	2	13
13.	NORTH EASTERN ELECTRIC POWER CORPORATION LTD.	2263	534	1796	546
14.	OIL & NATURAL GAS CORPORATION LTD.	0	0	2799	0

S. No.	NAME OF PSU	2005-2006 Gross Block	2005-2006 Employment	2004-2005 Gross Block	2004-2005 Employment
15.	OIL INDIA LTD.	6	0	6	0
16.	POWER GRID CORPORATION OF INDIA LTD	15529	305	15123	304
17.	RURAL ELECTRIFICATION CORPN. LTD.	1	4	6	5
18.	TEHRI HYDRO DEVELOPMENT CORP. LTD..	0	2	0	2
19.	TELECOMMUNICATIONS CONSULTANTS (INDIA) LTD.	0	2	0	2
20.	URANIUM CORPORATION OF INDIA LTD.	226	1	0	0
	TOTAL	**21261**	**1086**	**23055**	**1109**
MIZORAM					
1.	INDIAN OIL CORPORATION LTD.	309	2	309	2
2.	AIRPORTS AUTHORITY OF INDIA LTD.	745	21	742	27
3.	CENTRAL WAREHOUSING CORPN.	12	0	12	0
4.	ENGINEERING PROJECTS (INDIA) LTD.	0	5	0	3
5.	HOUSING & URBAN DEV. CORPN. LTD.	0	3	0	3
6.	IRCON INTERNATIONAL LTD.	29	10	5	16
7.	NATIONAL BLDG. CONSTN. CORPN. LTD.	0	61	1	55
8.	NORTH EASTERN ELECTRIC POWER CORPORATION LTD.	28093	72	28629	91
9.	OIL & NATURAL GAS CORPORATION LTD.	0	0	2182	0
10.	POWER GRID CORPORATION OF INDIA LTD	3939	45	3926	45
11.	TELECOMMUNICATIONS CONSULTANTS (INDIA) LTD.	0	1	0	3
	TOTAL	**33127**	**220**	**35806**	**245**
NAGALAND					
1.	INDIAN OIL CORPORATION LTD.	3088	31	3088	31
2.	AIRPORTS AUTHORITY OF INDIA LTD.	1405	48	1400	56

S. No.	NAME OF PSU	2005-2006 Gross Block	2005-2006 Employment	2004-2005 Gross Block	2004-2005 Employment
3.	CENTRAL WAREHOUSING CORPN.	8	7	8	12
4.	HINDUSTAN PETROLEUM CORPN. LTD.	0	0	74	0
5.	HOUSING & URBAN DEV. CORPN. LTD.	37	13	33	13
6.	NAGALAND PULP & PAPER COMPANY LTD.	7447	294	7446	298
7.	NATIONAL BLDG. CONSTN. CORPN. LTD.	0	39	0	27
8.	NATIONAL SMALL INDUSTRIES CORPN. LTD.	0	1	0	0
9.	NORTH EASTERN ELECTRIC POWER CORPORATION LTD.	75181	228	75123	225
10.	OIL & NATURAL GAS CORPORATION LTD.	8086	0	13548	0
11.	POWER GRID CORPORATION OF INDIA LTD	5988	83	5738	81
12.	TELECOMMUNICATIONS CONSULTANTS (INDIA) LTD.	0	4	0	1
	TOTAL	**101240**	**748**	**106458**	**744**
ORISSA					
1.	INDIAN OIL CORPORATION LTD.	83851	377	83851	377
2.	AIRPORTS AUTHORITY OF INDIA LTD.	6266	188	6210	191
3.	ARTIFICIAL LIMBS MFG. CORPN. OF INDIA	312	26	199	28
4.	BALMER LAWRIE & CO. LTD.	7	1	7	1
5.	BBJ CONSTRUCTION COMPANY LTD.	2	148	2	27
6.	BENGAL CHEMICALS & PHARMACEUTICALS LTD.	1	5	1	5
7.	BHARAT EARTH MOVERS LTD.	69	93	69	55
8.	BHARAT PETROLEUM CORPN. LTD.	20774	155	17689	158
9.	BHARAT REFRACTORIES LTD.	0	0	0	1
10.	BHARAT SANCHAR NIGAM LTD.	252743	5965	232479	6381
11.	BRIDGE & ROOF CO.(INDIA) LTD.	675	65	840	75
12.	CENTRAL MINE PLANNING & DESIGN INSTITUTE LTD.	781	299	965	237

S. No.	NAME OF PSU	2005-2006		2004-2005	
		Gross Block	Employment	Gross Block	Employment
13.	CENTRAL WAREHOUSING CORPN.	2434	121	2414	122
14.	CONTAINER CORPORATION OF INDIA LTD.	289	0	289	1
15.	COTTON CORPN. OF INDIA LTD.	6	0	6	11
16.	DREDGING CORPN.OF INDIA LTD.	3	16	4	20
17.	ENGINEERING PROJECTS (INDIA) LTD.	487	1	54	3
18.	ENGINEERS INDIA LTD.	0	24	0	10
19.	EXPORT CREDIT GUARANTEE CORPN.OF INDIA LTD.	14	3	5	3
20.	FERRO SCRAP NIGAM LTD.	3173	216	2574	213
21.	FERTILIZER CORPN. OF INDIA LTD.	29230	11	29233	12
22.	FOOD CORPN. OF INDIA	3402	1231	3290	1240
23.	GAIL (INDIA) LTD.	0	1	0	1
24.	HINDUSTAN AERONAUTICS LTD.	73186	3260	54688	3304
25.	HINDUSTAN LATEX LTD.	1	2	0	2
26.	HINDUSTAN PETROLEUM CORPN. LTD.	20146	122	18600	108
27.	HINDUSTAN STEEL WORKS COSTN. LTD.	612	91	826	94
28.	HOUSING & URBAN DEV. CORPN. LTD.	388	25	387	27
29.	I T I LTD.	3	27	2	28
30.	I.B.P. CO. LTD.	1257	6	1007	12
31.	INDIA TOURISM DEV. CORPN.LTD.	310	44	309	51
32.	INDIAN RAILWAY CATERING AND TOURISM CORPN. LT	0	222	0	0
33.	INDIAN RARE EARTHS LTD.	12556	1103	17680	1116
34.	INSTRUMENTATION LTD.	17	8	17	8
35.	IRCON INTERNATIONAL LTD.	82	38	7	36
36.	JUTE CORPN. OF INDIA LTD.	2	45	2	48
37.	KARNATAKA ANTIBIOTICS & PHARMACEUTICALS LTD.	0	5	0	3
38.	KUDREMUKH IRON ORE CO.LTD	2	2	0	1
39.	M M T C LTD.	400	190	405	192

S. No.	NAME OF PSU	2005-2006		2004-2005	
		Gross Block	Employment	Gross Block	Employment
40.	MAHANADI COALFIELDLS LTD.	285338	20856	271803	21277
41.	MECON LTD.	88	19	88	24
42.	NATIONAL ALUMINIUM COMPANY LTD.	910937	7248	890943	6926
43.	NATIONAL BLDG. CONSTN. CORPN. LTD.	46	2	218	38
44.	NATIONAL HANDLOOM DEVELOPMENT CORPORATION LTD	0	2	0	2
45.	NATIONAL MINERAL DEVELOPMENT CORPN. LTD.	0	5	0	6
46.	NATIONAL SCHEDULED TRIBES FINANCE & DEVP. COR	1	2	1	2
47.	NATIONAL SEEDS CORPN. LTD.	0	3	0	3
48.	NATIONAL SMALL INDUSTRIES CORPN. LTD.	0	9	0	0
49.	NTC(WEST BENGAL,ASSAM,BIHAR & ORISSA)LTD.	285	305	285	321
50.	NTPC LTD.	845480	2371	834762	2399
51.	OIL & NATURAL GAS CORPORATION LTD.	59	0	4446	0
52.	OIL INDIA LTD.	872	28	677	41
53.	ORISSA DRUGS & CHEMICALS LTD	160	83	150	0
54.	POWER GRID CORPORATION OF INDIA LTD	196069	252	194979	238
55.	RAIL VIKAS NIGAM LTD.	0	9	0	0
56.	RASHTRIYA ISPAT NIGAM LTD.	24	8	20	9
57.	RITES LTD.	89	54	13	54
58.	RURAL ELECTRIFICATION CORPN. LTD.	12	17	14	16
59.	SCOOTERS INDIA LTD.	0	1	0	1
60.	STEEL AUTHORITY OF INDIA LTD.	675684	22297	664608	22991
61.	TEHRI HYDRO DEVELOPMENT CORP. LTD..	0	13	0	12
62.	UTKAL ASHOK HOTEL CORPN. LTD.	289	55	289	55
63.	WATER & POWER CONSULTANCY SERVICES(INDIA) LTD	0	4	4	5
	TOTAL	**3428914**	**67779**	**3337411**	**68622**

S. No.	NAME OF PSU	2005-2006		2004-2005	
		Gross Block	Employment	Gross Block	Employment
PUNJAB					
1.	INDIAN OIL CORPORATION LTD.	88511	376	88511	376
2.	AIR INDIA LTD.	8	3	8	3
3.	AIRPORTS AUTHORITY OF INDIA LTD.	7014	228	1095	207
4.	ARTIFICIAL LIMBS MFG. CORPN. OF INDIA	0	1	33	0
5.	BHARAT EARTH MOVERS LTD.	2	4	2	5
6.	BHARAT HEAVY ELECTRICALS LTD.	660	102	586	104
7.	BHARAT PETROLEUM CORPN. LTD.	26756	106	22355	210
8.	BHARAT SANCHAR NIGAM LTD.	538620	11265	498758	11811
9.	BRIDGE & ROOF CO.(INDIA) LTD.	887	57	227	19
10.	BRITISH INDIA CORPORATION LTD.	2010	1242	1937	1281
11.	CEMENT CORPN. OF INDIA LTD.	399	2	1405	2
12.	CENTRAL WAREHOUSING CORPN.	5485	287	5473	327
13.	CONTAINER CORPORATION OF INDIA LTD.	4001	43	2481	29
14.	COTTON CORPN. OF INDIA LTD.	55	75	53	76
15.	ENGINEERING PROJECTS (INDIA) LTD.	0	1	0	0
16.	EXPORT CREDIT GUARANTEE CORPN.OF INDIA LTD.	134	11	90	11
17.	FOOD CORPN. OF INDIA	13411	6428	13583	6821
18.	GAIL (INDIA) LTD.	0	1	0	7
19.	GURU GOBIND SINGH REFINARIES LTD.	26964	1	26776	2
20.	HINDUSTAN INSECTICIDES LTD.	1513	297	1501	318
21.	HINDUSTAN LATEX LTD.	0	3	0	5
22.	HINDUSTAN PETROLEUM CORPN. LTD.	34117	87	28320	95
23.	HINDUSTAN STEEL WORKS COSTN. LTD.	3	0	3	0
24.	HINDUSTAN VEGETABLE OILS CORPN. LTD.	346	0	346	0
25.	HMT LTD.	92	0	148	0
26.	I.B.P. CO. LTD.	5711	17	711	11

S. No.	NAME OF PSU	2005-2006		2004-2005	
		Gross Block	Employment	Gross Block	Employment
27.	INDIAN RAILWAY CATERING AND TOURISM CORPN. LT	0	19	0	0
28.	IRCON INTERNATIONAL LTD.	1104	34	719	21
29.	KARNATAKA ANTIBIOTICS & PHARMACEUTICALS LTD.	0	6	0	7
30.	M M T C LTD.	0	9	0	12
31.	MECON LTD.	0	3	0	0
32.	NATIONAL BLDG. CONSTN. CORPN. LTD.	10	39	34	38
33.	NATIONAL FERTILIZERS LTD.	86494	2438	85730	2467
34.	NATIONAL HANDLOOM DEVELOPMENT CORPORATION LTD	0	3	0	3
35.	NATIONAL HYDROELECTRIC POWER CORPN.LTD.	0	87	0	0
36.	NATIONAL SEEDS CORPN. LTD.	110	10	106	12
37.	NATIONAL SMALL INDUSTRIES CORPN. LTD.	248	24	250	35
38.	NTC(DELHI,PUNJAB & RAJASTHAN) LTD.	880	180	878	1279
39.	NTPC ELECTRIC SUPPLY COMPANY LTD.	0	0	0	2
40.	POWER GRID CORPORATION OF INDIA LTD	172886	259	132043	258
41.	PUNJAB ASHOK HOTEL COMPANY LTD.	266	0	231	0
42.	RASHTRIYA CHEMICALS AND FERTILIZERS LTD.	0	5	0	3
43.	RASHTRIYA ISPAT NIGAM LTD.	88	16	72	10
44.	RITES LTD.	0	10	0	3
45.	SEMI-CONDUCTOR COMPLEX LTD.	24526	602	24074	608
46.	STATE TRADING CORPN. OF INDIA LTD.	0	13	0	15
47.	STEEL AUTHORITY OF INDIA LTD.	499	86	517	90
48.	TEHRI HYDRO DEVELOPMENT CORP. LTD..	0	6	0	7
49.	TELECOMMUNICATIONS CONSULTANTS (INDIA) LTD.	20	7	0	1
50.	TRIVENI STRUCTURALS LTD.	0	0	0	1
	TOTAL	1043830	24493	939056	26592

S. No.	NAME OF PSU	2005-2006 Gross Block	2005-2006 Employment	2004-2005 Gross Block	2004-2005 Employment
RAJASTHAN					
1.	INDIAN OIL CORPORATION LTD.	160898	869	160898	869
2.	AIR INDIA LTD.	6	2	6	2
3.	AIRPORTS AUTHORITY OF INDIA LTD.	11075	375	10027	369
4.	BENGAL CHEMICALS & PHARMACEUTICALS LTD.	1	3	1	5
5.	BHARAT EARTH MOVERS LTD.	6	15	6	5
6.	BHARAT PETROLEUM CORPN. LTD.	32108	299	27547	306
7.	BHARAT SANCHAR NIGAM LTD.	549148	13606	527094	14136
8.	BRIDGE & ROOF CO.(INDIA) LTD.	92	15	0	0
9.	CENTRAL WAREHOUSING CORPN.	3847	146	3714	131
10.	COAL INDIA LTD.	3	14	3	16
11.	CONTAINER CORPORATION OF INDIA LTD.	2165	20	1973	18
12.	COTTON CORPN. OF INDIA LTD.	136	93	134	89
13.	ELECTRONICS CORPN. OF INDIA LTD.	2	3	1	3
14.	ENGINEERING PROJECTS (INDIA) LTD.	512	8	509	7
15.	ENGINEERS INDIA LTD.	0	46	0	0
16.	EXPORT CREDIT GUARANTEE CORPN.OF INDIA LTD.	68	9	49	8
17.	FCI ARAVALI GYPSUM & MINERALS (INDIA) LTD.	144	122	130	132
18.	FOOD CORPN. OF INDIA	4968	1577	4947	1545
19.	GAIL (INDIA) LTD.	109148	141	68362	118
20.	GURU GOBIND SINGH REFINARIES LTD.	80	2	0	0
21.	HINDUSTAN ANTIBIOTICS LTD.	2	22	2	23
22.	HINDUSTAN COPPER LTD.	30981	3045	41655	3080
23.	HINDUSTAN LATEX LTD.	0	6	0	5
24.	HINDUSTAN PAPER CORPORATION LTD.	4	5	4	5
25.	HINDUSTAN PETROLEUM CORPN. LTD.	44189	167	37234	204

S. No.	NAME OF PSU	2005-2006		2004-2005	
		Gross Block	Employment	Gross Block	Employment
26.	HINDUSTAN PHOTO FILMS MANUFACTURING CO. LTD.	2	2	2	2
27.	HINDUSTAN SALTS LTD.	31	34	30	34
28.	HMT MACHINE TOOLS LTD.	1623	520	1625	540
29.	HOUSING & URBAN DEV. CORPN. LTD.	273	22	272	23
30.	HSCC (INDIA) LTD.	0	1	0	0
31.	I.B.P. CO. LTD.	1851	8	826	12
32.	INDIA TOURISM DEV. CORPN.LTD.	453	60	451	64
33.	INDIAN RAILWAY CATERING AND TOURISM CORPN. LT	0	25	0	0
34.	INSTRUMENTATION LTD.	4843	1187	4832	1211
35.	IRCON INTERNATIONAL LTD.	2	0	3	2
36.	KARNATAKA ANTIBIOTICS & PHARMACEUTICALS LTD.	0	11	0	14
37.	M M T C LTD.	55	23	55	22
38.	MECON LTD.	0	2	0	2
39.	NATIONAL BLDG. CONSTN. CORPN. LTD.	6	183	4	110
40.	NATIONAL HANDLOOM DEVELOPMENT CORPORATION LTD	0	1	0	1
41.	NATIONAL MINERAL DEVELOPMENT CORPN. LTD.	0	0	240	4
42.	NATIONAL SCHEDULED TRIBES FINANCE & DEVP. COR	1	3	1	3
43.	NATIONAL SEEDS CORPN. LTD.	144	51	131	57
44.	NATIONAL SMALL INDUSTRIES CORPN. LTD.	78	12	91	14
45.	NEYVELI LIGNITE CORPN. LTD.	5803	60	4526	15
46.	NTC(DELHI,PUNJAB & RAJASTHAN) LTD.	897	349	900	1380
47.	NTPC LTD.	53702	220	53693	234
48.	NUCLEAR POWER CORPN. OF INDIA LTD.	561020	2618	339079	2690
49.	NUMALIGARH REFINARY LTD.	0	1	0	0
50.	OIL & NATURAL GAS CORPORATION LTD.	21067	198	34804	204
51.	OIL INDIA LTD.	25266	156	19551	148

S. No.	NAME OF PSU	2005-2006		2004-2005	
		Gross Block	Employment	Gross Block	Employment
52.	P E C LTD.	4	3	4	3
53.	POWER GRID CORPORATION OF INDIA LTD	59239	98	42464	97
54.	PYRITES, PHOSPHATES & CHEMICALS LTD.	3365	0	3365	0
55.	RAIL VIKAS NIGAM LTD.	0	3	0	0
56.	RAJASTHAN DRUGS & PHARMACEUTICALS LTD.	412	143	304	145
57.	RAJASTHAN ELECTRONICS AND INSTRUMENTS LTD.	1057	156	992	196
58.	RASHTRIYA ISPAT NIGAM LTD.	258	9	250	8
59.	RURAL ELECTRIFICATION CORPN. LTD.	10	20	10	21
60.	SAMBHAR SALTS LTD.	994	137	775	140
61.	SCOOTERS INDIA LTD.	0	2	0	2
62.	STATE FARMS CORPORATION OF INDIA LTD.	2544	1242	2397	1261
63.	STEEL AUTHORITY OF INDIA LTD.	221	37	212	40
64.	TEHRI HYDRO DEVELOPMENT CORP. LTD..	0	7	0	7
65.	TELECOMMUNICATIONS CONSULTANTS (INDIA) LTD.	6	25	6	15
66.	WATER & POWER CONSULTANCY SERVICES(INDIA) LTD	34	6	34	3
	TOTAL	**1694844**	**28245**	**1396225**	**29800**
SIKKIM					
1.	INDIAN OIL CORPORATION LTD.	5367	2	5367	2
2.	BHARAT PETROLEUM CORPN. LTD.	72	0	72	0
3.	FOOD CORPN. OF INDIA	2174	455	0	0
4.	HINDUSTAN PETROLEUM CORPN. LTD.	2	0	4	0
5.	I.B.P. CO. LTD.	77	2	77	2
6.	NATIONAL BLDG. CONSTN. CORPN. LTD.	11	43	0	20
7.	NATIONAL HYDROELECTRIC POWER CORPN.LTD.	233686	751	187779	779

S. No.	NAME OF PSU	2005-2006		2004-2005	
		Gross Block	Employment	Gross Block	Employment
8.	NATIONAL SMALL INDUSTRIES CORPN. LTD.	0	1	0	0
9.	NUCLEAR POWER CORPN. OF INDIA LTD.	335369	1565	0	0
10.	POWER GRID CORPORATION OF INDIA LTD	8385	16	5753	14
	TOTAL	585143	2835	199052	817
TAMILNADU					
1.	INDIAN AIRLINES LTD.	8496	2523	8496	2523
2.	NATIONAL JUTE MANUFACTURERS CORPORATION LTD.	4061	18494	4061	18494
3.	IDPL (TAMILNADU) LTD.	6156	31	6156	31
4.	INDIAN OIL CORPORATION LTD.	200657	1805	200657	1805
5.	KOCHI REFINERIES LTD.	0	0	11	4
6.	SETHUSAMUDRAM CORPN. LTD.	4325	24	0	0
7.	AIR INDIA LTD.	123524	646	61418	493
8.	AIRLINE ALLIED SERVICES LTD.	9	47	9	56
9.	AIRPORTS AUTHORITY OF INDIA LTD.	90033	2203	58593	2265
10.	ANDREW YULE & COMPANY LTD.	504	124	493	132
11.	BALMER LAWRIE & CO. LTD.	5502	257	5551	266
12.	BENGAL CHEMICALS & PHARMACEUTICALS LTD.	1	4	1	8
13.	BHARAT EARTH MOVERS LTD.	22	28	20	61
14.	BHARAT ELECTRONICS LTD.	2843	245	2562	250
15.	BHARAT HEAVY ELECTRICALS LTD.	72123	11264	69456	11248
16.	BHARAT HEAVY PLATE & VESSELS LTD.	1	4	1	2
17.	BHARAT PETROLEUM CORPN. LTD.	65184	839	58647	847
18.	BHARAT PUMPS & COMPRESSORS LTD.	1	3	1	3
19.	BHARAT SANCHAR NIGAM LTD.	1111150	37078	1043139	32698

S. No.	NAME OF PSU	2005-2006		2004-2005	
		Gross Block	Employment	Gross Block	Employment
20.	BHARATIYA NABHIKIYA VIDYUT NIGAM LTD.	33352	188	15541	92
21.	BIECCO LAWRIE LTD.	1	2	1	2
22.	BONGAIGAON REFINERY & PETROCHEMICALS LTD.	0	0	1	2
23.	BRIDGE & ROOF CO.(INDIA) LTD.	208	69	172	59
24.	BURN STANDARD COMPANY LTD.	5692	462	5669	472
25.	CENTRAL COTTAGE INDUSTRIES CORPN. OF INDIA LT	125	10	127	12
26.	CENTRAL WAREHOUSING CORPN.	5067	381	5120	407
27.	CHENNAI PETROLEUM CORPORATION LTD.	489256	1666	481231	1692
28.	COAL INDIA LTD.	3	14	3	14
29.	CONTAINER CORPORATION OF INDIA LTD.	5557	82	5469	79
30.	COTTON CORPN. OF INDIA LTD.	23	48	21	45
31.	DREDGING CORPN.OF INDIA LTD.	13	21	10	11
32.	ELECTRONICS CORPN. OF INDIA LTD.	23	88	33	91
33.	ENGINEERING PROJECTS (INDIA) LTD.	34	22	31	23
34.	ENGINEERS INDIA LTD.	510	66	870	85
35.	ENNORE PORT LTD.	68191	20	67521	21
36.	EXPORT CREDIT GUARANTEE CORPN.OF INDIA LTD.	734	82	538	83
37.	FERTILIZERS & CHEMICALS (TRAVANCORE) LTD.	34	60	33	52
38.	FOOD CORPN. OF INDIA	3501	2473	4404	2515
39.	GAIL (INDIA) LTD.	47	27	10632	14
40.	HANDICRAFTS & HANDLOOM EXPORTS CORP. OF INDIA	352	86	349	87
41.	HINDUSTAN ANTIBIOTICS LTD.	4	45	6	47
42.	HINDUSTAN INSECTICIDES LTD.	2	8	2	7
43.	HINDUSTAN LATEX LTD.	74	26	27	32
44.	HINDUSTAN PAPER CORPORATION LTD.	9	9	9	11
45.	HINDUSTAN PETROLEUM CORPN. LTD.	49862	525	43782	542

S. No.	NAME OF PSU	2005-2006 Gross Block	2005-2006 Employment	2004-2005 Gross Block	2004-2005 Employment
46.	HINDUSTAN PHOTO FILMS MANUFACTURING CO. LTD.	72032	1011	72030	1024
47.	HINDUSTAN STEEL WORKS COSTN. LTD.	24	13	95	28
48.	HINDUSTAN VEGETABLE OILS CORPN. LTD.	59	0	59	0
49.	HMT BEARINGS LTD.	0	3	0	4
50.	HMT MACHINE TOOLS LTD.	21	44	25	29
51.	HOUSING & URBAN DEV. CORPN. LTD.	1236	66	1238	63
52.	HSCC (INDIA) LTD.	8	1	5	2
53.	I T I LTD.	111	74	141	77
54.	I.B.P. CO. LTD.	20114	175	20268	176
55.	INDIA TOURISM DEV. CORPN.LTD.	66	18	55	22
56.	INDIA TRADE PROMOTION ORGANISATION	70	10	78	10
57.	INDIAN RAILWAY CATERING AND TOURISM CORPN. LT	81	768	61	355
58.	INDIAN RARE EARTHS LTD.	4261	475	4004	488
59.	INDIAN RENEWABLE ENERGY DEVT.AGENCY LTD.	0	2	0	1
60.	INSTRUMENTATION LTD.	12	16	11	14
61.	IRCON INTERNATIONAL LTD.	216	51	103	33
62.	KARNATAKA ANTIBIOTICS & PHARMACEUTICALS LTD.	0	24	0	22
63.	KUDREMUKH IRON ORE CO.LTD	10	5	10	6
64.	M M T C LTD.	184	160	176	168
65.	M S T C LTD.	37	21	36	21
66.	MADRAS FERTILIZERS LTD.	88160	937	88217	976
67.	MANGALORE REFINARY & PETROCHEMICALS LTD.	747	0	685	0
68.	MECON LTD.	51	19	47	15
69.	NATIONAL ALUMINIUM COMPANY LTD.	52	10	52	11
70.	NATIONAL BLDG. CONSTN. CORPN. LTD.	0	39	10	74
71.	NATIONAL FILM DEV. CORPN. LTD.	125	42	115	42

S. No.	NAME OF PSU	2005-2006		2004-2005	
		Gross Block	Employment	Gross Block	Employment
72.	NATIONAL HANDLOOM DEVELOPMENT CORPORATION LTD	44	34	44	28
73.	NATIONAL HYDROELECTRIC POWER CORPN.LTD.	0	2	0	2
74.	NATIONAL MINERAL DEVELOPMENT CORPN. LTD.	0	12	0	14
75.	NATIONAL SEEDS CORPN. LTD.	0	13	0	12
76.	NATIONAL SMALL INDUSTRIES CORPN. LTD.	1256	80	1280	107
77.	NEYVELI LIGNITE CORPN. LTD.	955200	18919	915780	18812
78.	NORTH EASTERN HANDICRAFTS & HANDLOOM DEV.COR	2	11	2	7
79.	NTC(TAMILNADU & PONDICHERRY) LTD.	30091	4118	31060	4320
80.	NTPC LTD.	32	31	29	33
81.	NUCLEAR POWER CORPN. OF INDIA LTD.	0	0	327352	1456
82.	OIL & NATURAL GAS CORPORATION LTD.	206102	808	463087	838
83.	P E C LTD.	18	9	18	9
84.	POWER FINANCE CORPORATION	0	4	0	4
85.	POWER GRID CORPORATION OF INDIA LTD	110289	196	87135	194
86.	PRAGA TOOLS LTD.	0	3	0	3
87.	PROJECTS & DEVELOPMENT INDIA LTD.	6	13	5	13
88.	RAIL VIKAS NIGAM LTD.	0	15	0	0
89.	RASHTRIYA CHEMICALS AND FERTILIZERS LTD.	16	11	16	13
90.	RASHTRIYA ISPAT NIGAM LTD.	1397	30	1310	33
91.	RICHARDSON & CRUDDAS(1972) LTD.	346	0	128	0
92.	RITES LTD.	45	76	55	79
93.	RURAL ELECTRIFICATION CORPN. LTD.	6	15	8	12
94.	SCOOTERS INDIA LTD.	0	3	0	6
95.	SHIPPING CORPORATION OF INDIA LTD.	80531	55	66286	53
96.	SPONGE IRON INDIA LTD.	0	1	0	1
97.	STATE FARMS CORPORATION OF INDIA LTD.	270	4	286	3

S. No.	NAME OF PSU	2005-2006		2004-2005	
		Gross Block	Employment	Gross Block	Employment
98.	STATE TRADING CORPN. OF INDIA LTD.	87	54	83	56
99.	STCL LTD.	6	4	3	4
100.	STEEL AUTHORITY OF INDIA LTD.	107180	1342	106231	1344
101.	TAMIL NADU TRADE PROMOTION ORGANISATION	4305	20	2126	20
102.	TEHRI HYDRO DEVELOPMENT CORP. LTD..	0	5	0	4
103.	TELECOMMUNICATIONS CONSULTANTS (INDIA) LTD.	93	21	92	30
104.	WATER & POWER CONSULTANCY SERVICES(INDIA) LTD	0	1	0	0
	TOTAL	4042265	111993	4350811	108854
TRIPURA					
1.	INDIAN OIL CORPORATION LTD.	5289	47	5289	47
2.	AIRPORTS AUTHORITY OF INDIA LTD.	5344	142	5249	146
3.	CENTRAL WAREHOUSING CORPN.	138	17	138	22
4.	ENGINEERING PROJECTS (INDIA) LTD.	1	4	1	5
5.	FOOD CORPN. OF INDIA	0	0	1991	636
6.	GAIL (INDIA) LTD.	4873	22	4825	22
7.	HINDUSTAN STEEL WORKS COSTN. LTD.	1	1	0	0
8.	HOUSING & URBAN DEV. CORPN. LTD.	1	3	0	3
9.	I.B.P. CO. LTD.	94	2	94	2
10.	JUTE CORPN. OF INDIA LTD.	1	29	1	30
11.	NATIONAL BLDG. CONSTN. CORPN. LTD.	0	298	0	223
12.	NATIONAL HANDLOOM DEVELOPMENT CORPORATION LTD	0	1	0	1
13.	NATIONAL SMALL INDUSTRIES CORPN. LTD.	0	1	0	0
14.	NORTH EASTERN ELECTRIC POWER CORPORATION LTD.	37586	208	37454	278
15.	NORTH EASTERN REGIONAL AGRI. MARKETING CORP.L	394	23	394	23

S. No.	*NAME OF PSU*	*2005-2006*		*2004-2005*	
		Gross Block	*Employment*	*Gross Block*	*Employment*
16.	OIL & NATURAL GAS CORPORATION LTD.	61600	1035	107817	1054
17.	POWER GRID CORPORATION OF INDIA LTD	4808	33	4696	37
18.	RITES LTD.	0	3	0	0
	TOTAL	**120130**	**1869**	**167949**	**2529**
UTTAR PRADESH					
1.	HINDUSTAN PREFAB LTD.	0	2	0	2
2.	BROADCAST ENGG.CONSULTANTS INDIA LTD.	205	3	73	0
3.	INDIAN OIL CORPORATION LTD.	727631	3526	569728	3526
4.	BHARAT LEATHER CORPN. LTD.	0	0	197	0
5.	AIR INDIA LTD.	5	2	5	2
6.	AIRPORTS AUTHORITY OF INDIA LTD.	150014	742	41610	828
7.	ARTIFICIAL LIMBS MFG. CORPN. OF INDIA	1518	418	1604	425
8.	BALMER LAWRIE & CO. LTD.	205	37	203	42
9.	BENGAL CHEMICALS & PHARMACEUTICALS LTD.	162	20	54	25
10.	BHARAT ELECTRONICS LTD.	17941	2596	16196	2616
11.	BHARAT HEAVY ELECTRICALS LTD.	15087	2415	14438	2441
12.	BHARAT IMMUNOLOGICALS & BIOLOGICALS CORP. LTD	3965	124	3955	120
13.	BHARAT PETROLEUM CORPN. LTD.	122800	996	79503	954
14.	BHARAT PUMPS & COMPRESSORS LTD.	3813	1202	3799	1216
15.	BHARAT SANCHAR NIGAM LTD.	993893	25323	956958	26620
16.	BHARAT YANTRA NIGAM LTD.	137	30	137	31
17.	BIECCO LAWRIE LTD.	0	2	0	2
18.	BRAHMAPUTRA VALLEY FERTILIZER CORPN. LTD.	0	4	0	4
19.	BRIDGE & ROOF CO.(INDIA) LTD.	759	150	61	28

S. No.	NAME OF PSU	2005-2006		2004-2005	
		Gross Block	Employment	Gross Block	Employment
20.	BRITISH INDIA CORPORATION LTD.	2656	1487	2518	1485
21.	BRUSHWARE LTD.	29	0	29	0
22.	CENTRAL COTTAGE INDUSTRIES CORPN. OF INDIA LT	0	0	41	0
23.	CENTRAL ELECTRONICS LTD.	3288	680	2246	691
24.	CENTRAL INLAND WATER TRANSPORT CORPN. LTD.	0	3	0	5
25.	CENTRAL WAREHOUSING CORPN.	8350	885	7960	905
26.	COAL INDIA LTD.	13	23	13	25
27.	CONTAINER CORPORATION OF INDIA LTD.	15859	119	16278	92
28.	EDUCATIONAL CONSULTANTS (INDIA) LTD.	872	89	859	88
29.	ELECTRONICS CORPN. OF INDIA LTD.	3	4	8	5
30.	ENGINEERING PROJECTS (INDIA) LTD.	67	14	106	7
31.	ENGINEERS INDIA LTD.	0	22	0	29
32.	EXPORT CREDIT GUARANTEE CORPN.OF INDIA LTD.	229	26	144	27
33.	FCI ARAVALI GYPSUM & MINERALS (INDIA) LTD.	0	2	0	2
34.	FERTILIZER CORPN. OF INDIA LTD.	7773	11	7773	12
35.	FOOD CORPN. OF INDIA	10965	5859	11095	6193
36.	GAIL (INDIA) LTD.	521381	1145	525080	1150
37.	HANDICRAFTS & HANDLOOM EXPORTS CORP. OF INDIA	53	3	636	3
38.	HINDUSTAN AERONAUTICS LTD.	62705	5748	62721	5843
39.	HINDUSTAN ANTIBIOTICS LTD.	2	34	2	33
40.	HINDUSTAN CABLES LTD.	9707	210	9707	210
41.	HINDUSTAN LATEX LTD.	81	10	1	9
42.	HINDUSTAN PAPER CORPORATION LTD.	4	5	4	5
43.	HINDUSTAN PETROLEUM CORPN. LTD.	54105	257	47103	273
44.	HINDUSTAN PHOTO FILMS MANUFACTURING CO. LTD.	2	5	2	5
45.	HINDUSTAN STEEL WORKS COSTN. LTD.	474	51	355	60

S. No.	NAME OF PSU	2005-2006 Gross Block	2005-2006 Employment	2004-2005 Gross Block	2004-2005 Employment
46.	HINDUSTAN VEGETABLE OILS CORPN. LTD.	625	0	625	0
47.	HMT MACHINE TOOLS LTD.	3	6	4	6
48.	HOUSING & URBAN DEV. CORPN. LTD.	176	20	175	26
49.	HSCC (INDIA) LTD.	1141	112	681	107
50.	I T I LTD.	125620	8647	47346	9407
51.	I.B.P. CO. LTD.	11987	126	10482	131
52.	INDIA TOURISM DEV. CORPN.LTD.	55	41	47	45
53.	INDIAN RAILWAY CATERING AND TOURISM CORPN. LT	3	348	0	0
54.	INDIAN STRATEGIC PETROLEUM RESERVES LTD.	56	1	0	1
55.	INSTRUMENTATION LTD.	23	42	20	42
56.	IRCON INTERNATIONAL LTD.	870	191	1566	175
57.	KARNATAKA ANTIBIOTICS & PHARMACEUTICALS LTD.	0	18	0	16
58.	M M T C LTD.	0	17	0	14
59.	MECON LTD.	0	5	1	5
60.	NATIONAL BLDG. CONSTN. CORPN. LTD.	193	40	488	105
61.	NATIONAL FERTILIZERS LTD.	469	441	0	0
62.	NATIONAL HANDLOOM DEVELOPMENT CORPORATION LTD	254	109	250	109
63.	NATIONAL HYDROELECTRIC POWER CORPN.LTD.	0	18	0	37
64.	NATIONAL MINERAL DEVELOPMENT CORPN. LTD.	2397	11	2397	12
65.	NATIONAL SCHEDULED CASTES FINANCE & DEVP. COR	45	3	45	3
66.	NATIONAL SEEDS CORPN. LTD.	389	113	342	120
67.	NATIONAL SMALL INDUSTRIES CORPN. LTD.	435	83	466	74
68.	NORTHERN COALFIELDS LTD.	270639	6910	266746	7020
69.	NTC(UTTAR PRADESH)LTD.	1208	587	1209	2051
70.	NTPC ELECTRIC SUPPLY COMPANY LTD.	4	0	0	1
71.	NTPC HYDRO LTD.	16	0	16	0

S. No.	NAME OF PSU	2005-2006 Gross Block	2005-2006 Employment	2004-2005 Gross Block	2004-2005 Employment
72.	NTPC LTD.	1413124	6475	1329041	6437
73.	NUCLEAR POWER CORPN. OF INDIA LTD.	268081	1251	90242	1298
74.	NUMALIGARH REFINARY LTD.	0	1	0	1
75.	OIL & NATURAL GAS CORPORATION LTD.	45792	2820	74146	3006
76.	OIL INDIA LTD.	44	18	35	21
77.	POWER GRID CORPORATION OF INDIA LTD	425180	589	355730	565
78.	PROJECTS & DEVELOPMENT INDIA LTD.	1399	167	1531	175
79.	RAJASTHAN ELECTRONICS AND INSTRUMENTS LTD.	0	3	0	0
80.	RASHTRIYA CHEMICALS AND FERTILIZERS LTD.	80	33	80	32
81.	RASHTRIYA ISPAT NIGAM LTD.	316	20	297	21
82.	RITES LTD.	46	41	11	34
83.	RURAL ELECTRIFICATION CORPN. LTD.	10	45	11	42
84.	SCOOTERS INDIA LTD.	5196	1618	5027	1702
85.	STATE FARMS CORPORATION OF INDIA LTD.	602	217	599	228
86.	STATE TRADING CORPN. OF INDIA LTD.	0	26	0	28
87.	STEEL AUTHORITY OF INDIA LTD.	6628	46	6679	48
88.	TEHRI HYDRO DEVELOPMENT CORP. LTD..	339	551	0	559
89.	TELECOMMUNICATIONS CONSULTANTS (INDIA) LTD.	0	7	14	18
90.	TRIVENI STRUCTURALS LTD.	2015	307	2014	308
91.	TYRE CORPORATION OF INDIA LTD.	0	0	1	0
92.	WATER & POWER CONSULTANCY SERVICES(INDIA) LTD	0	1	0	1
	TOTAL	**5322213**	**86409**	**4581566**	**90070**
UTTARANCHAL					
1.	INDIAN DRUGS & PHARMACEUTICALS LTD.	6565	231	6565	231

S. No.	NAME OF PSU	2005-2006 Gross Block	2005-2006 Employment	2004-2005 Gross Block	2004-2005 Employment
2.	HINDUSTAN PREFAB LTD.	0	3	0	1
3.	INDIAN OIL CORPORATION LTD.	3799	40	3799	40
4.	AIRPORTS AUTHORITY OF INDIA LTD.	515	27	505	26
5.	BALMER LAWRIE & CO. LTD.	0	1	0	1
6.	BHARAT ELECTRONICS LTD.	7750	618	5558	631
7.	BHARAT HEAVY ELECTRICALS LTD.	78923	7495	73289	7778
8.	BHARAT PETROLEUM CORPN. LTD.	1812	0	1810	0
9.	BHARAT SANCHAR NIGAM LTD.	108821	2595	100220	2677
10.	BRIDGE & ROOF CO.(INDIA) LTD.	0	0	0	3
11.	CENTRAL WAREHOUSING CORPN.	0	57	0	52
12.	ENGINEERING PROJECTS (INDIA) LTD.	0	5	0	1
13.	FOOD CORPN. OF INDIA	682	509	674	509
14.	HANDICRAFTS & HANDLOOM EXPORTS CORP. OF INDIA	0	0	12	12
15.	HINDUSTAN LATEX LTD.	0	0	0	1
16.	HINDUSTAN PETROLEUM CORPN. LTD.	1752	7	2304	7
17.	HINDUSTAN SALTS LTD.	3	5	2	6
18.	HMT WATCHES LTD.	7347	597	7357	597
19.	HOUSING & URBAN DEV. CORPN. LTD.	10	11	8	11
20.	I.B.P. CO. LTD.	993	21	953	21
21.	INDIAN MEDICINES & PHARMACEUTICAL CORPN. LTD.	0	0	181	127
22.	INSTRUMENTATION LTD.	0	0	0	1
23.	KARNATAKA ANTIBIOTICS & PHARMACEUTICALS LTD.	0	1	0	0
24.	M M T C LTD.	0	2	0	0
25.	MECON LTD.	0	1	0	3
26.	NATIONAL BLDG. CONSTN. CORPN. LTD.	0	0	0	4
27.	NATIONAL HYDROELECTRIC POWER CORPN.LTD.	216086	1175	213957	1150

S. No.	NAME OF PSU	2005-2006		2004-2005	
		Gross Block	Employment	Gross Block	Employment
28.	NATIONAL MINERAL DEVELOPMENT CORPN. LTD.	24	10	0	0
29.	NATIONAL RESEARCH DEVP. CORPN.	9	0	9	0
30.	NATIONAL SEEDS CORPN. LTD.	0	13	0	14
31.	NATIONAL SMALL INDUSTRIES CORPN. LTD.	28	0	27	7
32.	NEPA LTD.	152	7	121	7
33.	NTPC ELECTRIC SUPPLY COMPANY LTD.	0	0	0	1
34.	NTPC HYDRO LTD.	28	0	26	0
35.	NTPC LTD.	18683	102	12290	55
36.	POWER GRID CORPORATION OF INDIA LTD	55441	38	37470	27
37.	PYRITES, PHOSPHATES & CHEMICALS LTD.	3444	0	3444	0
38.	RASHTRIYA ISPAT NIGAM LTD.	3	3	2	3
39.	STEEL AUTHORITY OF INDIA LTD.	5	0	0	0
40.	TEHRI HYDRO DEVELOPMENT CORP. LTD..	781141	1585	708845	1592
41.	TELECOMMUNICATIONS CONSULTANTS (INDIA) LTD.	0	15	0	0
42.	WATER & POWER CONSULTANCY SERVICES(INDIA) LTD	1	1	0	0
	TOTAL	**1294017**	**15175**	**1179428**	**15596**
WEST BENGAL					
1.	INDIAN AIRLINES LTD.	9078	3512	9078	3512
2.	INDIAN OIL CORPORATION LTD.	473008	3880	473008	3880
3.	INDIAN IRON & STEEL CO. LTD.	0	0	65735	11657
4.	INDIAN OIL BLENDING LTD.	0	0	2443	178
5.	AIR INDIA LTD.	3185	285	3185	285
6.	AIRLINE ALLIED SERVICES LTD.	130	206	129	248

S. No.	NAME OF PSU	2005-2006		2004-2005	
		Gross Block	Employment	Gross Block	Employment
7.	AIRPORTS AUTHORITY OF INDIA LTD.	66752	2229	66752	2349
8.	ANDAMAN & NICOBAR ISL. FOREST & PLANT.DEV.COR	23	8	23	7
9.	ANDREW YULE & COMPANY LTD.	10018	7773	9816	7846
10.	ARTIFICIAL LIMBS MFG. CORPN. OF INDIA	2	4	0	3
11.	BALMER LAWRIE & CO. LTD.	8003	688	7948	709
12.	BBJ CONSTRUCTION COMPANY LTD.	655	262	595	112
13.	BENGAL CHEMICALS & PHARMACEUTICALS LTD.	2118	737	1795	754
14.	BHARAT BHARI UDYOG NIGAM LTD.	71	26	70	27
15.	BHARAT COKING COAL LTD.	10540	2716	10206	3203
16.	BHARAT EARTH MOVERS LTD.	417	119	422	128
17.	BHARAT OPHTHALMIC GLASS LTD.	591	6	591	6
18.	BHARAT PETROLEUM CORPN. LTD.	46254	952	41448	976
19.	BHARAT PUMPS & COMPRESSORS LTD.	1	5	1	4
20.	BHARAT REFRACTORIES LTD.	0	8	0	8
21.	BHARAT SANCHAR NIGAM LTD.	641872	21984	576749	11780
22.	BHARAT WAGON & ENGG. CO. LTD.	5	4	5	3
23.	BIECCO LAWRIE LTD.	1528	484	1526	507
24.	BIRDS JUTE & EXPORTS LTD.	268	131	268	131
25.	BONGAIGAON REFINERY & PETROCHEMICALS LTD.	57	12	37	14
26.	BRAHMAPUTRA VALLEY FERTILIZER CORPN. LTD.	0	4	0	4
27.	BRAITHWAITE & CO. LTD.	4781	544	4595	550
28.	BRIDGE & ROOF CO.(INDIA) LTD.	2776	345	2807	551
29.	BURN STANDARD COMPANY LTD.	7481	1077	7436	1084
30.	CENTRAL COALFIELDS LTD.	69	158	69	169
31.	CENTRAL COTTAGE INDUSTRIES CORPN. OF INDIA LT	35	11	35	12
32.	CENTRAL INLAND WATER TRANSPORT CORPN. LTD.	13346	820	13451	1055

S. No.	NAME OF PSU	2005-2006		2004-2005	
		Gross Block	Employment	Gross Block	Employment
33.	CENTRAL MINE PLANNING & DESIGN INSTITUTE LTD.	430	342	606	299
34.	CENTRAL WAREHOUSING CORPN.	6613	515	6513	537
35.	COAL INDIA LTD.	22395	869	22332	911
36.	CONTAINER CORPORATION OF INDIA LTD.	2464	43	2215	40
37.	COTTON CORPN. OF INDIA LTD.	280	23	278	23
38.	DREDGING CORPN.OF INDIA LTD.	49	48	42	49
39.	EASTERN COALFIELDS LTD.	318421	87106	315487	90668
40.	ELECTRONICS CORPN. OF INDIA LTD.	49	129	50	127
41.	ENGINEERING PROJECTS (INDIA) LTD.	202	83	145	82
42.	ENGINEERS INDIA LTD.	200	37	222	22
43.	EXPORT CREDIT GUARANTEE CORPN.OF INDIA LTD.	773	42	596	41
44.	FERRO SCRAP NIGAM LTD.	2992	231	2625	234
45.	FOOD CORPN. OF INDIA	5200	3149	5158	3301
46.	GAIL (INDIA) LTD.	9290	16	52	15
47.	GARDEN REACH SHIPBUILDERS & ENGINEERS LTD.	16565	4759	16385	5168
48.	HANDICRAFTS & HANDLOOM EXPORTS CORP. OF INDIA	12	11	0	0
49.	HEAVY ENGINEERING CORPN. LTD.	95	10	91	10
50.	HINDUSTAN AERONAUTICS LTD.	1204	285	751	316
51.	HINDUSTAN ANTIBIOTICS LTD.	7	0	7	0
52.	HINDUSTAN CABLES LTD.	31533	1833	31530	1858
53.	HINDUSTAN COPPER LTD.	757	128	738	128
54.	HINDUSTAN FERTILIZER CORPN. LTD.	30110	31	30028	39
55.	HINDUSTAN INSECTICIDES LTD.	2	11	2	10
56.	HINDUSTAN LATEX LTD.	5	7	4	10
57.	HINDUSTAN PAPER CORPORATION LTD.	505	180	512	183
58.	HINDUSTAN PETROLEUM CORPN. LTD.	33109	717	30917	753

S. No.	NAME OF PSU	2005-2006		2004-2005	
		Gross Block	Employment	Gross Block	Employment
59.	HINDUSTAN PHOTO FILMS MANUFACTURING CO. LTD.	2	7	2	8
60.	HINDUSTAN STEEL WORKS COSTN. LTD.	1311	82	1271	91
61.	HINDUSTAN VEGETABLE OILS CORPN. LTD.	494	40	494	0
62.	HMT BEARINGS LTD.	0	4	0	4
63.	HMT MACHINE TOOLS LTD.	7	19	9	19
64.	HOOGHLY DOCK AND PORT ENGINEERS LTD.	2113	718	2093	746
65.	HOOGHLY PRINTING COMPANY LTD.	167	60	166	63
66.	HOUSING & URBAN DEV. CORPN. LTD.	251	37	256	39
67.	HSCC (INDIA) LTD.	0	0	10	0
68.	I T I LTD.	139	124	121	81
69.	I.B.P. CO. LTD.	19070	328	19070	338
70.	INDIA TOURISM DEV. CORPN.LTD.	19	7	19	8
71.	INDIA TRADE PROMOTION ORGANISATION	174	8	174	8
72.	INDIAN RAILWAY CATERING AND TOURISM CORPN. LT	46	1163	32	222
73.	INSTRUMENTATION LTD.	21	30	21	35
74.	IRCON INTERNATIONAL LTD.	702	69	711	59
75.	JUTE CORPN. OF INDIA LTD.	339	897	348	924
76.	KARNATAKA ANTIBIOTICS & PHARMACEUTICALS LTD.	0	28	0	26
77.	M M T C LTD.	227	163	224	172
78.	M S T C LTD.	942	167	334	155
79.	MAHANADI COALFIELDLS LTD.	23	20	23	21
80.	MECON LTD.	358	24	358	26
81.	NATIONAL ALUMINIUM COMPANY LTD.	59	26	59	29
82.	NATIONAL BACKWARD CLASSES FINANCE & DEVELOPME	6	2	6	2
83.	NATIONAL BLDG. CONSTN. CORPN. LTD.	46	97	82	101
84.	NATIONAL FILM DEV. CORPN. LTD.	16	22	22	25

S. No.	NAME OF PSU	2005-2006 Gross Block	2005-2006 Employment	2004-2005 Gross Block	2004-2005 Employment
85.	NATIONAL HANDLOOM DEVELOPMENT CORPORATION LTD	18	16	18	16
86.	NATIONAL HYDROELECTRIC POWER CORPN.LTD.	30401	384	16025	306
87.	NATIONAL INSTRUMENTS LTD.	899	68	900	67
88.	NATIONAL MINERAL DEVELOPMENT CORPN. LTD.	0	0	24	10
89.	NATIONAL SCHEDULED CASTES FINANCE & DEVP. COR	14	3	14	3
90.	NATIONAL SEEDS CORPN. LTD	126	25	118	25
91.	NATIONAL SMALL INDUSTRIES CORPN. LTD.	531	95	623	102
92.	NEYVELI LIGNITE CORPN. LTD.	34	1	35	1
93.	NORTH EASTERN HANDICRAFTS & HANDLOOM DEV.COR	3	11	3	7
94.	NORTH EASTERN ELECTRIC POWER CORPORATION LTD.	402	12	378	10
95.	NORTHERN COALFIELDS LTD.	29	17	29	20
96.	NTC(WEST BENGAL,ASSAM,BIHAR & ORISSA)LTD.	1063	789	1697	1583
97.	NTPC ELECTRIC SUPPLY COMPANY LTD.	1	0	0	0
98.	NTPC HYDRO LTD.	1	0	0	0
99.	NTPC LTD.	317931	1693	312868	1712
100.	NUMALIGARH REFINARY LTD.	20	8	8	4
101.	OIL & NATURAL GAS CORPORATION LTD.	16433	931	108780	979
102.	OIL INDIA LTD.	4504	146	3111	238
103.	P E C LTD.	15	11	15	11
104.	POWER GRID CORPORATION OF INDIA LTD	126895	529	124769	487
105.	PROJECTS & DEVELOPMENT INDIA LTD.	13	3	13	4
106.	RAJASTHAN ELECTRONICS AND INSTRUMENTS LTD.	0	2	0	0
107.	RASHTRIYA CHEMICALS AND FERTILIZERS LTD.	6	5	6	3
108.	RASHTRIYA ISPAT NIGAM LTD.	1104	29	1079	23
109.	RITES LTD.	955	259	1008	263
110.	RURAL ELECTRIFICATION CORPN. LTD.	15	22	18	20

S. No.	NAME OF PSU	2005-2006 Gross Block	2005-2006 Employment	2004-2005 Gross Block	2004-2005 Employment
111.	SCOOTERS INDIA LTD.	0	7	0	6
112.	SHIPPING CORPORATION OF INDIA LTD.	113671	141	99429	160
113.	SOUTH EASTERN COALFIELDS LTD.	28	80	27	84
114.	STATE TRADING CORPN. OF INDIA LTD.	137	72	131	70
115.	STCL LTD.	0	0	0	1
116.	STEEL AUTHORITY OF INDIA LTD.	750869	40519	667690	25730
117.	TEHRI HYDRO DEVELOPMENT CORP. LTD..	0	16	0	16
118.	TELECOMMUNICATIONS CONSULTANTS (INDIA) LTD.	96	27	54	11
119.	TRIVENI STRUCTURALS LTD.	0	2	0	1
120.	TYRE CORPORATION OF INDIA LTD.	11771	276	11763	307
121.	URANIUM CORPORATION OF INDIA LTD.	0	1	0	0
122.	WATER & POWER CONSULTANCY SERVICES(INDIA) LTD	33	10	28	16
	TOTAL	**3190876**	**199947**	**3144075**	**192074**
ANDAMAN & NICOBAR ISLANDS					
1.	INDIAN OIL CORPORATION LTD.	3942	13	3942	13
2.	AIRPORTS AUTHORITY OF INDIA LTD.	474	23	248	15
3.	ANDAMAN & NICOBAR ISL. FOREST & PLANT.DEV.COR	1846	1648	1872	1716
4.	BHARAT SANCHAR NIGAM LTD.	14635	242	13911	258
5.	CENTRAL WAREHOUSING CORPN.	115	0	0	0
6.	HOUSING & URBAN DEV. CORPN. LTD.	1	4	1	4
7.	NATIONAL BLDG. CONSTN. CORPN. LTD.	0	4	0	0
8.	NATIONAL HYDROELECTRIC POWER CORPN.LTD.	7	8	6	5
9.	OIL & NATURAL GAS CORPORATION LTD.	0	0	13	0
10.	RITES LTD.	0	1	0	1

S. No.	NAME OF PSU	2005-2006		2004-2005	
		Gross Block	Employment	Gross Block	Employment
11.	SHIPPING CORPORATION OF INDIA LTD.	5	15	0	0
	TOTAL	**21025**	**1958**	**19993**	**2012**
CHANDIGARH					
1.	INDIAN OIL CORPORATION LTD.	4176	192	4176	192
2.	AIRPORTS AUTHORITY OF INDIA LTD.	475	33	472	33
3.	BHARAT PETROLEUM CORPN. LTD.	364	34	274	34
4.	CENTRAL WAREHOUSING CORPN.	101	73	101	66
5.	COAL INDIA LTD.	14	24	14	25
6.	EXPORT CREDIT GUARANTEE CORPN.OF INDIA LTD.	9	3	5	2
7.	GAIL (INDIA) LTD.	0	14	65	13
8.	HINDUSTAN LATEX LTD.	0	2	0	0
9.	HINDUSTAN PAPER CORPORATION LTD.	3	2	3	3
10.	HINDUSTAN PETROLEUM CORPN. LTD.	1682	70	2335	36
11.	HINDUSTAN PHOTO FILMS MANUFACTURING CO. LTD.	2	2	2	2
12.	HOUSING & URBAN DEV. CORPN. LTD.	62	27	55	30
13.	I.B.P. CO. LTD.	1318	6	1318	26
14.	KARNATAKA ANTIBIOTICS & PHARMACEUTICALS LTD.	0	3	0	4
15.	NATIONAL BLDG. CONSTN. CORPN. LTD.	8	0	24	2
16.	NATIONAL FERTILIZERS LTD.	0	0	479	457
17.	NATIONAL HYDROELECTRIC POWER CORPN.LTD.	676	96	0	86
18.	NATIONAL SCHEDULED CASTES FINANCE & DEVP. COR	1	3	1	3
19.	NATIONAL SEEDS CORPN. LTD.	0	21	0	23
20.	NATIONAL SMALL INDUSTRIES CORPN. LTD.	5	7	0	0
21.	NTC(DELHI,PUNJAB & RAJASTHAN) LTD.	0	13	6	15

S. No.	*NAME OF PSU*	*2005-2006*		*2004-2005*	
		Gross Block	*Employment*	*Gross Block*	*Employment*
22.	NTPC ELECTRIC SUPPLY COMPANY LTD.	2	0	0	0
23.	POWER GRID CORPORATION OF INDIA LTD	251	17	197	22
24.	RAJASTHAN ELECTRONICS AND INSTRUMENTS LTD.	0	1	0	0
25.	RASHTRIYA CHEMICALS AND FERTILIZERS LTD.	0	1	14	7
26.	RASHTRIYA ISPAT NIGAM LTD.	320	4	312	7
27.	RITES LTD.	0	5	0	3
28.	SCOOTERS INDIA LTD.	0	2	0	1
29.	STEEL AUTHORITY OF INDIA LTD.	111	0	130	0
30.	TEHRI HYDRO DEVELOPMENT CORP. LTD..	0	2	0	2
	TOTAL	**9580**	**657**	**9983**	**1094**
DELHI					
1.	INDIAN AIRLINES LTD.	502663	6501	502663	6501
2.	HINDUSTAN PREFAB LTD.	615	414	613	404
3.	KUMARAKUPPA FRONTIER HOTELS LTD.	1	4	1	4
4.	BROADCAST ENGG.CONSULTANTS INDIA LTD.	96	10	134	13
5.	INDIAN OIL CORPORATION LTD.	210692	1830	210692	2212
6.	KOCHI REFINERIES LTD.	0	0	53	9
7.	AIR INDIA LTD.	66140	1702	4025	1702
8.	AIRLINE ALLIED SERVICES LTD.	402	416	383	364
9.	AIRPORTS AUTHORITY OF INDIA LTD.	6582	5176	91742	5200
10.	ANDREW YULE & COMPANY LTD.	10	15	0	0
11.	ARTIFICIAL LIMBS MFG. CORPN. OF INDIA	5	7	0	10
12.	BALMER LAWRIE & CO. LTD.	295	78	288	78
13.	BBJ CONSTRUCTION COMPANY LTD.	0	14	0	103

S. No.	NAME OF PSU	2005-2006 Gross Block	2005-2006 Employment	2004-2005 Gross Block	2004-2005 Employment
14.	BENGAL CHEMICALS & PHARMACEUTICALS LTD.	1	6	0	0
15.	BHARAT BHARI UDYOG NIGAM LTD.	0	3	0	3
16.	BHARAT EARTH MOVERS LTD.	687	57	394	60
17.	BHARAT HEAVY ELECTRICALS LTD.	56913	873	56210	901
18.	BHARAT HEAVY PLATE & VESSELS LTD.	22	2	22	3
19.	BHARAT IMMUNOLOGICALS & BIOLOGICALS CORP. LTD	0	2	0	2
20.	BHARAT PETROLEUM CORPN. LTD.	21875	471	18669	513
21.	BHARAT PUMPS & COMPRESSORS LTD.	1	8	1	6
22.	BHARAT REFRACTORIES LTD.	0	6	0	6
23.	BHARAT SANCHAR NIGAM LTD.	0	0	0	6155
24.	BHARAT WAGON & ENGG. CO. LTD.	2	2	2	2
25.	BIECCO LAWRIE LTD.	13	4	13	3
26.	BONGAIGAON REFINERY & PETROCHEMICALS LTD.	440	28	559	27
27.	BRIDGE & ROOF CO.(INDIA) LTD.	72	25	208	24
28.	CEMENT CORPN. OF INDIA LTD.	569	172	3953	175
29.	CENTRAL COTTAGE INDUSTRIES CORPN. OF INDIA LT	1402	277	1350	284
30.	CENTRAL WAREHOUSING CORPN.	6563	786	6159	855
31.	CERTIFICATION ENGINEERS INTERNATIONAL LTD.	0	5	0	1
32.	CHENNAI PETROLEUM CORPORATION LTD.	71	6	71	7
33.	COAL INDIA LTD.	925	135	924	141
34.	CONTAINER CORPORATION OF INDIA LTD.	132146	391	110194	397
35.	COTTON CORPN. OF INDIA LTD.	35	25	37	22
36.	DREDGING CORPN.OF INDIA LTD.	46	1	45	2
37.	ELECTRONICS CORPN. OF INDIA LTD.	385	148	361	141
38.	ENGINEERING PROJECTS (INDIA) LTD.	615	188	634	194
39.	ENGINEERS INDIA LTD.	9406	1771	7924	1879

S. No.	NAME OF PSU	2005-2006		2004-2005	
		Gross Block	Employment	Gross Block	Employment
40.	EXPORT CREDIT GUARANTEE CORPN.OF INDIA LTD.	780	60	583	69
41.	FCI ARAVALI GYPSUM & MINERALS (INDIA) LTD.	0	3	0	3
42.	FERTILIZER CORPN. OF INDIA LTD.	212	13	213	17
43.	FERTILIZERS & CHEMICALS (TRAVANCORE) LTD.	8	3	8	2
44.	FOOD CORPN. OF INDIA	10625	2328	7196	2431
45.	GAIL (INDIA) LTD.	35838	533	16689	459
46.	GOA SHIPYARD LTD.	79	3	0	0
47.	GURU GOBIND SINGH REFINARIES LTD.	43	12	42	20
48.	HANDICRAFTS & HANDLOOM EXPORTS CORP. OF INDIA	992	101	333	103
49.	HEAVY ENGINEERING CORPN. LTD.	0	11	0	11
50.	HINDUSTAN AERONAUTICS LTD.	1645	16	260	18
51.	HINDUSTAN ANTIBIOTICS LTD.	12	36	13	37
52.	HINDUSTAN COPPER LTD.	323	17	327	17
53.	HINDUSTAN FERTILIZER CORPN. LTD.	94	12	137	10
54.	HINDUSTAN INSECTICIDES LTD.	509	97	511	98
55.	HINDUSTAN LATEX LTD.	0	7	28	13
56.	HINDUSTAN PAPER CORPORATION LTD.	248	26	234	30
57.	HINDUSTAN PETROLEUM CORPN. LTD.	23088	393	21931	489
58.	HINDUSTAN PHOTO FILMS MANUFACTURING CO. LTD.	6	9	6	10
59.	HINDUSTAN SHIPYARD LTD.	0	3	0	3
60.	HINDUSTAN STEEL WORKS COSTN. LTD.	17	17	13	21
61.	HINDUSTAN VEGETABLE OILS CORPN. LTD.	198	120	198	124
62.	HMT (INTERNATIONAL) LTD.	1	1	2	2
63.	HMT BEARINGS LTD.	0	2	0	4
64.	HMT CHINAR WATCHES LTD.	0	11	0	0
65.	HMT MACHINE TOOLS LTD.	19	31	22	24

S. No.	NAME OF PSU	2005-2006		2004-2005	
		Gross Block	Employment	Gross Block	Employment
66.	HOTEL CORPN. OF INDIA LTD.	4001	1301	3963	875
67.	HOUSING & URBAN DEV. CORPN. LTD.	6586	570	6568	562
68.	HSCC (INDIA) LTD.	0	9	0	3
69.	I T I LTD.	115	202	108	154
70.	I.B.P. CO. LTD.	11009	202	11009	194
71.	INDIA TOURISM DEV. CORPN.LTD.	9278	2421	8968	2210
72.	INDIA TRADE PROMOTION ORGANISATION	7655	1122	7613	1137
73.	INDIAN MEDICINES & PHARMACEUTICAL CORPN. LTD.	304	127	0	0
74.	INDIAN RAILWAY CATERING AND TOURISM CORPN. LT	2230	264	1753	219
75.	INDIAN RAILWAY FINANCE CORPORATION LTD.	1690	20	1685	16
76.	INDIAN RENEWABLE ENERGY DEVT.AGENCY LTD.	1117	114	1117	125
77.	INSTRUMENTATION LTD.	103	42	99	44
78.	IRCON INTERNATIONAL LTD.	15190	523	5867	607
79.	JUTE CORPN. OF INDIA LTD.	3	3	3	4
80.	KARNATAKA ANTIBIOTICS & PHARMACEUTICALS LTD.	0	11	0	9
81.	KONKAN RAILWAY CORPORATION LTD.	2	2	0	1
82.	KUDREMUKH IRON ORE CO.LTD	18	11	16	11
83.	M M T C LTD.	2553	707	2373	709
84.	M S T C LTD.	47	32	45	30
85.	MADRAS FERTILIZERS LTD.	0	1	0	1
86.	MAHANAGAR TELEPHONE NIGAM LTD.	760488	25423	727724	26158
87.	MANGALORE REFINARY & PETROCHEMICALS LTD.	395	13	347	13
88.	MANGANESE ORE(INDIA) LTD.	37	2	37	2
89.	MECON LTD.	1988	106	1902	118
90.	MINERAL EXPLORATION CORPN. LTD.	32	4	29	4
91.	MUMBAI RAILWAY VIKAS CORPORATION LTD.	0	2	0	2

S. No.	NAME OF PSU	2005-2006		2004-2005	
		Gross Block	Employment	Gross Block	Employment
92.	NARMADA HYDROELECTRIC DEVELOPMENT CORPN. LTD.	0	0	5	10
93.	NATIONAL ALUMINIUM COMPANY LTD.	187	45	196	43
94.	NATIONAL BACKWARD CLASSES FINANCE & DEVELOPME	179	48	179	48
95.	NATIONAL BLDG. CONSTN. CORPN. LTD.	1920	716	1636	855
96.	NATIONAL FERTILIZERS LTD.	3824	155	3829	151
97.	NATIONAL FILM DEV. CORPN. LTD.	15	14	11	17
98.	NATIONAL HANDLOOM DEVELOPMENT CORPORATION LTD	0	5	0	5
99.	NATIONAL INFORMATICS CENTRE SERVICES INCORPOR	1671	40	0	0
100.	NATIONAL INSTRUMENTS LTD.	2	1	0	0
101.	NATIONAL MINERAL DEVELOPMENT CORPN. LTD.	202	10	33	11
102.	NATIONAL MINORITIES DEVP. & FINANCE CORPN.	89	44	88	34
103.	NATIONAL PROJECTS CONSTRUCTION CORPN. LTD.	6424	2359	6873	2506
104.	NATIONAL RESEARCH DEVP. CORPN.	166	95	150	95
105.	NATIONAL SAFAI KARAMCHARIS' FINANCE & DEVPT.	36	21	31	6
106.	NATIONAL SCHEDULED CASTES FINANCE & DEVP. COR	0	0	706	67
107.	NATIONAL SCHEDULED TRIBES FINANCE & DEVP. COR	565	45	545	42
108.	NATIONAL SEEDS CORPN. LTD.	310	186	301	200
109.	NATIONAL SMALL INDUSTRIES CORPN. LTD.	1849	322	1804	386
110.	NATIONAL TEXTILE CORPN. (Holding Co.) LTD.	452	119	446	122
111.	NEPA LTD.	3	4	0	0
112.	NEYVELI LIGNITE CORPN. LTD.	384	34	381	36
113.	NORTH EASTERN HANDICRAFTS & HANDLOOM DEV.COR	5	7	4	5
114.	NORTH EASTERN ELECTRIC POWER CORPORATION LTD.	614	28	611	66
115.	NTC(DELHI,PUNJAB & RAJASTHAN) LTD.	79	144	82	148
116.	NTPC ELECTRIC SUPPLY COMPANY LTD.	0	0	0	48
117.	NTPC LTD.	11133	4095	11713	3850

S. No.	NAME OF PSU	2005-2006		2004-2005	
		Gross Block	Employment	Gross Block	Employment
118.	NTPC VIDYUT VYAPAR NIGAM LTD.	33	37	26	30
119.	NUMALIGARH REFINARY LTD.	39	7	32	5
120.	OIL & NATURAL GAS CORPORATION LTD.	44659	783	49313	809
121.	OIL INDIA LTD.	3911	155	3326	144
122.	ONGC VIDESH LTD.	13887	59	13854	77
123.	P E C LTD.	389	122	354	121
124.	PAWAN HANS HELICOPTERS LTD.	14124	210	42281	215
125.	POWER FINANCE CORPORATION	7606	283	5874	264
126.	POWER GRID CORPORATION OF INDIA LTD	26077	452	25824	438
127.	PRAGA TOOLS LTD.	0	3	0	3
128.	RAIL VIKAS NIGAM LTD.	371	72	1568	101
129.	RAILTEL CORPORATION INDIA LTD.	94721	193	88527	170
130.	RAJASTHAN DRUGS & PHARMACEUTICALS LTD.	0	2	0	2
131.	RASHTRIYA CHEMICALS AND FERTILIZERS LTD.	0	15	0	8
132.	RASHTRIYA ISPAT NIGAM LTD.	413	37	400	45
133.	RITES LTD.	0	109	0	166
134.	RURAL ELECTRIFICATION CORPN. LTD.	7439	362	3448	341
135.	SATLUJ JAL VIDYUT NIGAM LTD.	0	0	0	12
136.	SCOOTERS INDIA LTD.	0	19	0	12
137.	SEMI-CONDUCTOR COMPLEX LTD.	8	4	8	9
138.	SHIPPING CORPORATION OF INDIA LTD.	149	13	148	10
139.	SPONGE IRON INDIA LTD.	0	1	0	1
140.	STATE FARMS CORPORATION OF INDIA LTD.	170	109	168	94
141.	STATE TRADING CORPN. OF INDIA LTD.	3355	527	3312	526
142.	STCL LTD.	0	0	1	0
143.	STEEL AUTHORITY OF INDIA LTD.	8199	961	7827	960

S. No.	NAME OF PSU	2005-2006 Gross Block	2005-2006 Employment	2004-2005 Gross Block	2004-2005 Employment
144.	TEHRI HYDRO DEVELOPMENT CORP. LTD..	0	33	0	34
145.	TELECOMMUNICATIONS CONSULTANTS (INDIA) LTD.	2678	501	2322	362
146.	TRIVENI STRUCTURALS LTD.	0	1	0	1
147.	TYRE CORPORATION OF INDIA LTD.	2	1	2	1
148.	URANIUM CORPORATION OF INDIA LTD.	56	1	0	0
149.	WATER & POWER CONSULTANCY SERVICES(INDIA) LTD	39	372	25	373
	TOTAL	**2177702**	**72639**	**2126560**	**79711**
GOA					
1.	INDIAN OIL CORPORATION LTD.	5296	107	5296	107
2.	AIR INDIA LTD.	6	13	6	13
3.	AIRPORTS AUTHORITY OF INDIA LTD.	1631	76	1564	70
4.	BHARAT EARTH MOVERS LTD.	19	8	19	20
5.	BHARAT PETROLEUM CORPN. LTD.	3364	51	3170	50
6.	BRIDGE & ROOF CO.(INDIA) LTD.	0	0	71	6
7.	CENTRAL WAREHOUSING CORPN.	76	13	76	16
8.	DREDGING CORPN.OF INDIA LTD.	1	0	1	0
9.	GOA SHIPYARD LTD.	8848	1534	10030	1535
10.	HINDUSTAN LATEX LTD.	0	1	0	1
11.	HINDUSTAN PETROLEUM CORPN. LTD.	6489	70	5902	69
12.	HOUSING & URBAN DEV. CORPN. LTD.	0	2	0	2
13.	I.B.P. CO. LTD.	125	2	125	2
14.	INDIA TOURISM DEV. CORPN.LTD.	9	2	8	2
15.	IRCON INTERNATIONAL LTD.	8	10	0	0
16.	KARNATAKA ANTIBIOTICS & PHARMACEUTICALS LTD.	0	1	0	1

S. No.	NAME OF PSU	2005-2006 Gross Block	2005-2006 Employment	2004-2005 Gross Block	2004-2005 Employment
17.	KONKAN RAILWAY CORPORATION LTD.	1248	931	0	931
18.	M M T C LTD.	193	52	164	55
19.	M S T C LTD.	0	1	0	0
20.	NATIONAL SMALL INDUSTRIES CORPN. LTD.	0	3	23	3
21.	OIL & NATURAL GAS CORPORATION LTD.	4470	65	4084	66
22.	P E C LTD.	0	1	0	1
23.	POWER GRID CORPORATION OF INDIA LTD	13820	39	13126	41
24.	RITES LTD.	0	6	0	6
	TOTAL	**45603**	**2988**	**43665**	**2997**
PONDICHERRY					
1.	INDIAN OIL CORPORATION LTD.	5498	25	5498	25
2.	AIRPORTS AUTHORITY OF INDIA LTD.	308	9	215	9
3.	BALMER LAWRIE & CO. LTD.	0	2	0	1
4.	CENTRAL WAREHOUSING CORPN.	40	7	40	7
5.	CONTAINER CORPORATION OF INDIA LTD.	18	1	18	2
6.	GAIL (INDIA) LTD.	13313	15	1657	24
7.	HINDUSTAN PETROLEUM CORPN. LTD.	1252	1	1116	1
8.	HINDUSTAN PHOTO FILMS MANUFACTURING CO. LTD.	1	6	1	5
9.	HOUSING & URBAN DEV. CORPN. LTD.	1	4	1	4
10.	I.B.P. CO. LTD.	25	1	25	1
11.	KARNATAKA ANTIBIOTICS & PHARMACEUTICALS LTD.	0	1	0	1
12.	MADRAS FERTILIZERS LTD.	0	1	0	1
13.	NATIONAL BLDG. CONSTN. CORPN. LTD.	0	1	0	5
14.	NATIONAL SCHEDULED CASTES FINANCE & DEVP. COR	787	67	0	0

S. No.	NAME OF PSU	2005-2006 Gross Block	2005-2006 Employment	2004-2005 Gross Block	2004-2005 Employment
15.	NATIONAL SMALL INDUSTRIES CORPN. LTD.	34	10	86	8
16.	NTC(A.PRADESH, KARNATAKA, KERALA & MAHE)LTD.	472	333	459	384
17.	NTC(TAMILNADU & PONDICHERRY) LTD.	0	0	1164	731
18.	OIL & NATURAL GAS CORPORATION LTD.	0	1131	0	1139
19.	PONDICHERRY ASHOK HOTEL CORPN. LTD.	167	24	171	25
20.	POWER GRID CORPORATION OF INDIA LTD	1024	9	1855	13
	TOTAL	**22940**	**1648**	**12306**	**2386**
OTHERS AND UNALLOCATED					
1.	AIR INDIA LTD.	0	0	9051	153
2.	AIRPORTS AUTHORITY OF INDIA LTD.	12575	0	0	0
3.	BALMER LAWRIE & CO. LTD.	0	1	0	1
4.	BHARAT HEAVY ELECTRICALS LTD.	32662	3013	26982	3194
5.	BHARAT PETROLEUM CORPN. LTD.	0	4	0	0
6.	BHARAT SANCHAR NIGAM LTD.	1058554	29462	944057	38823
7.	BONGAIGAON REFINERY & PETROCHEMICALS LTD.	6139	0	0	0
8.	BRAHMAPUTRA VALLEY FERTILIZER CORPN. LTD.	570	0	0	0
9.	BRIDGE & ROOF CO.(INDIA) LTD.	18	30	110	30
10.	CENTRAL WAREHOUSING CORPN.	0	1	0	0
11.	CONTAINER CORPORATION OF INDIA LTD.	0	3	0	0
12.	ENGINEERS INDIA LTD.	61	148	60	133
13.	GAIL (INDIA) LTD.	497	2	0	0
14.	GOA SHIPYARD LTD.	1503	0	0	0
15.	HINDUSTAN AERONAUTICS LTD.	33117	0	0	0
16.	HINDUSTAN COPPER LTD.	29918	0	0	0
17.	HINDUSTAN LATEX LTD.	37	0	0	0

S. No.	NAME OF PSU	2005-2006		2004-2005	
		Gross Block	Employment	Gross Block	Employment
18.	HINDUSTAN STEEL WORKS COSTN. LTD.	18	1	144	3
19.	HINDUSTAN VEGETABLE OILS CORPN. LTD.	2	0	0	0
20.	HMT MACHINE TOOLS LTD.	7	0	91	0
21.	I.B.P. CO. LTD.	140	0	0	0
22.	INDIA TOURISM DEV. CORPN.LTD.	2	100	0	277
23.	INDIA TRADE PROMOTION ORGANISATION	72	6	61	6
24.	IRCON INTERNATIONAL LTD.	10940	274	17053	198
25.	KARNATAKA ANTIBIOTICS & PHARMACEUTICALS LTD.	0	3	0	3
26.	KONKAN RAILWAY CORPORATION LTD.	4243	453	0	0
27.	M M T C LTD.	0	2	0	0
28.	MECON LTD.	0	1	0	1
29.	NARMADA HYDROELECTRIC DEVELOPMENT CORPN. LTD.	5811	0	0	0
30.	NATIONAL BLDG. CONSTN. CORPN. LTD.	0	0	0	4
31.	NATIONAL HYDROELECTRIC POWER CORPN.LTD.	0	0	641	0
32.	NATIONAL MINERAL DEVELOPMENT CORPN. LTD.	1	0	1	0
33.	NATIONAL SEEDS CORPN. LTD.	38	0	0	0
34.	NATIONAL SMALL INDUSTRIES CORPN. LTD.	24	24	0	0
35.	NTC(TAMILNADU & PONDICHERRY) LTD.	1	0	0	0
36.	NTPC HYDRO LTD.	377	0	0	0
37.	NUMALIGARH REFINARY LTD.	30545	0	0	0
38.	OIL & NATURAL GAS CORPORATION LTD.	442457	0	416478	0
39.	OIL INDIA LTD.	9	1	0	0
40.	ONGC VIDESH LTD.	895407	31	622478	8
41.	P E C LTD.	0	1	0	1
42.	PUNJAB ASHOK HOTEL COMPANY LTD.	0	0	3	0
43.	RAIL VIKAS NIGAM LTD.	153489	0	69155	0

S. No.	*NAME OF PSU*	*2005-2006*		*2004-2005*	
		Gross Block	*Employment*	*Gross Block*	*Employment*
44.	RASHTRIYA CHEMICALS AND FERTILIZERS LTD.	18576	0	0	0
45.	RITES LTD.	757	77	708	68
46.	SHIPPING CORPORATION OF INDIA LTD.	33010	5221	32996	5499
47.	TEHRI HYDRO DEVELOPMENT CORP. LTD..	5523	10	0	5
48.	TELECOMMUNICATIONS CONSULTANTS (INDIA) LTD.	4160	189	4846	702
49.	WATER & POWER CONSULTANCY SERVICES(INDIA) LTD	30	25	53	29
	TOTAL	**2781290**	**39083**	**2144968**	**49138**
DADRA NAGARHAVLI					
1.	BALMER LAWRIE & CO. LTD.	2223	19	2211	14
2.	BHARAT EARTH MOVERS LTD.	0	0	0	6
3.	GAIL (INDIA) LTD.	0	1	0	0
4.	HINDUSTAN PETROLEUM CORPN. LTD.	3907	2	3916	8
5.	POWER GRID CORPORATION OF INDIA LTD	951	0	951	9
6.	WATER & POWER CONSULTANCY SERVICES(INDIA) LTD	0	0	0	1
	TOTAL	**7081**	**22**	**7078**	**38**
DAMAN AND DIU					
1.	AIRPORTS AUTHORITY OF INDIA LTD.	144	8	135	2
2.	BHARAT EARTH MOVERS LTD.	0	0	0	6
3.	BHARAT PETROLEUM CORPN. LTD.	58	1	63	1
4.	HINDUSTAN PETROLEUM CORPN. LTD.	76	0	78	0
5.	POWER GRID CORPORATION OF INDIA LTD	0	0	0	2
	TOTAL	**278**	**9**	**276**	**11**

S. No.	NAME OF PSU	2005-2006		2004-2005	
		Gross Block	Employment	Gross Block	Employment
LAKSHADWEEP					
1.	AIRPORTS AUTHORITY OF INDIA LTD.	209	24	282	23
2.	GOA SHIPYARD LTD.	0	0	79	3
3.	NATIONAL INSTRUMENTS LTD.	0	0	1	3
	TOTAL	209	24	362	29
	GRAND TOTAL	71281872	1648537	64924516	1699649

References

BOOKS

Baumol, W.J. (1959), *Business Behaviour, Value and Growth*, Macmillan, London.

Cantwell, J. (1989), *Technological Innovation and Multinational Corporations*, Basil Blackwell, Oxford.

Chapman, Colin (1990), *Selling the Family Silver: Has Privatization Worked?* Hutchinson Business Books Limited, London.

Chen, E.K.Y. (1983), *Multinational Corporations, Technology, and Employment*, McMillan, London.

Clarke, Thomas (ed), (1994), *International Privatisation: Strategies and Practices*, Walter de Gruyter & Co. Berlin.

Cyert, R.M. and March, J.G. (1963), *A Behavioural Theory of the Firm*, Prentice Hall, Hemel Hempstead.

Van De Walle, Nicholas (ed) (1993), *Methods and Practices of Privatization*, United Nations, New York.

Demsetz, Harold (1998), *Ownership, Control and the Firm*, Basil Blackwell, New York.

Desai, A.V. (1988), *Technological Absorption in Indian Industry*, Wiley Eastern Ltd, New Delhi.

Donahue, John D. (1989), *The Privatization Decision: Public Ends, Private Means*, Basic Books, New York.

Gelbraith, J.K. (1967), *The Industrial State*, New American Library, New York.

Godar, B.N. (1986): *Productivity Growth in Indian Industry*, Allied Publishers, New Delhi.

Gordon, R.A. (1945), *Business Leadership in Large Corporations*, Brookings, Washington.

Lal, Deepak (2006), *Reviving the invisible Hand; The Case for Classical Liberalism in the Twenty-first Century*, Academic Foundation, New Delhi.

Mandal, R. (1994), *Privatization in the Third World*, Vikas Publishing Home, New Delhi.

Marris R. (1964), *The Economic Theory of Managerial Capitalism*, Macmillan, London.

Martin, S. (1993), *Economics of Discretionary Behaviour: Managerial Objectives and a Theory of the Firm*, Kershaw, London.

Micklethwait, J., and A. Wooldridge (2003), *The Corporation*, AttenLane, London.

Prasad, P. (1957), *Some Economic Problems of Public Enterprises in India*, HE Stenfert Kroese, Leiden.

Ryon, John (1994), *Regional Innovation System in Europe: The Case of Baden-Wurttemberg and Wales* (minio), University of Manchester, Manchester.

Trivedi, Prajapati, ed. (1990), *Memorandum of Understanding: An Approach to Improving Public Enterprise Performance*, International Management Publishers, New Delhi.

Turvey, R.G. (1968), *Public Enterprise, Penguin Modern Economics*, London.

Williamson, Oliver E. (1985), *The Economic Institutions of Capitalism: Firms. Markets, Rational Contracting*. Free Press, New York.

World Bank. (1995), *Bureaucrats in Business: The Economics and Politics of Government Ownership*. Oxford University Press, Washington, D.C.

ARTICLES

Balakrishan, P.K. Pushpangadan and M. Suresh Babu (2000), 'Trade Liberalisation and Productivity Growth in Manufacturing: Evidence from Firm Level Panel Data' *Economic and Political Weekly*, October 7, 2000

Bartel, Ann. P. and Harrison Ann. E, Ownership Versus Environment: Disentangling the Sources of Public Sector Inefficiency, Columbia Business School and NBER

Cable, J. and Yasuki, H. (1985),'Internal Organization, business groups and corporate performance', *International Journal of Industrial Organization*, 3,(4)

Chaudhuri, S. (2002): Economic Reforms and Industrial Structure in India, *Economic and Political Weekly*, pp. 155-68, January 12, 2002

Christofides, L.N. and Tapon, (1979),' Discretionary expenditures and profit risk management: The Galbraith—Caves hypotheses. ' *Quarterly Journal of Economics*, 93.

Conyon, M. and Leech, D. (1994),'Executive compensation, corporate performance and ownership structure', Oxford Bulletin of Economics and Statistics, 56.

Das, D.K, 'Manufacturing Productivity Under Varying Trade Regimes: India in the 1980s and the 1990s', *Economic and Political Weekly*, September 2007, 2003

Dobek, M. Marusz (1993), Privatization as a Political Priority: The British Experience. *Political Studies*, Vol. 41, No. 1.

Domestz, H. (1967), "Towards a Theory of Property Rights", *American Economic Review* 57(2): 347-59.

Ehrlich, Isaac, et al (1994), Productivity Growth and Firm Ownership: An Analytical and Empirical Investigation, *Journal of Political Economy*, 1994

Galal, Ahmed, (1990), Public Enterprise Reform: A Challenge for the World Bank, The World Bank, Washington, April, 1990

Ghosh, Asha, (2005), Public-Private or a Private Public, *Economic and Political Weekly*; Mumbai, November 19, 2005

Goldar, B.N., V.S. Renganathan and R. Banga, (2003), 'Ownership and Efficiency in Engineering Firms in India', *Economic and Political Weekly*, 2003

Gordon, Roger H., and Wei Li. 1995, (1995), The Change in Productivity of Chinese State Enterprise, 1983-1987, *The Journal of Productivity Analysis*, 6, 5-26, 1995

Gregg, P., Machin, S. and Szymanski, S. (1993),'The disappearing relationship between directors' pay and corporate performance,' *British Journal of Industrial Relations*, 31.

Groves, Theodore, et al., (1995), Autonomy and Incentives in Chinese State Enterprises, *Quarterly Journal of Economics*, 109, 181-209, 1995

Linz, Susan, and Gary Krueger (1998), Enterprise Restructuring in Russia's Transition Economy: Formal and Informal Mechanisms, *Comparative Economic Studies*, 40: 5-52, 1998

Mary, Shirley and Lixin Colin Xu, (1997), Empirical Effects of Performance Contracts: Evidence from China, October 1997

Megginson, William, et al., (1994), The Financial and Operating

Performance of Newly Privatized Firms: An International impirical Analysis, *Journal of Finance*, 49:403-452, 1994

Morck, R., A Shleifer and R. Vishny, (1988), "Management Ownership and Market Valuation: An Empirical analysis," *Journal of Financial Economics* 20, 293-315, 1988

Naib, Sudhir, (2003), Partial Divestiture and Performance of Indian Public Sector Enterprises, *Economic and Political Weekly*; Mumbai, July 19, 2003

Palmer, A.M.F., (1960), On Public Accountability, *Socialist Commentary*, January, 1960.

Ryon, John (1994), Regional Innovation System in Europe: The Cases of Baden-Wurttemberg and Wales (minio), University of Manchester, Manchester

Sader, Frank (1993), Privatization and Foreign Investment in the Developing World, 1988-92. Working Paper, WPS 1202., World Bank, Washington, D.C.

Schoeffler, S. Buzzel, R.D. and Heavy, D.F. (1974), 'Impact of Strategic Planning on Profit Performance', *Harvard Business Review*, 52, March-April.

Shleifer, Andrei and Robert Vishny, (1986), "Large Shareholders and Corporate Control," *Journal of Political Economy*, 94: 461-488, 1986

Siddharthan, N.S. and A.E. Safarian (1997): 'Transnational Corporations, Technology Transfer and the Import of Capital Goods: The Recent Indian Experience', *Transnational Corporations Journal*, Vol. 6, 1997

Siddharthan, N.S. and K. Lal (2004), 'Liberalization, MNE and Productivity of Indian Enterprises', *Economic and Political Weekly*, January 31, pp. 448

Simon, H.A. (1959), Theories of decision making in economics and behavioural science, *American Economic Review*, 49.

Steer, P. and Cable, J. (1978), 'Internal organization and profit: An empirical analysis of large UK Companies,' *Journal of Industrial Economics*, 27.

Topalova, Petia, (2004), IMF Working Paper: Overview of the Indian Corporate Sector: 1989-2002, International Monetary Fund, Washington, April 2004

Williamson, O.E. (1971), 'Managerial discretion, organization form and the multidivisional hypothesis', in R. Marris and A. Wood (eds.), *The Corporate Economy*.

REPORTS

International Monetary Fund (2004), IMF Working Paper, Washington2004.

Ministry of Commerce and Industry, Government of India (1956), Industrial Policy Resolution, New Delhi, 1956

Ministry of Finance, Government of India (1991), Industrial Policy Statement, New Delhi, 1991,

Ministry of Heavy Industries and Public Enterprises, Guidelines to Corporate Governance, New Delhi, 2007.

Ministry of Heavy Industries and Public Enterprises, Public Enterprises Survey (various issues), New Delhi.

OECD, Economic Survey of India, Academic Foundation, New Delhi, 2007.

Planning Commission, Government of India (2002), Tenth Five Year Plan (2002-07), New Delhi, (2002)

Planning Commission, Government of India (2005), Public Private Partnership, New Delhi, 2005.

Planning Commission, Government of India (2007), Approach Paper to the Eleventh Five Year Plan (2008-2011), New Delhi, 2007

Planning Commission, Government of India (2007), Report of the Working Group on Competition Policy, New Delhi, 2007.

SAIL (1990), Corporate Planning Function: A Review and Approach, New Delhi 1990.

Index